The Gallant Cause

The Gallant Cause

CANADIANS
in the
SPANISH
CIVIL WAR
1936 ~ 1939

MARK ZUEHLKE

WHITECAP BOOKS
VANCOUVER / TORONTO

The information in this book is true and complete to the best of our knowledge. All recommendations are made without guarantee on the part of the author or Whitecap Books Ltd. The author and publisher disclaim any liability in connection with the use of this information. For additional information please contact Whitecap Books Ltd., 351 Lynn Avenue, North Vancouver, BC, V7J 2C4.

Edited by Carolyn Bateman
Proofread by Elizabeth McLean
Cover design by Val Speidel
Cover photo courtesy of National Archives of Canada (PA193629)
Interior design by Warren Clark
Typeset by Warren Clark

Printed and bound in Canada.

Canadian Cataloguing in Publication Data

Zuehlke, Mark
  The gallant cause

  Includes bibliographical references and index.
  ISBN 1-55110-488-1
  1. Spain—History—Civil War, 1936–1939—Participation, Canadian I. Title.
DP269.47C2Z83 1996   946.081   C96-910371-9

The publisher acknowledges the support of the Canada Council and the Cultural Services Branch of the Government of British Columbia in making this publication possible.

For Fiero,
who showed the Way.

Acknowledgements

While researching this book, I was assisted by many helpful staff at the National Archives of Canada (NAC) and National Library of Canada, the Baldwin Room of the Metropolitan Toronto Reference Library (MTRL), the Canadian Broadcasting Corporation's Radio Archives in Toronto (special thanks to Debbie Lindsey), the special collections departments of the University of British Columbia, Vancouver Public Library (VPL), and University of Victoria, and the British Columbia Archives and Records Service in Victoria.

In 1964 and 1965, Canadian Broadcasting Corporation researcher Mac Reynolds travelled across Canada to interview a number of Canada's Spanish Civil War volunteers. Those interviews are preserved at the CBC Radio Archives. Mac kindly consented to my drawing on them for this book. Myron Momryk of the National Archives of Canada's Manuscript Division shared his knowledge and insights into the motivation, ethnicity, and fate of the volunteers. Jolanta Sise approved the opening of Hazen Sise's personal records, and J. Wendell MacLeod opened his personal collection on Dr. Norman Bethune.

I would also like to thank the Canada Council for funding through its Short Term Grant program and the British Columbia Cultural Services Branch for a writing grant.

Books always require a long march from inception to conclusion. Throughout this journey, I was fortunate in having Fran Backhouse's sound counsel, unwavering support, and honest friendship.

Contents

Introduction

*T*ANGLED WEBS OF LOYALTIES

IN TORONTO'S QUEEN'S PARK, A LARGE RUSTY-WHITE BOULDER sits between a huge monument to William Lyon Mackenzie, the rebel who inspired and led the doomed 1837 Upper Canada Rebellion, and a narrow lane that provides vehicles with delivery access to the Ontario legislature. Thick shrubbery further shrouds the rock from the casual view of passersby.

It was shortly after midnight on a starry autumn night in 1995 when I first visited this boulder, which is a monument to the Canadians who fought for the Spanish Republic in a bloody civil war that raged from July 1936 to the early months of 1939. Stray threads of light cast by the street lamps and glimmers of starlight caused· mineral deposits in the rock to glitter and gently shimmer.

Sitting cross-legged on the grass before the stone, I read the official plaque mounted on its face by the National Historic Sites and Monuments Board. It read in part: "Despite their government's opposition, more than 1,500 Canadians volunteered to fight with the Republican forces. . . . They fought courageously for their ideals, suffering heavy losses in major battles."

The stone was brought to Canada by Canadian veterans of the Spanish Civil War. They had collected it in the early 1990s from a battlefield near Gandesa in Aragon province. Here many men and women who volunteered to fight in the International Brigades had perished in a vain attempt to defend democracy from fascism during a war that ultimately proved a dress rehearsal for World War II.

No one really knows the actual number of Canadians who went to Spain between 1936 and 1939. Most recent calculations put the number at about sixteen hundred, rather than the fifteen hundred stated on the memorial. Almost half of the volunteers never returned, coming to rest in shallow graves hastily dug into the Spanish earth.

For several days I had spent many hours in the CBC Radio Archives listening to the voices of some of the veterans who survived the war. I had heard their incredible war stories and thought perhaps I now understood their reasons for going to another people's war. Those voices echoed softly through my thoughts.

The world sixty years earlier was far different from the present twilight years of the twentieth century. So, too, were the people. In the 1930s, Canada, like most of the developed world, was in the throes of the Great Depression. One out of every nine Canadians was receiving federal government relief. Countless others were homeless, drifting from place to place in search of any kind of work they could find. The Prairie provinces were undergoing a terrible drought, the once fertile fields reduced to dustbowls.

Living in desperate times encouraged many Canadians to seek new roads that might lead to brighter futures. Beside the worn pathways of conservatism and liberalism, both having proved incapable of leading the way out of the depression's chaos, two new, dramatically different roads were visible. In Canada, as in most industrialized nations, many people chose to explore one or the other.

In one direction lay fascism, in the other communism. The anti-fascist poet, novelist, and teacher Alexander Maitland Stephen identified eleven fascist organizations operating in Canada during the mid-1930s. Some, like the Canadian Union of Fascists, were overt in advertising their beliefs. Others, like the Chalifoux Labour Club established in Montreal, tried to mask their connection to the world fascist movement. But Chalifoux members showed their true colours when they rallied behind an aldermanic candidate whose election platform advocated hanging a "Socialist and a Jew from every lamp-post" in the city.

Unlike in Germany, Italy, and other nations, where right-wing dictators rose to power, most Canadians failed to heed the siren call of fascism. A far larger number of Canadians were drifting leftward toward the glimmering hope offered by socialism and communism. Most of the socialists found a home in the Co-operative Commonwealth Federation (CCF) and the communists in the Communist Party (CP) of Canada, which had direct links to the International Comintern based in the Soviet Union.

At its peak in the late 1930s, the CP claimed only about twenty thousand card-carrying members. The low number of official members was hardly surprising considering that during much of its early history the party operated in defiance of laws intended to suppress leftist elements. While fascism was allowed virtually free rein in Canada, communists found themselves running afoul of Quebec's Padlock Law or Section 98 of the Canadian Criminal Code, which made it a punishable crime to be involved in an "unlawful association." Curiously, while the various fascist organizations were largely untouched by this latter legislation, several CP leaders were arrested and jailed under its provisions and the party was forced to operate underground.

As a consequence of this government repression, many Canadians sensibly chose to keep secret any communist sympathies they had. Several times a year, especially during May Day parades in the major cities, it was nevertheless evident that thousands of Canadians believed communism offered the best hope for a beleaguered nation. Every May Day, downtown streets were jammed with thousands of people marching under international communism's red flag.

Today, knowing that while these Canadians were marching under communist banners Joseph Stalin was executing and imprisoning millions of Soviet citizens, it is sometimes difficult to not think them naïve, ill-informed, or beguiled. But the twenty-twenty vision of historical hindsight can blinker our own understanding of the past. Comprehension of why people behaved as they did is usually best gained by assuming their viewpoint, so as to better understand their motivations, beliefs, and desires.

Many of the Canadians who went to Spain called themselves communists, and it may seem strange that they decided to fight for democracy. But in the 1930s it was not yet clear that communism would become an antidemocratic force. Marx's dictatorship of the proletariat was considered by many to be the ultimate democratic ideal, and in Spain it seemed that goal was being realized.

It is true, too, that most of the Canadians who went to Spain were more anti-fascist than anything else. They fervently believed that Spain was the first battleground in an inevitable world war between every other political belief and the world's fascist movements. In this conviction they correctly anticipated forthcoming world events. Had democratic governments responded with the same perceptiveness, it is possible that World

War II might have been prevented and millions of lives saved.

The Canadians who went to Spain didn't know, of course, that a world war would inevitably follow if the Republic fell to the fascists. In fact, given the complexity of Spanish politics, their understanding of the forces at work in Spain was often relatively confused. Even when they got to Spain, trying to sort out the differing political parties and movements was an unenviable task that few vigorously undertook.

Generally they knew that in 1931 King Alphonso XIII had gone into exile, effectively ending the Spanish monarchy. A republic (Spain's second) was declared. There followed a wave of reforms aimed at reducing the power of the large landowners, the military, and the Roman Catholic Church. These reforms redistributed the nation's wealth and greatly improved the average Spaniard's life at the cost of this triumvirate, which had traditionally possessed the lion's share of Spain's wealth.

The members of these three groups were, of course, ill pleased with the Republic. They plotted and agitated, seeking to exploit any opportunity to disrupt the democratic process.

Meanwhile, however, the Republic was drifting ever leftward as the leftist parties and movements gained a greater share of political power through co-operation rather than competition. In the February 1936 general election, the leftist parties went to the polls as an organized Popular Front and won a massive majority, electing 267 deputies to the right-wing parties' 132. The centre parties were virtually wiped off the political map.

Coalitions are always tenuous propositions at best. Composed of four parties ranging from moderate socialist to communist, the Popular Front government was as often in disagreement with itself as it was with the right-wing opposition parties.

Reforms, however, progressed, moving Spain rapidly from an almost feudal state toward a modernized nation. Literacy rates were rising, agricultural collectives were redistributing the land to the peasants, unions were being formed in all industries, and it seemed the government was determined to make Spain a better place for the common person.

In July 1936, however, the Popular Front and Spanish democracy were threatened when the Spanish army attempted to stage a coup. The military junta staging the coup expected to control all of Spain within a few days, but they failed. The Spanish Civil War began.

There were two obviously opposing sides—the fascists versus the Popular Front government, but this was confused by the tendency of both sides to adopt a range of labels. Fascists were called Nationalists, Royalists, or Monarchists. The Popular Front supporters were called Reds, Republicans, or Loyalists. Both sides claimed to represent the legitimate government.

Within the Popular Front was found a panoply of political ideologies and movements that were unfamiliar to most North Americans. One of the most confusing for the Canadian volunteers to understand were the Spanish anarchists, who were inspired by the Russian aristocrat Michael Bakunin. Bakunin once wrote: "I want the masses of humanity to be really emancipated from all authorities and from all heroes present and to come." Like most anarchists, those in Spain opposed the ownership of property in favour of loosely formed collectives that were run by consensus rather than any form of governing hierarchy. It is estimated that in 1936, 1.5 million Spaniards were anarchist in sympathy. Catalan province and its capital Barcelona were anarchist strongholds.

A subgroup and sometime offshoot of the anarchists were the Anarcho-Syndicalists. Syndicaliste is French for trade unionist. The Anarcho-Syndicalist movement was the trade union wing of the anarchist movement, but it also included many lower- and middle-class urban workers and shopkeepers. Consequently, most urban-based anarchists were Anarcho-Syndicalists. The rural and urban anarchists shared the same basic goals of desiring to create a classless society free of any kind of dogmatic creed or hierarchical authority structure. Their opposition to organized authority set the anarchists as far apart from the communists as it did from the fascists.

Highly critical of Soviet-style communism and generally sympathetic to, and sometimes aligned with, the anarchists was the Partido Obrero de Unificación Marxista (POUM). This small political party blended the philosophy of Russian communist Leon Trotsky with elements of anarchism. POUM particularly advocated Trotsky's call for constant revolution on an international front in order to achieve a world classless state. Trotsky and his political beliefs were by the mid-1930s anathema to the Soviet Communist Party, the Comintern, and most mainstream national communist parties (including the Communist Party of Canada). It would not be long before the Popular Front singled out POUM as an enemy of the Republic and set about suppressing it.

As the war progressed, the Spanish Communist Party became ever more closely aligned with, and controlled by, the Soviet Union. With most of the arms that were vitally needed to keep the Republic alive coming from the

Soviet Union, it was not long before the Spanish Communist Party rose from a minority position in the Popular Front to assume the forefront politically and militarily. The party soon proceeded to suppress the anarchists, POUM, and other groups in purges that imitated those being carried out in the Soviet Union. Most International Brigade members joined the Spanish Communist Party, and the brigades were generally Communist Party led.

Most of the Canadian volunteers were too concerned with fighting the war to be bothered developing more than this kind of thumbnail understanding of the political groups operating on the Republican side during the course of the war. Like most everyone else, they were often puzzled and dismayed by the Popular Front's increasing tendency as the war went on to engage in internecine rivalry and conflict instead of remaining united and focussed on defeating Franco's fascists. But the Popular Front was a marriage of convenience, and the unity that appeared to operate so well at the war's beginning was largely illusory. As conditions worsened, both domestically and on the battlefront, the union fractured and ultimately collapsed into disarray.

That the Republic was doomed from the outset due to the refusal of the western democracies, particularly Britain, France, and the United States, to support its fight against Franco is now a matter of historical record. The other fascist nations ensured Franco had all he needed to eventually defeat the Republic. That it took three years for the fascists to succeed illustrates the commitment of the majority of Spaniards to the fledgling democracy and their determination to defend it.

The same can be said of the members of the International Brigades. The forty-two thousand brigaders suffered heavy casualties. Like the Canadians, it was common for international contingents to have by war's end lost more than half their numbers. This fact alone belies later claims that the volunteers were little short of soldiers of fortune. The Internationals fought and all too often died for a cause they strongly believed was worth defending.

In this book I have attempted to tell the story of the Canadian volunteers in a way that will enable the modern reader to understand why so many would go to fight in a foreign land despite their own government's opposition to the undertaking. I have also sought to take the reader into the very heart of their experiences by drawing extensively from their writings and recorded memories to re-create the war as they lived it.

This book is a work of literary non-fiction. As such it adopts certain stylistic conventions that require shaping the narrative around the limited point of view of the participants. In this sense the form mimics fictional technique. The fundamental premise of historical literary non-fiction is that the limited point of view and meticulous research required to make the form effective will transport the reader directly into the historical events related. This happens not only in descriptive terms but, more important, by putting the reader inside the minds of the participants who lived the events. The reader, then, is distinctly aware of the motives, beliefs, and emotions that psychologically and intellectually influenced the historical participants to do what they did.

It should be noted that literary non-fiction is *not* fiction or what is sometimes called "faction." The details surrounding the characters, the actions they take, and the thoughts they have are all drawn as faithfully as possible from the historical record. If the sky is described as being blue on the day of a particular battle, then the historical record shows this was the case. No literary licence is taken or assumed.

One limitation of literary non-fiction is that the writer cannot inject his or her own thoughts into the narrative. There is virtually no room for the omnipotent irony, cynicism, and other commentary that so often punctuates modern treatments of past events. Sometimes it may seem that the participants are amazingly naïve or doctrinaire in their emotions and beliefs, and it is tempting for the writer to point this out in a casual aside. But to do so is to deny the influence of the times and the validity of the participants' personal interpretations of events.

The decision to use the literary non-fiction technique to tell the story of the Canadians in the Spanish Civil War was made that autumn night in Toronto as I sat before the Queen's Park monument to the veterans. It seemed to me that, more than any other Canadian veterans of war, those who served in Spain had been denied the opportunity to have their experiences related. This book is an attempt to give their history a voice.

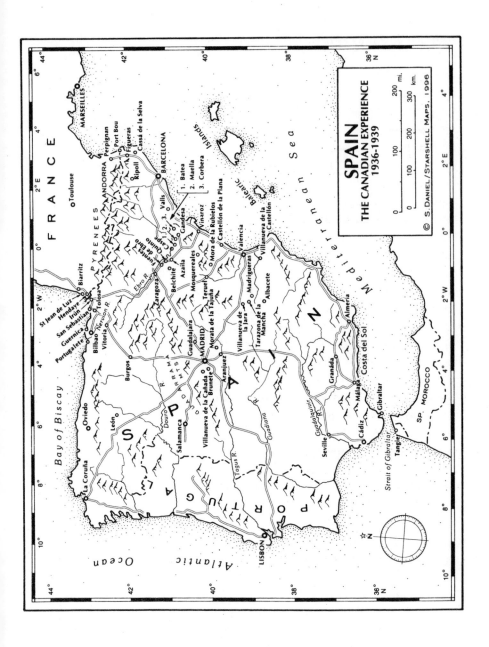

SPAIN
THE CANADIAN EXPERIENCE
1936-1939

© S. DANIEL / STARSHELL MAPS, 1996

1. Batea
2. Maella
3. Corbera

Prologue

*T*HE BITTERSWEET FAREWELL

THE CANADIANS WALKED ON FLOWERS. IT SEEMED EVERY MAN, woman, and child in the crowd past which the Canadian volunteers of the XVth International Brigade marched had a limitless supply of flowers to cast forth. Like a soft snow of brilliant reds, whites, pinks, and yellows, flowers showered down upon their shoulders and berets, dribbled redolently down their tattered uniforms, fell away to deepen the blossomy carpet beneath their worn and broken boots.

Along sycamore-lined El Diagonal—that broad avenue that slashes through Barcelona's heart—they marched in rows eight abreast. Before and behind the small clutch of about two hundred Canadians paraded volunteers from all the national battalions that constituted the International Brigades. Two thousand brigaders marched. They were but a mere fragment of the forty-two thousand Internationals who, since the outbreak of the Spanish Civil War on July 17, 1936, had fought for Spanish democracy. On October 29, 1938, however, only two thousand were able to muster for this farewell parade.

For some of the Canadians present it was the first time they had ever marched as part of the legendary Mackenzie-Papineau Battalion, fondly known as the Mac-Paps. Although many Canadians back home thought of the Mac-Paps as *their* unit, it had always been a mongrel comprising Canadians, Americans, a few Cubans, a scattering of other Internationals, and many Spaniards. For their part, some sixteen hundred Canadians had served in the American, British, German, Ukrainian, Czech, French, and other

International and regular Spanish battalions. Today, however, for the first and last time the Canadians marched as a single entity.

The Internationals marched toward a massive reviewing stand erected in the Plaça de la Gloria. A Spanish military honour guard stood rigidly at attention on either side of El Diagonal. Overhead, the small Russian-made Republican fighter planes circled like a ragged flock of so many noisy ravens, ensuring that the parade proceeded undisturbed by fascist bombers.

Behind the honour guard, the people of Barcelona pressed forward by the thousands. They crowded the balconies of the facing buildings, massed upon the rooftops, perched by the dozens in every tree.

Like so many of the soldiers, Canadian volunteer William Beeching was overwhelmed with emotion. It was the singing that struck him, that indelibly touched his heart. "The Internationale"—the anthem of popular fronts the world over—rang joyously from every mouth.

Finnish-Canadian Carl Syvänen had never seen so many people. Their singing and cries of *Viva* thundered louder than any artillery barrage he had endured during the brutal months of combat. But this was no hostile barrage. This, he thought, was the sound of a people's love. And it was a love directed toward all those who had travelled from distant lands to fight in this terrible war.

The crowd was not content to be kept apart from their brave foreign compatriots. They surged forward and the honour guard parted, unwilling to use force to sustain something as un-Spanish as disciplined ranks. Syvänen, Beeching, all the Internationals were swept up like fall leaves and carried forward in the crowd's current. Stunningly beautiful women with flashing brown eyes kissed Syvänen's cheeks, embraced him, and only re-luctantly passed him forward into the arms of another equally beautiful woman. The people gathered the soldiers up and marched arm in arm with them to the reviewing stand. By the time the Internationals reached the stand they were blended, folded, mixed inseparably with the people of Barcelona.

Syvänen's Finnish-Canadian compatriot John Keitaanranta saw the tears in the women's eyes. He listened to them sing "The Internationale" again in voices cracking with emotion. "It is their battle song," he thought. For a moment he allowed himself the foolish, fervent hope that the defiance and devotion pouring forth in song might be transformed into a righteous vio-lence that could shatter Franco's advancing fascist armies and even now save the Republic. Keitaanranta lent his voice to the song, as did the other Canadians.

On the reviewing stand, Republican prime minister Dr. Juan Négrin and his war cabinet signalled for the people to quieten. Gradually a gentle hush settled, a silence broken only by the perpetual drone of the overflying aircraft. Dr. Négrin spoke. He spoke softly and with careful formality. He spoke of why his government had withdrawn the Internationals from combat at a time when the Republic's need was so dire. He explained the decision to send them home, even though they had not asked to leave. He told of the government's hope that this would lead Franco to withdraw the countless thousands of German and Italian troops who fought on the fascist side. If the Germans and Italians also left, he said, the war would again become an entirely Spanish affair. Left to their own future, Dr. Négrin said, the Spanish people could yet triumph, the Republic be saved, and democracy preserved.

The Internationals tried to hide their scepticism. Listening to his words, Syvänen and Beeching both tasted the bitter salt of failure. Dr. Négrin spoke with courage and resolve. But he offered only fanciful words. The truth was a plainer, harsher thing. *La causa,* the cause so many friends had died fighting for, was lost. At best, the Republic could hold another few months. Then, El Diagonal would ring with the jackboots of the fascist troops of General Francisco Franco, Adolf Hitler, and Benito Mussolini. They would sneer their defiance at the world's democracies, who had offered Spain as a sacrifice before the altar of appeasement.

As the Spanish Communist Party leader and spiritual light of the Republican cause, Dolores Ibarruri, "La Pasionaria" herself, approached the microphone, Syvänen felt tears trace down his cheeks and tried to set aside these bitter thoughts. He did not cry alone. It seemed they all cried. Hard men no more. Her words to the women of Spain wrung his heart and evoked images of the more than eight hundred Canadian comrades who had fallen during the years of battle.

"Mothers! Women! When the years pass by and the wounds of war are staunched," she said in her powerful, deliberate voice, "when the cloudy memory of the sorrowful, bloody days returns in a present of freedom, love and well-being . . . speak to your children. Tell them of the International Brigades. Tell them how, coming over the seas and mountains, crossing frontiers bristling with bayonets . . . these men reached our country as crusaders for freedom. They gave up everything, their loves, their country,

3

home and fortune—fathers, mothers, wives, brothers, sisters, and children—and they came and told us: 'We are here. Your cause, Spain's cause, is ours. It is the cause of all advanced and progressive mankind.' Today they are going away. Many of them, thousands of them, are staying here with the Spanish earth for their shroud."

To the men of the Internationals she said, "You can go proudly. You are history. You are legend. You are the heroic example of democracy's solidarity and universality. We shall not forget you. And, when the olive tree of peace puts forth its leaves again, come back!. . . All of you will find the love and gratitude of the whole Spanish people who now and in the future will cry out with all their hearts, 'Long live the heroes of the International Brigades.'"

And around the brigaders the people of Barcelona again sang "The Internationale," the song that in 1938 was sung by millions the world over. In Canada, tens of thousands knew the words. They sang it in the union halls, in the hobo jungles, in the church basements, and at the political rallies. They sang it and believed. They believed the future the song promised humankind. They believed the people could be set free—all people everywhere. Standing in the fading afternoon light of Spanish autumn, Beeching still believed. Just as he had believed on an autumn day in 1936 when he had made the fateful decision to go to Spain and fight for the Republican cause.

One

IN SOLIDARITY

THE FASCIST UPRISING IN SPAIN AGAINST THE FRACTIOUS five-year-old democracy started on July 16, 1936, in the Spanish colony of Morocco. The following day the uprising spread across the Strait of Gibraltar to Spain itself. That was the same day Bill Beeching first read of the uprising. The news stories in the Regina *Leader-Post* reported how some of Spain's generals had launched an attempted military coup. Gunfire had been exchanged in the Andalusian port city of Seville, and Morocco was under military rule.

Since the Popular Front coalition had won the recent Spanish general elections of February 16, 1936, Beeching had been keenly following Spain's news. The government's programs of extensive land reform, peasant emancipation, bank nationalization, and introduction of universal education all encouraged Beeching to believe that similar hopeful initiatives might eventually come to Canada.

If a country that had suffered hundreds of years of oppression could establish a functioning, thriving, progressive, and democratic republic, then anything was possible. Could not Canada undergo changes similarly as radical and hitherto inconceivable? Beeching believed the need for change in Canada was every bit as urgent as it had been in Spain. For seven years the Great Depression had dragged on unabated. All Canada's federal and provincial governments could offer was impotent hand-wringing, while the nation's wealthy capitalists prospered and a nation's hope and its youth bled away in the misery of relief camps and massive unemployment.

Yes, Spain was hope. And now that hope was imperilled by fascist goons. Beeching was sick with dismay, but he was also angry. He wanted to strike back; to somehow help prevent the tragedy that would occur if the Republic was destroyed.

But what could he do? Beeching was a repairman for the Western Butchers Supply Company, which was itself an agent for International Business Machines. He repaired and maintained the weigh scales of Regina and the surrounding farm towns. In addition, he was the Saskatchewan First Labour Council's secretary and a card-carrying member of the Communist Party of Canada. As far as he could see, neither his job nor his union and political affiliations offered much opportunity to help save Spanish democracy.

July 18, 1936, was a Saturday. In Toronto, the humidity was such that sweat oozed from every pore. Joseph Baruch Salsberg was at the Communist Party headquarters on Adelaide Street, just west of Bay. In his role as the party's chief organizer among Ontario trade unions, Salsberg was drafting a speech he would deliver the following day before a workers' rally in Hamilton. The heat was making the speech writing a slow, tedious process. He was about to give up until it cooled down in the evening when the radio news announced that Spain's government was on the brink of being overthrown by a military coup. For the rest of the day, wherever he went, Salsberg kept close to the radio, feverishly following events.

Each report was bleaker than the last. Madrid's military garrison was in revolt. Units of the army were clashing in the streets with hastily organized citizen militias. Reports from Barcelona were more confused. Some claimed there was fighting, others that the streets were calm and peace prevailed. Almost all of Morocco was in the rebel generals' hands. But who were these generals? Who supported them? Would the bulk of the army rally to their rebellion? Or would it splinter, with some elements backing the generals, others supporting the government? All the news was contradictory, uncertain. Sitting next to a radio in Toronto it was impossible to draw a clear picture of events.

One thing, however, was crystal clear. "This," he said to a party office worker, "is the decisive turning point in Europe, and, therefore, the world. The establishment of a fascist regime in Spain will strengthen the fascist forces in the very heart of Europe and thus endanger what is left of democratic Europe. Make no mistake about it." [All quotes are drawn directly from written or taped accounts given by the person quoted. These sources appear in the bibliography.]

Salsberg thought he merely stated the obvious. In August 1934, Adolf Hitler had been anointed dictator of Germany. Since then the Nazis had busied themselves creating what was arguably the world's most powerful military juggernaut. Dictator Benito Mussolini had ruled Italy for almost eleven years. In 1935, Mussolini had unleashed his vast army against Abyssinia, and the League of Nations had done nothing to curb the invasion. If Spain fell, the European continent would be reconfigured into a fascist triangle. Spain and Italy would be at opposite points of the triangle's base, and Germany would stand at the triangle's apex. Europe would face a fascist triumvirate.

It was too late to stop the rise of German or Italian fascism. Only a Spanish democratic victory could prevent the fascist domination of Europe. A failure in Spain, Salsberg was certain, would guarantee Europe's slide into the very war that Europe's democracies were desperately trying to forestall through the policy of appeasement. It was a war the democracies could quite conceivably lose, opening the spectre of fascism's triumph throughout the world.

Salsberg's sleep that night was deeply troubled. In the morning the news from Spain had only worsened. The streets of Barcelona were strewn with dead killed in a continuing pitched battle. Rebel soldiers, now calling themselves Nationalists, were trying to overwhelm anarchist, syndicalist, socialist, and communist militias that had rushed to the Republic's defence. The militias were armed with a hodgepodge of weapons ranging from shotguns and clubs to machine guns and artillery pieces looted from military supply depots. The Telefonica Building, housing Catalan province's major telephone and communication terminus, was the focal point around which the struggle continued to turn.

In Madrid, men, women, and even children were hastily blocking the major thoroughfares with barricades constructed of paving bricks, overturned cars, furniture, and doors torn from their hinges. From behind these dubious shelters, the people met the advances of machine-gun-toting troops with barrages of rocks, bottles, and paving stones. Remarkably, it was the people who were winning. Rebel soldiers were retreating, and in some places they were surrendering en masse to the militias and soldiers who had remained loyal to the Republic.

Driving from Toronto along the shore of Lake Ontario toward Hamil-

The 1936 fascist attempt to capture Madrid was thrown back by thousands of citizens who organized themselves into militias and manned barricades throughout the city. (NAC PA194589)

ton, Salsberg listened to the radio reports. It was another insufferably hot day. In Spain, the common people—workers, peasants, students—were fighting and dying. These were people who were like those he would presently address.

He would be speaking in the province's industrial heartland, in a city of steel mills and iron foundries. It was a city that lay under an almost perpetual cloud of sooty black smoke. Hamilton's work force was composed of immigrant workers from the United Kingdom, Italy, and Poland, boosted, since the 1920s, by refugees from central Europe and the Baltic states. Many of these people had often known oppression in their homelands. Here in Canada—in the midst of the never ending depression—they again knew suffering.

As Salsberg drove into Hamilton's outskirts, he saw the parallels between what the workers there were going through and what was developing in Spain. Today, he decided, local issues could wait. Instead, Salsberg would speak of Spain. He would speak of the need for Canadians to show solidarity with the Spanish people in their struggle against fascism. Salsberg would urge those at the rally to support the universal cause of anti-fascism.

And so he did. Salsberg stood on a podium in Market Square with Hamilton City Hall at his back. He faced a mass rally of thousands of men, women, and children. Standing there in hot sunshine, Salsberg called for organization, for alliances to support the Spanish people. He urged the setting aside of petty political differences in favour of a concerted effort to send aid to Spain's Popular Front government. When he finished the people cheered. It occurred to Salsberg that he was probably the first public person in Canada to speak on the Spanish Civil War. Although the thought pleased him, Salsberg was also troubled because he had no idea how to turn words into action.

James Walsh cared precious little for words. Without the presentation of a realizable course of action, all the lofty speeches and ideas in the world constituted nothing. It was this very lack of purposeful action that had brought Walsh to Ocean Falls, on British Columbia's mainland coast. James "Red" Walsh was thirty-three years old and had been a labour organizer all his working life. He was a veteran of the Relief Camp Workers' Union and of the On to Ottawa Trek. Both in the union and on the trek he had been intensely active in fighting for workers' rights, but in the middle of 1936 there seemed little hope that action by common Canadians could lead to any improvement in their condition. The capitalists, the government, and the police had tightened down the lid of repression so effectively that there was nothing much anyone could do. So Walsh had come to Ocean Falls to earn a paycheque, rather than organize. And on July 18, 1936, Walsh was deeply concerned about the news coming out of Spain but doubted there was much anyone in Canada could do to help the Spanish brethren resist the fascist oppressors.

He worked on the boom gang at the Pacific Mills' wharf—loading and unloading freighters—and his life there was a hell of an improvement over that of the relief camps. Walsh earned fifty cents a day, instead of receiving the camps' daily allowance of twenty cents. Fifty cents a day could buy anything a worker needed. A work shirt was only two bits, a pair of dungarees seventy-five cents, a meal in the fanciest restaurant twenty cents. Not that Ocean Falls had a fancy restaurant.

Walsh could hardly believe Ocean Falls. This was the quintessential company town. Even the light bulbs in all the houses bore the company logo. The workers drew their clothes, food, and other needs from the company store. Most lived in company housing. There was no union and little chance of organizing one.

But Walsh wasn't there to organize. He had come to work and was still amazed that Pacific Mills had actually hired him. Obviously they had failed to check his background. No doubt this was a result of how he had come to get the Ocean Falls job. It had actually been a friend of his who had got the job offer, but the man had thought Ocean Falls too isolated and there was no provision for taking his wife and young child along. So he suggested Walsh take his place.

At the time Walsh was living in a Vancouver flophouse. He was living on $3.05 a week relief and whatever change he could tag from passersby on the streets of Hastings and Cordova.

Walsh had been blacklisted after the On to Ottawa Trek in the summer of 1935. A stamp on his identification papers prohibited him from going into the camps. The only reasons for anyone being barred from the relief camps was that they were either known labour organizers, communists, or both. When he got off the boat in Ocean Falls, Walsh had been worried the company foreman would want to see his papers. The presence of the stamp would have led to his immediate expulsion on the next boat out.

Although Walsh was nicknamed Red because of the colour of his hair, a lot of people said it was because of his political views. They could be forgiven the mistaken impression. Hidden in Walsh's belongings was his Communist Party card, and he always paid the party's five cents a month dues on time. Walsh was also a Relief Camp Workers' Union organizer through and through. If he could, Walsh would organize Ocean Falls. But there was no opening for labour organization there. The pay was too good, the conditions fair, and so much as breathing the word union would lead to immediate dismissal. Like all company towns, Ocean Falls had a covey of stool pigeons who helped the foremen watch for any signs of unionists infiltrating the community. Walsh was actually quite content to work, stash away some cash, and eventually go back to Vancouver with enough money to get by without relief for a while. It was hard to resist the ways of a lifetime, though, and not start talking union at the coffee breaks, during lunch, or in the beer halls over a glass of sour beer.

Walsh had been union since he was eighteen, starting out as a steel-worker. He had travelled up and down the eastern seaboard, slamming up high buildings and punching bridges across rivers. Having grown up in the

Bronx, Walsh had an accent that sounded as if he was chewing on gravel when he spoke.

Since coming to Canada in March 1934, Walsh had been working as a Relief Camp Workers' Union organizer. The union offered no pay and covered few expenses, but it did offer about the only hope there was for single men trying to survive in depression-ridden Canada. The camps were little more than prisons, where, in exchange for an allowance of twenty cents a day and a hardboard bed in a tarpaper shack, the internees built roads with picks, shovels, and wheelbarrows. Although the federal government liked to say entry into the camps was voluntary, failure to volunteer for the camps resulted in a denial of relief benefits. The choice was between the camps or living on the bum. After a few months of riding the trains and begging for work or food, the camps usually started looking good. So the men alternated between the camps and bumming, shifting from one type of existence to the other as the reality of the present circumstance paled in relation to the other's dim prospects.

But eventually the camps and being on the bum all grew stale. Walsh and the others had worked hard organizing the camps, building the union. But he was beginning to wonder if there was any point. The country was dying. A generation of youth was rotting away in the camps. All Prime Minister Richard Bedford "Bloody" Bennett could think of as a solution to the depression was the camps. There was no money for a public works program, like the one the United States had launched in 1933 under the New Deal banner.

By March 1935, there were more than two hundred camps hidden away in the bush of B.C.'s Interior. The camps were run by the Department of National Defence. They held some two thousand men. Men who were getting increasingly angry and restless. Deciding some kind of action had to be taken, the union called a conference in Kamloops. Delegates slipped out of the camps to attend. Everyone agreed the conditions were getting worse, and it was beginning to look as if they could either do something about the situation or spend the rest of their lives stagnating in the camps. They decided to call a strike in April. Work and wages would be the battle cry. If they all went out together, Bennett would have to listen.

After the meeting, Walsh travelled to Princeton. There were camps throughout the Cascade Mountains, and the men were conscripted to build the Hope-Princeton Highway. Walsh rented a little shack in town. To avoid being arrested, as had happened to an earlier organizer, Walsh had to stay

Across Canada, a young generation was rotting away in relief camps—the government's only answer to the devastating unemployment caused by the Great Depression. (VPL 8834)

hidden in the shack. At night, the camp organizers slipped into town for meetings. Some travelled 115 kilometres in the back of supply trucks to attend.

Five days before the strike, Walsh left his shack and headed for the camps. He was pretending to be a prospector, and even carried a prospecting licence. By alternating lifts bummed on the trucks with overland hiking, Walsh reached the top camp the day before the strike was to be called. He slipped into the camp that night and slept in a spare bed.

Next morning he ordered the men out. They commandeered the camp's two trucks, filled them to the brim with their personal effects and food, and then walked out alongside them to Princeton. It took two days, and all along the way the men from the other camps were joining up. By the time they came into Princeton they were 450 strong.

Princeton was a mining town, lousy with bars and brothels. Walsh ordered a picket guard set up around both types of establishments to keep the men out. They needed organization, not a drunken rabble. The men bedded down in the Legion Hall that night. It would be two days before a freight train came through.

The local newspaper branded all the strike leaders communists. Even though the editor was right about Walsh, he stomped into the man's office and threatened to pull the building down around his ears unless he printed a retraction. The next day the paper carried a lamely worded apology, which Walsh read as he boarded the freight bound for Vancouver.

From all over the province the freights rolled into Vancouver and the strikers got off. About fifteen hundred of the two thousand in the camps joined the strike. They marched, they demonstrated, they made sure the city fathers knew they were there. They held an illegal tag day, putting two thousand men on the streets who rattled their tin cans and collected $5,000 in donations from passersby. The money went to buy food and shelter for the men. They occupied the Vancouver Museum, held rallies in the middle of the Spencer's and Woodward's department stores. Then they did the same thing at the Hudson's Bay Company store. Things went sour there when about a hundred club-waving police tried to forcibly evict the strikers. The ensuing riot turned into a bloody battle in Victory Square. The Vancouver police were reinforced by Mounties and provincial police. After that fracas, a wary truce smouldered between the police and the strikers.

It was becoming clear that, after two months, the strike was slowly withering away. About two hundred strikers had already left—hopping freights out of the city. The rest were tired and dispirited. They were in Vancouver, the government was in Ottawa. If anyone was going to listen to the plight of the unemployed, it would have to be the politicians in Ottawa who did the listening and the acting.

It was Stan Lowe who came up with a proposal to turn that realization into action. A lad in the Young Communist League, he stood up at a meeting of the central strike committee held at the Avenue Theatre. Arthur "Slim" Evans was in the chair. Ronald Liversedge, Steward "Paddy" O'Neill, Walsh, and most of the other core organizers were present. Evans was one of the strike leaders and a man who, like Canadian Communist Party general secretary Tim Buck before him, had been imprisoned under the notorious Section 98 law that allowed the government to brand any labour organizing activity as seditious conspiracy. "Comrades, we've got to get militant!" he said, banging one fist into the palm of his opposite hand. This was greeted with a roar of laughter. One fellow said, "What do you think we've been doing, Slim, ever since the strike started?" Evans shrugged. It was either up the ante, he replied, or "admit defeat."

That was when young Lowe stood up. "I think we are through in

The Relief Camp Workers' Union strike emptied the camps and pulled thousands of men into Vancouver, but after several months the marching and demonstrations continued to be ignored by an indifferent federal government. (VPL 8811)

Vancouver," he said, "but I don't think our struggle is finished. All the time since the slave camps were established, we have been trying to get to the people who run the slave camps. Our oldest slogan is a demand for negotiations with the federal government. They won't come to us, so I say, let us go to them. I hereby move that we go to Ottawa, to discuss work and wages with the federal cabinet."

At first they all just gaped at him. The effrontery of it. Silence hung in the room until Evans quietly seconded the motion. Walsh smiled then, thinking about two thousand ragged hobos showing up on Parliament Hill and making the politicians listen to their demands.

They didn't bother with a lot of planning or organizing. Within days they were gone. The first group was about eight hundred strong. They went down to the foot of Gore Street where the Canadian Pacific Railway freight stopped, and they all climbed up on the Seaboard Freight boxcar roofs at 10:30 P.M. on June 3, 1935. Walsh was on that freight. Two other groups boarded different freights the following day. When the last of these

On June 3 and 4, fifteen hundred men left Vancouver on the tops of trains bound for Ottawa. The On to Ottawa Trek had begun. (NAC C24834)

trains rolled out of Vancouver, almost fifteen hundred men were bound for Ottawa. At each departure, several thousand Vancouverites came to cheer the Trekkers on their way. The men were bundled in whatever clothes they had managed to scrounge. Many had taken chalk and scrawled "On to Ottawa" on their coat sleeves.

By the time his train rolled out, Walsh was sceptical about the whole venture. Sitting on the freight train roof, being buffeted by a chill wind, he kept thinking that when they stopped in Kamloops most of the guys would just disappear. It was cold and there was little food or warm clothing. But when they hit Kamloops, instead of people jumping off there were men waiting to get on. The trek organizers took the time then to think things through and send an advance committee ahead to make sure the communities up the track knew there were a lot of hungry men on the way who would need food.

The ride through Rogers Pass from Revelstoke to Golden happened at night. They went over the high mountains and through Connaught Tunnel in inky blackness. Everyone was hellishly worried about this stretch. They worried they would not be able to breathe in the eight-kilometre-long tunnel. Though the smoke from the engines roiled around them in a thick, choking cloud that one man said reminded him of the gas attacks in the Great War, they got through safely. At four in the morning the train rolled into Golden. Walsh was so stiffened by the cold that after climbing off the roof he almost fell down on the gravel siding.

Somehow he managed to stagger along with the other men into the little park fronting the tracks. There, in the emerging dawn light, Walsh saw clusters of people and smelled something delicious. His gaze settled

15

on one woman standing before a claw-footed bathtub beneath which a fire of wooden logs blazed. The tub brimmed with a vast, simmering stew that she stirred with a yard-long stick. The woman's name was Mrs. Sorley and she told Walsh to get the men lined up. "There's some tables there. We'll give them a hot meal," she said.

That was how it went all the way to Regina. Everywhere they stopped more men joined the trek, and the townsfolk came out in force with food, clothing, and whatever else they could spare to help the men survive the journey. Three thousand men were waiting in Winnipeg. The organizers estimated they would be fifty thousand strong by the time they reached Ottawa. For the Trekkers, Regina was just another whistle stop on the way to Parliament Hill.

But Bennett had ordered the police to stop the trek in Regina. Bennett refused to face off against fifty thousand Trekkers in Ottawa. Nor, for that matter, would he allow twenty-five hundred Trekkers from the West to link up with the three thousand waiting in Winnipeg. When the Trekkers arrived in Regina they found the city police heavily reinforced by the RCMP. No freights were allowed to run east from Regina. Without the freights for transport the trek was stalemated.

The Trekkers refused to give up. They bedded down in the Exhibition Grounds, and soon five hundred more men walked out of the nearby Dundurn Relief Camp to join up. There was also one small cause for cautious optimism. Bennett had agreed to bring a delegation of Trekkers to Ottawa for a meeting. Although the organizers distrusted Bennett's intentions, they had to accept the invitation. Negotiation was what the trek was all about and now Bennett was offering a meeting.

The government agreed to provide relief to the Trekkers in Regina until the delegation returned. Eight men climbed onto a passenger train and rode to Ottawa. Evans was the leader. Paddy O'Neill, R. "Doc" Savage, Peter Neilson, Edward Martin, Mike McCauley, John Cosgrove, and Red Walsh were also along. [Of these Walsh, O'Neill, Savage, and Neilsen would go to Spain, as would more than four hundred other Trekkers.]

The meeting took place on Saturday, June 22, at 11:30 A.M. in the prime minister's office in the East Block. Attending were the eight Trekkers, Bennett, and eleven of his cabinet ministers. The floor was covered in a red carpet. Bennett commanded the centre of a large table that glistened with polishing wax. His secretary, H. Oliver, perched at one end with pad and pencil poised. Cabinet ministers flanked Bennett. Walsh and the other Trekkers sat opposite, facing the politicians. Outside, the hallways were bustling with Mounties and reporters.

Bennett wore a swallowtail coat and dotted tie. His shirt collar had little wings on it that greatly amused Walsh. He was sure the prime minister was so stiffly starched his clothes would squeak if he moved. Walsh wore overalls. Nobody had offered any of the Trekkers suits and ties for this momentous occasion of workingmen meeting their betters. Not that Walsh would have worn a suit if it had been offered. Evans also wore overalls, and his underwear showed at the cuffs and throat. The Trekkers sat in the meeting like a bunch of tramps, but they were unbowed.

Bennett asked each man where he had been born. "Ireland," Walsh said. It wasn't true, but Walsh didn't care what he said. If it mattered, his forefathers had come from Galway.

The meeting was a disaster. Evans stated the complaints of the men as succinctly as possible. Bennett hectored and chided, ridiculed and redbaited. Communism, he said, would not be tolerated. "Agitators went into these camps, agitators representing a form of government that we will not tolerate in Canada, agitators representing Communism which we will stamp out in this country with the help of the people of Canada."

Bennett made his statements and filed his accusations. The Trekkers shot back challenges. The meeting broke off with neither side giving a bit.

On his way out, Walsh's eyes were drawn to the corner of the room where heavy drapes covered the windows. There, peeking out from under the drapes, was a big pair of black, polished Mountie boots. He wondered whether the Mounties were hiding behind the drapes to listen in or because Bennett was afraid these representatives of the Red Hordes might jump across the table and start a workers' revolution by seizing the prime minister.

On Sunday evening Evans spoke to a rally at the Rialto Theatre in Ottawa, and then the men caught the train for Regina. On the way back they stopped in Sudbury, Port Arthur, Fort William, Winnipeg, and Brandon. In Winnipeg, they were joined by Tim Buck. Evans and Buck spoke to a huge crowd near the train depot. At 7:00 A.M. on June 26, Walsh and the rest got back to Regina. Walsh learned that about 350 Mounties were now deployed in the city. The following days were increasingly frustrating, as the committee tried to figure out what to do next. A motorcade to take the Trekkers to Winnipeg was proposed, but it failed to materialize and the police made it clear they would allow no convoys to leave Regina.

July 1 dawned hot and tense. Police were everywhere. Regina city officers dressed in blue uniforms and wearing cardboard-lined "bobby" helmets lurked in the shadows and on street corners. Walsh was nervous. Nobody knew what the police were planning, especially the Mounties, but it was obvious something was up.

That evening a rally was planned for Market Square, one of the main focal points of the community. For the first time Evans would report publicly on the meeting with Bennett. In the southeast corner of the square stood the police station and fire department. By late afternoon a truck mounting a public address system had been set up in the square. Because of the heat and the Trekkers' deteriorating morale, only about three hundred Trekkers bothered coming in from the Exhibition Grounds where they had camped since their arrival in Regina. About twelve hundred Regina citizens, including many families, attended the rally.

Walsh went over to the Unemployed Hall two blocks from Market Square to write a press release. For this reason he missed the riot's start.

Evans was up on the truck with George Black, Gerry Winters (whose real name was Tellier and whose brother Lucien was also present), and John Toothill of the Regina Citizens' Emergency Committee. There were a few opening remarks and then Winters made an appeal for funds. He was still talking when a whistle blew from within the middle of the crowd. Then a bunch of RCMP officers rushed up onto the truck and grabbed Black and Evans literally out of midair while they were trying to escape into the crowd. Suddenly police were everywhere trying to arrest people.

The police station's garage doors flew open and out came Regina's finest wielding baseball bats. Earlier some vans had pulled up, and from these poured more RCMP officers. They were all wearing knee-high boots, breeches, brown serge jackets, .45 Colt revolvers in holsters, steel helmets, and swinging twenty-one-inch-long leather batons. The Mounties lined up single file and faced the crowd.

Men started urging the women to grab the children and flee the square, as many of the men themselves were refusing to run. The men, about half Trekkers and half Regina residents, began picking up rocks, pieces of brick, anything they could lay a hand on to throw at the approaching police line.

Just as the police and the men went head to head, someone reported to the Unemployment Hall that the police had attacked the crowd. Walsh pelted out into the street and rushed up to the square. It was full of dust, smoke, and gas from the grenades the police were hurling into the crowd.

Glass was scattered across the street. Walsh saw men scooping up the gas grenades and chucking them back at the police. People were running in every direction and police were running around too. It seemed to Walsh that everyone was running, but nobody was thinking about where he was actually going.

Organize them. That was Walsh's first thought. He jumped up on a garbage can standing against a wall and started shouting for the men to fall back and rally at the Exhibition Grounds. Then someone next to him started yelling, "They're using guns." Walsh heard a succession of sharp popping sounds but rejected the man's claim. He refused to believe the police would fire on civilians. Glaring the wide-eyed man down, Walsh said, "There's no guns. If they are using guns, then they're firing blanks." No sooner were the words out of his mouth than the concrete wall above his head started splintering away and dust poured down Walsh's neck. It dawned on him that the only thing that could be chipping away the wall above his head were bullets.

Walsh got the lid off the garbage can and climbed inside. When the concrete stopped falling, he crawled out and joined the others in the four-hour scrap that followed. The riot ran until midnight when the crowds

On July 1, Regina police and the Royal Canadian Mounted Police attacked a rally in Regina's Market Square, brutally ending all hopes of the On to Ottawa Trek ever reaching its destination. (Sasketchewan Archives Board R-B171-1)

19

finally dispersed. Walsh and the Trekkers fell back on the Exhibition Grounds.

In the morning, Walsh woke up and looked over at the Grain Exchange tower being built across the way. Up on the roof he could see Mounties with rifles and machine guns. Other Mounties with bayonet-fixed rifles were patrolling the Exhibition Grounds perimeter. They wore helmets and were acting as if they were in the middle of a war.

Walsh learned that about 250 people had been injured. At least twenty were in hospital with gunshot wounds, and a police bullet had killed a plainclothes Regina officer. There was a disturbing rumour that there were others—Trekkers—who had been gunned down, their bodies buried in secret graves by the police. Walsh, after seeing the police fire on the crowd, believed the rumour might be true. Nobody knew the identities of all the Trekkers; they came and went of their own free will. Somebody could easily disappear without a trace and nobody would be the wiser.

The riot spelled the end of the trek. It was obvious after the bloody events of the previous day that the government would stop at nothing to prevent the Trekkers continuing to Ottawa. Now all the organizers could do was try to keep the movement together. That meant retreating to Vancouver where they had a strong base of public support. A delegation met with Saskatchewan premier James Gardiner and asked for two trains and sufficient food to get the men back to Vancouver. Gardiner agreed and the federal government went along with the proposal. Prime Minister Bennett tried one gambit, though, to break the organization's strength. He offered free second-class tickets to anyone who wanted to go east, even as far as Halifax. A few accepted the offer, but most opted for Vancouver.

They left a few days later. All the time they remained in Regina the police kept making more arrests. They picked up about one hundred men. Evans, John Cosgrove, and George Black were all arrested and charged under Section 98 with, among other things, inciting a riot. But the charges had no substance and all were eventually freed. Walsh heard there was a warrant out for his arrest, too, but he avoided the police and hopped on the first of the two Vancouver-bound trains.

In Vancouver things were bleak. The longshoremen were out in a long, bitter strike. The people of the city were unable to feed the Trekkers, the longshoremen, and themselves too. Most of the Trekkers bitterly returned to the camps, and the Relief Workers' Union kept them organized, worked to bring the government down in the forthcoming federal election, and used passive resistance to force the camp administrators to improve conditions.

Bennett was swept from office on October 23, 1935, by William Lyon Mackenzie King, who had campaigned with the slogan "King or Chaos." King's Liberal government changed the camps to public works camps with slightly improved pay and conditions. That helped some, but as far as Walsh could see, chaos was winning the day. The depression ground on, slowly wearing away at everyone's spirits.

Walsh finally went to Ocean Falls, where he toted and packed in the boom gang, just escaping for a while from the union, the organization, and the depression. But soon enough the world intervened again on his respite. When Walsh heard the news of the military uprising in Spain he sat down and wrote a note to the Relief Camp Workers' Union office at 52 1/2 Cordova Street asking for information on what plans the union or the Communist Party had to help their Spanish brethren. Clearly the fascist threat in Spain called for a profound demonstration of working-class international solidarity against fascism. If there was anything he could do, Walsh figured he would dump the Ocean Falls job and head directly to the new battlefront.

Not a ruffle of a breeze touched the water of the Bay of Biscay in the early evening of July 19. It was a beautiful summer's evening and from where he stood on the deck of an old Spanish freighter, looking out at the broad mouth of the River Nérvion, Bill Williamson could see the lights of Portugalete slowly approaching. About sixteen kilometres beyond the port community, the denser lights of Bilbao were visible.

Williamson barely believed it possible that he was on the verge of joining the fight to preserve Spanish democracy. A big, rawboned twenty-nine-year-old, Williamson had only three days earlier read about the military uprising and decided to immediately go to Spain.

He had been in England, one leg of a winding, spontaneously planned route that was designed to eventually take him to the Soviet Union. There he hoped to find either Sergei Eisenstein or Eisenstein's brilliant cinematographer Eduard Tisse, whose film *Potemkin* had given Williamson a fascination with photography, and ask either of them to take him on as an apprentice. Williamson had never, of course, met either Eisenstein or Tisse, but he fervently believed that the men who produced films telling of the history of the peoples' struggle to build a workers' paradise would not turn him away.

Williamson was no empty-headed dreamer. He considered his career plan eminently sensible and felt himself capable of bringing it to fruition. For sixteen years Williamson had been on his own, coping in a harsh world. Orphaned soon after his birth in Winnipeg's East Kildonan neighbourhood, Williamson had been taken in by an aunt. When he was thirteen he had struck out on his own, for the woman could no longer support him.

Drifting back and forth across Canada, Williamson had worked every conceivable type of job. In the Maritimes, Quebec, northern Ontario, and on Vancouver Island he had toiled as a faller. He had worked for the railroads, deck-handed on the Great Lake freighters, harvested wheat on prairie farms, wrangled on Alberta ranches, erected steel buildings as a steelworker in southern Ontario, been a longshoreman, and a truck driver.

While he was in the West, Williamson had met some of the old-time Wobblies, the Industrial Workers of the World men who still dreamed of organizing One Big Union. That was when he got involved in the labour movement. A few years later, Williamson joined the Communist Party and helped organize, first for the Marine Workers Industrial League and then the Lumber Workers Industrial Union. As the depression worsened, Williamson had found himself unemployed, idling away in the relief camps in B.C. Soon he was organizing there for the Relief Camp Workers' Union. Then came the On to Ottawa Trek and the bloody Regina riot.

After that Williamson could see no sense in going back to Vancouver and continuing the camp struggle. So he took the offered train ticket east to Winnipeg. In Winnipeg, many of the three thousand men who had been waiting to join the trek were still around. Williamson joined some of them in a new, smaller trek they started toward Ottawa. Several hundred men rode the rails all the way to Kenora, but their numbers kept dwindling with every stop, and soon it was obvious the spirit of the first trek was gone. Williamson switched freights and went instead to Halifax.

There he met Eddie Sarman, an organizer for the Young Communist League. Sarman had just returned from two years in the Soviet Union, where he had been employed as a factory worker. As he talked of his experiences in the Worker's State, Williamson decided to go see for himself. Once he got there, Williamson thought, finding Eisenstein and Tisse would prove manageable.

Getting work on a ship to England had been the first and easiest step toward the Soviet Union. He had gone across the Atlantic as a deck hand on a Norwegian freighter in January 1936. In England, however, finding a

22

job as a deck hand on a ship bound for the Soviet Union had proved an exercise in frustration.

Williamson was still looking for passage when he read of Spain's fascist uprising. Impulsively, he decided the Soviet Union could wait and travelled to Cardiff in the Bristol Channel because several Spanish ships were tied up there in a strike. Williamson sought out the Spanish Merchant-men's Strike Committee, finding them in the nick of time on July 17—one day after the fascist coup attempt had started. The strike committee leader told Williamson the sailors were ending their strike and sailing for home on the coming early morning tide. He could offer Williamson no work, but the sailors would turn a blind eye to any stowaways.

That evening, just as the longshoremen finished loading the ship, Williamson slipped aboard. He sneaked down into the bunkers and buried himself in the coal. Shortly after midnight he felt the ship move. Williamson was bound for Spain.

When the boat was well under way, Williamson surrendered himself to the ship's captain, who decided there was no reason the Canadian should not be allowed to fight for the Spanish Republican cause if he wished. He was given a berth and allowed to move about freely. This meant that, as the ship sailed into Portugalete—which was Latin for galley-slave port—Williamson was able to be topside instead of hidden away in the coal bunkers. What he saw reminded him of the scene from his beloved *Potemkin*, where the naval ship draws into harbour to a tumultuous welcome. On the two-kilometre-long mole protecting the inner harbour a great mass of people were gathered.

As the vessel drew abreast of the breakwater, the captain ordered a huge Republican flag unfurled from the main mast. He was testing the loyalty of the city before committing his ship to the confining inner waters. The crowd, which had been silently watching the approaching vessel, loosed a massive volley of cheers and shouts. Republican flags were flourished and waved wildly over the heads of the people. The captain ordered the ship into the harbour.

No sooner were they tied up than the captain cheerfully turned his stowaway over to a committee of local militia. Williamson explained to the committee that he had come to Spain to join their fight against fascism. When he said this the committee members gave him a great welcome, some of them coming forward to embrace him. They told him he was free to wander Bilbao at will and assigned a "Joven Comunista" militiawoman named Dolores, who spoke passable English, as his guide. Williamson had picked up a smattering of Spanish over the years, so the two were able to converse fairly well.

They walked together through a town transformed by the struggle against fascism. Horn-honking automobiles and trucks raced through the streets. Every vehicle trailed a flag—either the blue, red, and yellow banner of the Republic or the black and red of such anarchist groups as the Federación Anarquista Iberica (FAI) and the Confederación Nacional del Trabajo (CNT). The most prevalent flag by far, however, was the Red flag of the Soviet Union with its distinctive hammer and sickle, which was commonly raised by workers' movements around the world as their banner. Every building was blanketed with flags. Sometimes a building wore the Republican colours, or that of the anarchists, but everywhere he looked were buildings blanketed in a sea of red. He and Dolores wandered into the Plaza Mayor where masses of people danced to music blaring from loud-

Dolores (left), a young Communist militiawoman, took Bill Williamson—Canada's first volunteer to fight for the Spanish Republic—under her wing and they became fast friends. Two months after this photo was taken Dolores was killed in action. (NAC PA194602)

24

speakers. From time to time people would address the crowd, urging them to flock to the defence of the Republic.

It was a Sunday, a day of rejoicing, Dolores told Williamson. A fiesta and dance had been planned, and it was to continue no matter what the fascists tried. The crowd thronged with men and women from the militias. Some wore the blue denim overalls known as a *mono,* but most were identified as militia only by a red armband that bore the hammer and sickle, or by armbands bearing the insignias of either the UGT, CNT, or JSU. The initials meant nothing to Williamson, and Dolores's attempts to explain what differentiated one group from another only left him more puzzled. It was more interesting to watch the people. Many of the dancers had rifles and shotguns slung on their shoulders. Even the militiawomen, wearing bright summer dresses and high-heeled shoes, shouldered shotguns or rifles while they danced.

The army in Bilbao, Dolores told Williamson, had stayed loyal to the Republic. To ensure this remained the case the government had ordered the armouries and gunshops opened and the arms given to the people.

Late that evening, Williamson and the young woman returned to a local palace commandeered by the militia command to serve as regional general headquarters. In the main parlour, a huge antique table was strewn with a half-dozen incessantly ringing phones. Shotguns and rifles were stacked in every available corner. Dolores showed Williamson to an upstairs bedroom where a vast, ornate, four-poster bed with silk sheets and thick covers dominated the centre of the room. She told Williamson he could sleep there.

Having had virtually no sleep for forty-eight hours, Williamson needed little prodding. Although still excited by all he had seen in his first few hours in Spain, he climbed happily into bed. Outside, the cars continued to honk their horns, downstairs the phones rang and went unanswered. Williamson closed his eyes and drifted off to sleep, feeling a perverse pleasure in the certainty that he was the first Canadian to arrive in Spain to fight for what was already known throughout the world as The Cause.

Two

THE CAUSE OF ALL PROGRESSIVE MANKIND

A FEW DAYS AFTER SPEAKING OUT IN SUPPORT OF SPAIN'S RE-
publican government at the Hamilton rally, Joseph Salsberg realized common Canadians were rallying to The Cause. Even as the battle lines in
Spain became more clearly drawn, an organization by which sympathetic
Canadians could send money and aid to the Spanish government had started
to evolve.

That the civil war in Spain was a fight of democratic forces against
fascism might have eluded the majority of North America's mainstream
press, but Salsberg knew this fact obviously had not escaped the average
person. While the American Hearst newspaper chain persisted in portray-
ing the Popular Front as Catholic church burners, killers of priests, rapers
of nuns, and looters of small businesses, it was evident that few people
were duped by these reports. The stories appearing in such Canadian publications as *Maclean's* and *Le Devoir* were equally laden with distortion.

As Salsberg would tell anyone willing to listen, the rebels trying to
topple the freely elected Spanish Popular Front government were led by
General Francisco Franco, a would-be tyrant. The military forces he commanded were being armed and equipped by the Nazis in Germany and by
Mussolini in Italy. There was conclusive evidence that Italian and German
specialized military forces were appearing in Spain. Fascist Portugal had
sent units of its army to support Franco. Even many of Franco's so-called
Nationalist troops were Moorish mercenaries rather than Spaniards.

Given the international character of Franco's forces, it was evident to

Salsberg that the Spanish people fought not only the Nationalists but also a powerful international fascist movement that sought to spread its loathsome ideology throughout the world. Consequently, the war in Spain was not a domestic matter—it was an international war of democracy against fascism.

If the League of Nations failed to recognize this and hesitated to come immediately to Spain's aid, that was its blindness. If Britain and France chose to advocate an immediate embargo on shipments of humanitarian and military aid to the Republic, that was their shame. And if Mackenzie King's government obediently followed Britain's lead in supporting such an embargo, that was its ignominy.

Perhaps the world's democratic governments were willing to let Spain's Republic perish, but their citizens obviously were of a different mind. This was as evident in Canada as anywhere else. In most every Canadian city, people were meeting in labour temples, church halls, and private homes to discuss the developing war in Spain. Most of the meetings were organized by the Canadian League Against War and Fascism.

Since its formation on October 6, 1934, at the Oddfellow's Hall in Toronto, the League had emerged as Canada's major anti-fascist voice. Salsberg admired how the League united people from across the progressive social spectrum into one body. In all, 211 organizations were involved in the League's establishment. The membership of these organizations comprised 337,000 Canadians. Among the member organizations were the Co-operative Commonwealth Federation (CCF); the Trades and Labor Congress; the All-Canadian Congress of Labor; the Federation of Catholic Workers of Canada; the Ex-Service Men's League; such unions as the International Fur Workers' Union, the Cutters' Local Industrial Needle Workers' Union, the Amalgamated Clothing Workers, and the Auto Workers' Union; the Toronto and Edmonton boards of education; and the Workers' Party of Canada. Absent from the list of forming organizations was the Communist Party of Canada, which had been forced underground by federal legislation in 1931. During this period it operated under the cover name of the Workers' Party of Canada. [Among the delegates to the founding conference were Canadians who would rise to prominence in the years to come. Two of these were the poet Dorothy Livesay and the intellectual Stanley Ryerson. Livesay would win two Governor General's Awards in the 1940s and emerge as one of Canada's most respected women writers in the 1960s and 1970s. Ryerson would become a leader in the Communist Party and the author of

various "people's histories" published in the 1960s. Also present was Edward
Cecil Smith, who would eventually command the Mackenzie-Papineau
Battalion in Spain. He represented the Progressive Arts Club and was quoted
in the First Canadian Congress Against War and Fascism Report as saying
that the "intellectual suffers as much as the worker under capitalism and
artists and writers must prostitute their art in order to earn a living."]

Despite the formal absence of the Communist Party from the list of
founding organizations, the League organizers had pointedly acknowledged
Tim Buck's message of good wishes for the League's success. The Communist Party's general secretary sent his message from his cell in Kingston
Penitentiary, where he was serving a five-year sentence after being convicted of a Section 98 charge. In 1932, Buck and seven others associated
with the Communist Party had been convicted and imprisoned within
months of Parliament empowering Prime Minister R.B. Bennett to use the
Relief Act to repress the Communist Party and other left-wing organizations. Bennett demanded this authority so he could maintain "peace, order,
and good government." Not until 1936 was Section 98 repealed and the
Communist Party again allowed to operate more or less openly.

Salsberg vehemently denied that the Canadian people had ever supported the Communist Party's repression. The unrelenting public outcry
against Buck's imprisonment made a lie of Bennett's claim that his actions
were legitimized by public consensus. Finally, unable to ignore public sentiment, Bennett ordered Buck's parole and he was released on November
24, 1934. Eight days later, at Maple Leaf Gardens in Toronto, a standing-
room-only crowd of seventeen thousand people crammed into the arena to
formally welcome Buck home. Another eight thousand stood outside in
the cold of a winter night to show their support. Behind the speakers' podium a massive portrait of Soviet leader Joseph Stalin had been erected.
Although this and other signs openly identified the rally with the Communist Party, the police stayed away and the event proceeded peacefully.

Salsberg had broken with Buck in the 1920s over what he perceived as
a leader-inspired national party drift toward the same cult-of-personality
dogma that was crippling the Soviet party. It was becoming increasingly
difficult to retain a people's movement in the face of ever mushrooming
rumours of Joseph Stalin's tyranny in the Soviet Union. But Salsberg was
careful in the face of the current fascist crisis to never openly criticize the
party leader. Secretly he thought that Buck, like Stalin, was guilty of subli-
mating the advancement of the party and the lower classes in favour of

Seventeen thousand Torontonians packed Maple Leaf Gardens to celebrate Canadian Communist Party leader Tim Buck's release from prison. Another eight thousand stood outside in the winter cold to show their support.
(NAC PA124370)

building his own "cult of personality." To make such a criticism publicly, however, would create internal dissension that could only weaken party solidarity and discipline, so Salsberg held his silence.

That solidarity and discipline was particularly needed now to galvanize Canadian support for the Spanish Republic. Encouraged by the Communist Party and the CCF, the Canadian League Against War and Fascism spawned an organization dedicated exclusively to supporting the Spanish Republic—the Canadian Committee to Aid Spanish Democracy. United Church minister Ben Spence, who was also a prominent Ontario CCFer, was elected the committee's first chairman. Its secretary was Communist Party member Norman Freed. Vice-chairmen were Tim Buck and Ontario CCF leader Graham Spry. Although the CCF and Communist Party provided the fulcrum upon which the committee turned, it counted in its membership virtually all the League's original founding organizations.

Despite the diversity of political views represented in the committee, Buck, A.A. MacLeod, and Salsberg were determined that it play a duel role. The Spanish-related committee would, of course, first provide the conduit for support of the Republic. Just as important, however, it would serve as a means for recruiting people into the Communist Party. So, while working closely with the CCFers in the committee, the Communist leaders also ensured the Communist Party was seen as the dynamic, driving force behind Canada's support for Spain's Popular Front. To this end, the Communist Central Committee, which determined the party's strategic operations, assigned A.A. MacLeod to work full time on the Spanish issue.

One of the first Canadians to return from Spain after the outbreak of the war was Bill Kashtan. He went directly to Adelaide Street and reported to the Communist Central Committee. Kashtan thought himself extraordinarily lucky in being in the right place at the right time. In July, as the fighting broke out, he had been one of seventy young Canadians attending a world congress of youth organizations sponsored by the League of Nations in Geneva. The congress was devoted to uniting "the young generation of the world against the threat of fascism and war arising from the emergence of fascism in Germany." Kashtan attended as a representative of the Young Communist League.

Also attending the conference was a delegation of Spanish communists. A group of these delegates approached Kashtan and asked if he would return to Spain with them as part of a fact-finding mission. Flattered and intrigued, Kashtan immediately agreed. He was joined by two other Canadians—Roy Davis and Margaret Crandall.

In a whirlwind visit the three toured Madrid, Barcelona, and Valencia. They met with youth representatives in each city, discussing with them the progress of the war in Spain. They also witnessed many of the Popular Front's programs of emancipation, such as literacy training for peasants, development of agricultural co-operatives, and the formation of industrial collectives in the cities.

A few days later the young Canadians caught a fast steamer home from Le Havre. After reporting on his visit to the party leadership, Kashtan embarked on a cross-Canada public speaking tour. He urged everyone to support the Spanish people and to lobby the Canadian government to officially recognize and assist the Spanish Republic.

Bill Williamson's first twenty-four hours in Spain left him more determined than ever to do all he could to defeat Franco's fascists. On the morning of July 20, Williamson was taken by his militiawoman guide Dolores to a meeting with the local Communist Party secretary. Although the party secretary warmly welcomed Williamson to Spain, he also pointedly wondered aloud why the Canadian had come.

Williamson replied that he wanted to fight alongside the Spanish comrades resisting the fascists. Having hunted all his life, Williamson hurried on, he had a lot of experience with rifles and shotguns. "I'm a first-class sharpshooter," he concluded.

Sceptical, the secretary ordered Williamson taken to a rifle range set up in the basement of the party headquarters. Williamson hefted an old carbine, checked its ammunition load, adjusted the sights, and methodically punched one perfect shot after another into a target. The duly impressed party secretary enrolled Williamson into the militia column preparing to march to battle. Williamson was happy to hear that his young friend Dolores had also joined the column.

The Columna Stalin, as the militia was named, marched the next day from Bilbao toward San Sebastian, a popular resort community located in the heart of Basque territory. Williamson thought the militia, armed as it was with a diversity of rifles and shotguns, was a glorious, if somewhat ragtag, force. Many of the militia recruits were women, some of these marching off to war in long dresses and high-heeled shoes. Though ill equipped, the column's morale was seemingly unsurpassable. As they marched, the militia soldiers sang patriotic songs. With Dolores at his side, Williamson happily—and much to the amusement of his companions—joined in with his broken Spanish.

For their part, the Spaniards struggled with the pronunciation of Williamson. Dolores started calling him Juan Villa, and the others soon adopted the sobriquet. A few thought this too long, however, and referred to him instead as Pancho. Williamson much preferred Juan Villa.

As the long line marched down dusty roads, Dolores and the others briefed Williamson on the purpose of their advance on San Sebastian. On July 19, two colonels named Carrasco and Vallespín had led the army garrison into rebellion. The Loyola barracks outside the city were in their hands, as were the Maria Cristina Hotel and Gran Casino Club. The hotel was held by a cabal of right-wing sympathizers, the club by rebel civil guards. The barracks were in the hands of the army who were equipped with at least two cannon. Although a strong militia force from the arms centre of Eibar had reinforced the San Sebastian loyalists, they had been unable to overcome the rebel strongholds. The militia had, however, successfully surrounded the rebels, but not before one of the colonels—

Wearing everything from high heels and dresses to the mono of the anarchist movement, women joined the militias in Bilbao and set off to war. Many died in the fighting. (NAC PA195505)

Vallespín—managed to escape the city. He was now rumoured to be in the province of Navarre, which, because of its pro-monarchy and Catholic Carlist population, was a rebel bastion. The Columna Stalin was marching north-east from Bilbao to assist the local militias in smashing the rebel forces besieged in San Sebastián.

The march took the column the better part of two days. Upon their arrival they immediately joined the battle—a nasty street fight with the rebels and the militias firing at each other from behind hastily erected barricades. When the guns stilled for a moment, there were equally heated exchanges of shouted propaganda and pleas as each side tried to convince the other to defect to the opposing cause. After a couple of days of this, many of the soldiers inside the barracks started sneaking out of their positions to surrender to the militias whenever their officers' backs were turned. Most of these defectors were conscripts, who were primarily pro-Republican. If they failed to obey the Nationalist officers' commands, however, they would be shot. So they put on a show of firing their guns and following orders while waiting for an opportunity to defect.

The San Sebastian rebels surrendered on July 28, but by that time the major elements of the militias were already marching south on the city of Vitoria. As Vitoria was just inland from Bilbao, Williamson had a sense of marching in circles. But it was marching with a purpose. He confidently expected Vitoria's rebel forces would crumble as easily as had those in San Sebastian. This seemed even more likely as the column that marched for Vitoria was at least twice the size of that which had left Bilbao. To reflect its new form, and to garner the support of the many non-Communist Basques, the militia's name was changed from Columna Stalin to Columna Perezagua.

Vitoria was the capital of the Basque province of Álava. Unlike San Sebastian, where the rebels had only gained a toehold before being counterattacked by forces loyal to the Republic, the entire city was reportedly in the hands of the rebels. Local opposition had been quashed when the Basque political party—Partido Nacionalista Vasco (PNV)—urged the populace to submit to the military forces to avoid a fratricidal bloodbath in the city streets. The appeal was successful and the popular resistance that had overwhelmed the rebels in Barcelona, San Sebastian, Bilbao, and Madrid failed to materialize in Vitoria.

As the column found itself meeting ever stiffening resistance the closer it came to Vitoria, Williamson realized how little glory there was in war. Just as those in the militia were willing to die for the Republic, it was becoming clear there were Spaniards equally determined to die for the Nationalist cause. No sooner had the column reached the outskirts of Vitoria than they were ordered to break off the assault. The militia quick-marched north again, heading this time for the mountains surrounding the ancient Basque town of Tolosa. From the east, a Nationalist column of about three thousand men was advancing in an attempt to regain control of Tolosa. Whoever took the mountain town would hold a major strategic point in the battle for dominance of the western Basque provinces.

Just as the militia finished digging into its positions on the road before Tolosa, the fascist column launched its assault. For eleven days the Republicans fought bitterly to hold Tolosa against superior numbers. But on August 11, desperately short of ammunition and having suffered many casualties, they were ordered to retreat. Six days later, the militia— now a tattered and bloodied remnant of its former self—stumbled wearily into San Sebastian. They were sent to Playa de la Concha's beaches for a rest.

34

On the first day, Williamson and his comrades delighted in sprawling on the sand and soaking up the sun. On the second day, however, their recuperative sunning was dramatically interrupted when three Spanish naval cruisers steamed into view and opened fire on San Sebastian with a general bombardment. One of the militiamen, who had served in the navy, studied the ships through binoculars and said they were the *España, Almirante Cervera,* and *Velasco.* He also swore that the flashes of guns on the edge of the horizon came from a ship with the distinctive outline of a German pocket battleship. It was too far away, however, to identify which Nazi ship had joined the fray. With shells falling all over the city and near the beach, Williamson and the others dashed for cover.

Luckily everyone had been quick to take shelter in basements. Civilian casualties were consequently quite light—four killed and thirty-eight wounded. The ships returned the next day, however, and the day following that.

On the third day of bombardment, the ships were joined in their attacks on San Sebastian by aerial bombers that continued to raid the city daily thereafter. Although Williamson knew there was little likelihood of anyone proving that the Spanish ships had been supported in their shelling by a German battleship, there was no doubt whatsoever that the bombing raids were the work of foreign fascists. He clearly saw the Italian markings on the flanks of the aircraft.

On August 25, Williamson's militia column, reconstituted to its original size by new enlistees, moved out of their "rest" position in San Sebastian to join a hasty defensive line thrown up before the border town of Irún. Three thousand Republicans were dug into the line. They faced only two thousand fascists, but the enemy was heavily supported by artillery. Virtually every fascist cannon in Spain was reportedly arrayed against them. The fascists also deployed light tanks mounted with machine guns and a small pack of armoured cars. All the fascist armour had *Viva España* scrawled in white chalk on their sides.

The Republicans facing the fascists had no artillery and just a scattering of machine guns for which there was little ammunition. Their rifles were ancient relics, most dating from well before the Great War.

Under a dazzling blue sky, the first day of battle opened with a fierce rebel artillery barrage on the Republican positions. This was followed by a strong infantry advance, supported by the tanks and armoured cars. When the enemy drew close, the militia abandoned its position and allowed the

35

Within weeks of joining the fighting in Spain, Bill Williamson (centre) was a seasoned veteran of several bloody engagements against Franco's fascists.
(NAC PA194603)

fascists to pour into the empty pocket their retreat created. As the fascists started milling about and reorganizing, the militia counterattacked with a bayonet charge. Vicious hand-to-hand fighting ensued until the fascists retreated in confusion.

The following day the same scenario was replayed under an identical hot sun with the same results. In fact, each day, from August 26 to September 2, followed true to form. But slowly the militias had to yield ground as casualties mounted and their supplies drained away. On September 2, from a position in the overlooking mountains, Williamson watched a long line of refugees flee from Irún toward the French frontier. They went up the road toward the International Bridge at Hendaye. People fled on foot, in cars, on horses, in wheelchairs. They took with them farm and domestic animals and an amazing assortment of furniture and paintings. When the refugees were gone and Irún was a virtual ghost town, the fascists came on again in a new assault on September 3.

The militia faced a fascist force of more than fifteen hundred. And now the fascists were no longer outnumbered by the Republicans. The fighting was so close to the border that large clusters of French civilians gathered on the border's verge to witness the battle.

By the end of the day the militia retreated through the city in disorder. It was a retreat that shortly turned into a rout as everyone tried to escape from the closing pincers of the fascist advance. Most fled north into France. But Williamson's militia slipped west toward San Sebastian, remaining intact as a fighting unit. As the militia withdrew from the burning ruin of Irún they carried with them the bodies of their fallen comrades. One of the bodies was that of Dolores, Williamson's first Spanish friend and closest comrade in arms.

In San Sebastian, the militia joined other Republican forces in forging what the leaders called the Iron Ring. But it was a ring built entirely of human flesh; there was no iron or steel. The militia had no tanks and precious little artillery to counter the fascist armour. Further, the Republican forces in the Bay of Biscay's coastal provinces were cut off from the rest of Republican Spain by a deep Nationalist wedge that at its narrowest point was about 250 kilometres deep. The only way they could be resupplied was by ship or by air, neither of which was practicable.

Even as he reached San Sebastian and took up a position within the Iron Ring, Williamson could see the battle for the city was hopeless. Outnumbered, lacking any artillery, constantly bombed by fascist planes, and desperately short of supplies, he doubted they could hold for long. Ten days later the militia retreated again, leaving San Sebastian to its fate without firing so much as a shot. They withdrew to Bilbao. Almost two months to the day from when Williamson had marched east with such high hopes he returned defeated at his starting point.

But there was to be no rest. Immediately, the survivors began reorganizing and building up their ranks in preparation for another campaign. After weeks of retreat, they were going over to the offensive. To Williamson's surprise, his comrades quickly shrugged off the cloak of defeat in favour of the glistening armour of potential victory. Soon, he was infected with their optimistic contagion. Some of his renewed enthusiasm resulted from being assigned to a machine-gun squad. This time when he went into battle it would be with sufficient firepower to do some real damage to the fascists. Perhaps the forthcoming battle might even prove a turning point.

Although the August World Peace Conference in Brussels had been organized to address the challenge of sustaining world peace, everyone was talking about war—the war in Spain to be exact. For his part, Tim Buck spent increasingly more days and nights locked in informal discussions with the Spanish Communist Party's conference delegates. José "Pepe" Diaz, Spanish Communist Party general secretary, kept urging Buck to come to Spain after the conference, rather than returning immediately to Canada. Dolores Ibarruri (known throughout Spain and the world as La Pasionaria or in English, Passion Flower) and French Communist Party member André Marty also pressed him on the point.

Buck was tempted. The conference had been organized by British lord Cecil of Chetworth, one of the principal draftsmen of the League of Nations Covenant in 1919 and an outstanding proponent of world peace. There had been high hopes that it might signal a sea change in the league's continued tolerance of fascist aggression. But it was soon obvious that neither the sixteen-member Canadian delegation nor any of the other five thousand delegates could achieve much with speeches made and resolutions passed. Immediately across the Belgian border the Nazi army was rearming at an alarming pace, the Italians were basking in the glory of their conquest of Abyssinia, and calls from conferences such as this and from diplomats like Lord Chetworth for the League of Nations to take collective action to contain the muscle-flexing of the fascists were being ignored.

So why not go to Spain and see firsthand what was happening there? Buck, who had heard the report from young Bill Kashtan a month earlier, was intrigued by the chance to see what might actually be an emerging people's government. He had, after all, devoted most of his adult life to making this a reality in Canada. He had been involved in left-wing politics almost since the day he arrived in Canada from Britain in 1910 at the age of nineteen. Although he earned his living as a machinist, Buck spent as much time living and breathing politics as working for wages. In 1921, he and a few others had gathered in a small barn near Guelph and formed the Communist Party of Canada. Buck became the chief architect of its trade-union policies. In 1929, he was elected the party's general secretary, a post he had held continuously ever since.

Tim Buck (far left) was closely wedded to the Soviet-directed international Communist movement. This picture was taken in Russia following the Eighth Plenum of the Comintern in 1927. Buck and Earl Browder, general secretary of the American Communist Party (far right) would be instrumental in raising the volunteer forces from Canada and the United States that joined the International Brigades in Spain. (NAC PA195506)

When the conference ended, Buck and his fellow Canadian Communist delegate A.A. MacLeod accepted the Spanish invitation to return with them to Spain. Communist delegates from several other countries also joined the trip. The group's first stop was Madrid, where they toured the battlefront near the city. Buck was impressed by all he saw. Most of all he noted with some surprise that the struggle in Spain against fascism was not exclusively a Communist effort. It seemed a true expression of the common Spaniard who, regardless of political affiliation or sympathy, was determined to defeat the uprising by the fascist rebel forces. Buck saw peasants standing shoulder to shoulder in the trenches around Madrid with petty bourgeoisie, professionals, and university lecturers. He also witnessed German and Italian planes bombing parts of Madrid.

Diaz, Ibarruri, and Marty arranged for Buck to have a personal meeting with Republican president Manuel Azáña and the prime minister, José Giral. Both stressed the importance of the outside world understanding the international significance of Spain's struggle. Only days after the meeting Giral resigned his post, however, and in the flurry of allegation and counter-allegation over incompetence, Buck also gained insight into how difficult it was for the government to hold the shaky alliance of liberals, socialists, anarchists, Trotskyites, communists, and others together in a united effort. The Popular Front was standing firm against fascism, but it had a lot of small cracks in its foundation that could turn into vast fissures at any time.

While Buck was visiting the Villaverde-Entrevias column, which was entrenched on the outskirts of Madrid and under the command of Enrique Lister, he received an invitation from José Diaz to attend a meeting at the railway town of Aranjuez, just south of Madrid. Many of the people who were in the country representing foreign organizations were invited. The purpose of the meeting, Diaz told them, was to examine ways and means of increasing foreign assistance to the Republic. It was increasingly obvious that unless the Republic received massive foreign aid there was a good chance the fascists would overpower them through sheer superiority of military hardware and numbers.

Although the Soviet Union had started shipping large amounts of equipment to Spain, these counted as little compared to the largesse Germany and Italy were showering upon Franco. The fascists had also been bolstered by elite German armour and air units, and by entire divisions of the Italian army. Even as Buck and the others were meeting, Mussolini broadcast an ominous threat. To Spain, the dictator said, ". . . I raise a large olive branch. This olive branch rises from an immense forest; it is a forest of eight million bayonets, well sharpened." Was Mussolini pledging to commit the entire Italian army? Although probably the kind of grand-standing for which Mussolini was famous, it was still worrisome. How could the Republic match the numbers of Italian troops already deploying in Spain?

Diaz proposed raising an international force of volunteers. Already, he said, many foreigners fought in Spanish units. The majority of these were serving in small units organized by nationality and attached to the Communist Party of Spain's Quinto Regimento. Many of these volunteers had been fighting beside the Spanish since the war broke out in Barcelona. They had been athletes attending a People's Olympics held there as a symbolic alternative for those leftist athletes who refused to attend the official Olympics hosted by Germany that same summer in Berlin. Others, especially Italian and German volunteers, had come to Spain to join in a fight they hoped would be the first step down the road to defeating the fascist governments ruling their own countries.

The conference quickly approved organizing international volunteers as an independent entity instead of grafting them to existing units. The new volunteer force would be called the International Brigades. The brigades would be built around the core of foreign volunteers serving in the Quinto Regimento. Optimistically a maximum strength of between twenty and twenty-five thousand was predicted.

When asked how many Canadians might volunteer, Buck hesitated and then tentatively suggested it might be possible to recruit 250. Diaz and the others were impressed. If every country represented by the meeting, they said, could enlist a similar per capita ratio of their population as the Canadians were pledging the force would be very effective indeed. Buck silently hoped he could deliver the promised number.

After the meeting, Diaz, Ibarruri, and Marty travelled to Paris and on to Moscow to start the organization of the brigades on a world scale. Buck and MacLeod also went to Paris, where they lingered a few days to check on developments within the French Communist Party. Buck also wrote a brief leaflet entitled "Defend Democracy in Spain, Tim Buck's Message from the War Front," to distribute upon his return to Canada. The two then boarded a ship in Le Havre bound for New York. From New York they caught a train to Toronto. At the Black Rock border crossing they were approached by a reporter from the *Toronto Daily Star*, who told Buck Spain was already a major issue throughout Canada. Buck was amazed. Despite the work he knew that Kashtan and the Committee to Aid Spanish Democracy were doing, he had expected few people to already know or care.

Buck gave the reporter an exclusive interview on his experiences in Spain because the *Daily Star* was one of the few large newspapers in Canada with a liberal, rather than deeply conservative, reputation. He wanted the initial splash of publicity to be as favourable and extensive as possible and this seemed the best route to ensure that result.

He then met with the Communist Party Central Committee in Toronto and briefed them on the need to raise a volunteer force. They immediately endorsed the plan. A few days later the party called a public rally at Toronto's Mutual Street Arena. The place was packed. After Buck finished speaking, people started coming forward to inquire about volunteering. Although he had been back in Canada for less than a week, Buck could see the campaign for volunteers was up and running. The only question now was who would come forward?

Three

CRUEL AND
IRREVERSIBLE DECISIONS

SHOULD HE GO TO SPAIN? ON A CHILL MONTREAL EVENING IN
early October, forty-six-year-old Dr. Norman Bethune struggled with this
question. That afternoon a spokesman for the Committee to Aid Spanish
Democracy had visited him at Sacré Coeur Hospital, where Bethune held
the post of chief of thoracic surgery. The committee, the man said, was
sending a medical unit to Madrid, the Spanish capital. Already, Henning
Sorenson, a young Danish-Canadian, was there paving the way for the team's
arrival. The medical unit vitally needed the leadership of a versatile and
talented surgeon. Would Bethune take the job? Bethune must understand,
of course, that he would receive no salary—the unit would be made up
entirely of volunteers.

That the committee should want him over all other Canadian physicians came as no surprise to Bethune. He was, after all, the renegade left-
wing doctor who advocated socialized medical care. In April 1936, Bethune
had stunned the Canadian medical profession by delivering a paper to the
Montreal Medico-Chirurgical (Surgical Medicine) Society entitled "Take the
Profit Out of Medicine."

"Twenty-five years ago it was thought contemptible to be called a
socialist," Bethune had told the society's members. "Today it is ridiculous
not to be one." He argued that Canada must implement a medical system
that would emulate the best features of the Soviet Union's universalized
healthcare.

During the summer of 1935, while attending the International Physi-

43

ological Congress in Leningrad, Bethune had personally witnessed the workings of the Soviet Union's health system. He had toured hospitals and sanitariums, keenly studying the way in which the Soviets treated tuberculosis. Bethune was greatly impressed. Starting virtually from scratch following the 1917–1922 revolution, the Soviet government had constructed the world's most sophisticated universalized healthcare system— a system where all received the same quality of medical care despite individual financial means.

Proof of the system's strength could be found in the incidences of tuberculosis in the Soviet Union, which had been slashed by 50 percent. As one of Canada's leading experts on tuberculin treatment, Bethune was surprised to see many treatment and diagnostic procedures he had unsuccessfully advocated in Canada considered routine by Soviet physicians. The sanitariums were far more advanced in terms of medical technology and provision of patient comfort than anything offered at home.

Back in Montreal, Bethune presented another talk on December 20, 1935, to the Montreal Medico-Chirurgical Society about his impressions of Soviet healthcare. He noted that general Canadian wisdom held that the Soviet Union's Communist government posed an international threat to law, order, and the world's democratic governments. Canada had no formal relations with the Soviet Union because the Canadian government maintained the Soviet government had illegally overthrown the Imperial Czar. Such a position, Bethune said, was ludicrously indefensible. What was happening in the Soviet Union was the formation of a government and society that reflected the desires and wishes of the Russian people. And, yes, for the will of the people to be expressed in Russia, it had been necessary to spill blood.

He likened Russia's revolution to a woman giving birth. Russia, Bethune said, was going through its delivery, and all that non-Russians found distasteful or threatening about the Soviet system was similar to the bloody mess that accompanied any birth.

It is this mess . . . which affronts the eyes and elevates the noses of those timid male and female virgins suffering from frigid sterility of the soul, who lack the imagination to see behind the blood the significance of birth. Creation is not and never has been a genteel gesture. It is rude, violent and revolutionary. But to those courageous hearts who believe in the unlimited future of man, his divine destiny which lies in his own hands to make of it what he will, Russia presents today the most exciting spectacle of the evolutionary, emergent and heroic spirit of man which has appeared on this earth since the Reformation.

Having publicly declared his new political faith, Bethune followed words with action by joining the Communist Party of Canada.

His conversion to communism was as much motivated by events in Canada as by his experiences in the Soviet Union. In March 1935, he had been caught by surprise in a police attack on a group of peaceful demonstrators. As the police moved in on the crowd of several thousand, a white banner bearing the words: "Milk for our Children! Bread for our Wives! Jobs, not Breadlines!" had caught Bethune's eye. Then all hell had broken loose as the police crashed into the crowd. Grabbing his medical bag from his car, Bethune threw himself into the fray, offering what assistance he could to the many demonstrators injured by the policemen's swinging clubs and the hooves of their horses.

The day after the police attack, Bethune walked into the Montreal Unemployed Association headquarters and pledged to provide free medical care to anyone who was poor and sick. Since then Bethune had worked tirelessly in Montreal's slums. He had also opened the Children's Art School of Montreal in his home. The first such project in Canada, the school accepted only children from the slums. Bethune paid all the school's expenses from his own pocket. When he visited the neighbourhoods where these children lived, he often found himself called Comrade Bethune instead of the customary Dr. Bethune. "It is an honourable title," he confided to his diary. "I feel I have set my feet on a new road. Where will it lead?"

Was Spain the next stop on that new road? Certainly the committee's proposal corresponded with his own growing interest in the Spanish conflict. Only a few weeks earlier he had started gathering background material on the Spanish war. Each day he gleaned the newspaper for news. Bethune was deeply sickened by the stories of the fascist air raids on Madrid. These indiscriminate attacks against a civilian populace, he thought, were the most blatant example of how far international fascism would go to achieve world domination. "They've begun in Germany, in Japan, now in Spain, and they're coming out in the open everywhere. If we don't stop them in Spain while we still can, they'll turn the world into a slaughterhouse," he lectured friends.

As he wrestled with the decision over whether to go to Spain, his home still bore the marks of an attack by Canadian fascists. A couple of weeks earlier, Bethune had come home to find his apartment badly vandalized. The furniture had been broken, his self-made collection of finely sculpted heads had all been smashed, and the slum children's paintings were torn into strips and strewn across the floor. On the walls of every room fresh paint dribbled down from black swastikas.

The police had come, wryly suggested he might have some personal enemies, and gone. They ignored his request that they investigate by interviewing some of the self-declared fascist legionnaires who acted as bully boys for Adrien Arcand's National Social Christian Party. There was no shortage of these thugs on the streets, strutting about in their paramilitary blue shirt uniforms and gathering in meeting halls—where the walls were plastered with swastika flags—to listen to Arcand's anti-Semitic and anti-socialist rantings. All over Montreal they were systematically smashing up Jewish shops and attacking leftist meetings. If the unemployed tried to hold a demonstration, the Montreal police were always on hand to wade in with truncheons and boots. But when the fascists marched they stood by and nodded their approval. As far as Bethune could see, the Quebec government and the police were in bed with the fascists. So, perhaps, was the federal government.

If the fascists won in Spain, their victory would only embolden Canada's fascists. Fascism was an insanity, he thought, an insanity spreading too quickly. Was it not the duty of all sane people everywhere to combat this sickness?

Could he do that most effectively in Spain? That was the question. Bethune scribbled a note to himself as he struggled with the decision. "I have to decide whether I go to Spain. I am surprised, honored—and perplexed. Am I the right person? Am I ready? Yesterday's answers seem to prepare new questions for today. And tomorrow—what? The times impose cruel and irreversible decisions on us!"

At last, in the night's darkest hours, Bethune decided. He would go. The decision behind him, Bethune wrote letters of resignation from his various medical positions. He then drafted a will and issued instructions that until the art school was able to acquire public funding it should be funded with money drawn from his personal accounts. He notified the committee that he could depart for Spain within three weeks.

The last thing he wrote that night was a short poem entitled "Red Moon Over Spain."

And this same pallid moon tonight,
Which rides so quiet, clear and high,
The mirror of our pale and troubled gaze,
Raised to a cool Canadian sky.

Above the shattered Spanish mountain tops
Last night, rose low and wild and red,
Reflecting back from her illumined shield
The blood-bespattered faces of the dead.

To that pale disc we raise our clenched fists
And to those nameless dead, our vows renew:
'Comrades, who fought for freedom and the future world
Who died for us—we will remember you.'

A fire! That is how William Krehm visualized it, a fire raging inside his head—the incendiary blaze of ideas. He was twenty-two years old, a young Canadian in Spain. Here, in Barcelona, Krehm was certain he lived on the cusp of a new political millennium soon to gloriously transform the world.

Krehm had come to Spain in October after first spending five days in Brussels at a conference of international leftist groups. These groups had broken away from the Soviet-backed Communist Party and the mainstream socialist parties because the old parties were frozen, rigid, corrupt, as equally incapable of imagination as their capitalist predecessors. In Brussels, the discussion had focussed on sustaining leftist purity. Debaters had wrestled with the problem of how to realize through political and social action the ideal vision of a classless society in which all people were truly equal. The discussions were heady, but all rather disappointingly inconclusive.

It was that very lack of conclusiveness that prompted Krehm's trip to Spain. In Spain, he thought, the Popular Front was acting—doing exactly what the conference delegates had only discussed. A follow-on conference to the one in Brussels was being planned for Barcelona, which helped Krehm feel confident that his decision was the correct one.

Krehm was impoverished. To shuttle back and forth between Canada and Europe for these conferences was beyond both his personal means and that of the cash-strapped political organization to which he belonged. The trouble with being on the extreme outer edge of the leftist spectrum, Krehm ruefully noted, was it meant self-imposed isolation. Raising funds was very difficult for the League for a Revolutionary Workers' Party, which was a splinter group from the too-conservative Trotskyists, who had themselves splintered off the Communist Party. In joining the league, Krehm had drifted as far left as was possible in Canada.

He had become involved in communist politics at university, where the pall of the depression hung just as heavily over the heads of the students as it did over the rest of the nation. The depression, Krehm sensed, had demoralized Canadians to the very marrow of their bones. At the university, the students pondered the utility in attaining an education. What use was an education when there were no jobs to be found and no reason to hope the depression would ever end? Eventually the depression struck Krehm directly when his parents could no longer afford his university tuition and he had to drop out. Krehm found a niche for himself as a seldom paid journalist writing for various left-wing publications. He wrote about leftist ideology, the inertia of the federal government in fighting the depression, and the spectre presented by the rising international fascist movement.

Fascism deeply worried Krehm. In Italy, Germany, even on the streets of Toronto, the fascists marched. Although Krehm was a non-practising Jew, he found it hard not to consider his Jewish racial origins and wonder when he might become a target for fascist violence.

Out of the eastern horizon that was occupied by the Soviet Union, however, shone forth a promising rosy dawn—the light of communism, blinding and dazzling in its brilliance. Krehm saw the light and believed. He basked in the sunshine of leftist politics. Soon, however, he rejected the Communist Party. It seemed closely wedded to the Soviet Union, and Krehm had learned of the gulags, of the bloody purges of hordes of people charged with harbouring anti-Stalinist attitudes, and of the repression and persecution of Leon Trotsky and his followers.

Krehm admired the Trotskyites. Their belief that for communism to succeed as an economic system it had to be applied on a worldwide scale made sense. That this entailed the necessity of permanent international revolution until communism won the field did too. Stalin's concentration on transforming the Soviet Union into an international power, rather than spreading the flames of revolution throughout the world, seemed wrongheaded. That strategy seemed to create merely another totalitarian regime that, although different in name, substantially mirrored the fascist states of Germany and Italy.

When the Brussels conference was announced, the league members decided that the zealot and journalist Krehm should be their single delegate. The party leadership delved into its operating budget of a few hundred dollars and found fifty dollars to spare for Krehm's passage by freighter to Le Havre. Krehm and a young American from a related party made the voyage together.

The American returned to North America a few days after the two of them arrived in Spain. Krehm, convinced he was witnessing the unfolding of a significant chapter in world history, refused the young man's entreaties that he should also return home.

Spain was where the future was unfolding and he must stay. Catalonia province and its capital Barcelona were the heartland of Spanish anarchism. Walking the streets of the city, Krehm thought himself in the middle of a lyrical springlike affair where everything was coming to pass that a radical had ever dreamed possible. In Barcelona there was no depression; the ills of capitalism seemed cured. There was also no evidence of the heavy-handed tyranny of Soviet-style communism or Nazi-like fascism. Drifting on the air, like the scent of blossoms in spring, was the promise of a true workers' democracy bursting into full bloom. For Krehm, it was utterly magical.

The city's industries were all being run by the workers—by spontaneously organized anarchist co-operatives. The tall white skyscraper of the telephone exchange, the fulcrum of the fighting between the anarchists and fascists in July, was operated by the anarchists. Anarchist militias departed daily for the front, men and women marching shoulder to shoulder off to war. The city buses were painted in the bold anarchist colours of black and red. In the barber shops—long a bastion of Catalonian anarchist organization—signs emphatically declared that barbers were no longer slaves but the equals of their customers. The most common attire seen on the street was the *mono,* the blue overalls that were the uniform of anarchist solidarity. There was nary a business suit to be seen. Indeed, to wear such an outfit was to risk your life. The bourgeoisie were finished in Barcelona, as were the priests, the nobility, and the elegantly attired mistresses of the rich. Even the prostitutes were being urged to abandon their profession and renounce the sale of their bodies for money.

Krehm was drawn to the anarchist philosophy and particularly to the Partido Obrero de Unificación Marxista, popularly known by its acronym POUM. One of POUM's founders was Andrés Nin, who had once served as Trotsky's private secretary. Despite this association with Trotsky, Krehm soon realized that POUM was not inherently Trotskyist. It did, however, advocate continuous socialist revolution and the dictatorship of the proletariat, which included virtually all mankind and so when triumphant must yield the ultimate form of democracy as an enlightened populace determined its own political and social destiny. How these philosophical ideals would evolve in practice was only vaguely hinted at by either Trotsky or the POUMists. Given the fall of the Soviet model into Stalin's strongman dictatorship, the path to proletarian democracy was rife with perilous turning points. Nevertheless, Krehm still believed any intelligent, progressive thinker had to embrace these ideals.

Counting only about thirty thousand members, POUM was also small when compared to the large Anarcho-Syndicalist parties, such as the Confederación Nacional del Trabajo (CNT), that dominated Catalonian politics. POUM's very smallness drew Krehm. Being internationalist in focus, the POUM leadership welcomed Krehm into the party's ranks and gave him the opportunity to do meaningful work.

He prepared radio broadcasts and articles for use in POUM's English-language publication, which was edited by an American socialist named Charles Hoar. Krehm also sent occasional articles home to a small leftist publication.

Several non-Spaniards working with POUM were housed together in a large mansion that POUM had expropriated from a wealthy German. Among those living in the mansion with Krehm were Americans, Greeks, and Albanians. Nobody received a salary. Krehm and the other international POUMists were granted cafeteria privileges at a POUM-operated hotel. In the Barcelona of fall 1936, money was of little relevance. Krehm always had enough to eat, wine was plentiful, he had clothing, a place to rest, and a purpose. What did money matter in this new society?

Hans Ibing knew well what it was like to live without money. It was that knowledge that gave him the strength to work twelve-hour days for six days a week, every week, for twenty cents an hour. Ibing considered himself fortunate to have a job, even one he hated, so he seldom complained. Instead, he rose early—long before dawn—went to his truck, and set out on his delivery rounds through the streets of Winnipeg. The merchant who employed him expected punctuality, so Ibing made a point of always being early. There was a long line of unemployed men outside Winnipeg's unemployment hall who would gladly replace him were he not to do his job well. In the late fall of 1936, the mornings were cold, snow blew down the streets, and the darkness seemed to hang over the city for hours before dawn lighted up Ibing's days.

The depression blanketed Canada, but it was a cloak that pressed down less suffocatingly upon this country than had been the case in his native Germany. Born in the Rhineland in 1908, Ibing had come to Canada in 1930 at the age of twenty-two.

He had been twice an outsider in Germany—a Protestant in a Catholic region, and a boy with an outspoken socialist for a father. Both had led to young Ibing being viciously bullied in the schoolyards. At the end of the Great War, things worsened when his father's politics got him arrested by the French occupation forces. The French forcibly evicted the family from their home, expelling them from the Rhineland to unoccupied Germany.

These experiences gave Ibing a deep sense of sympathy for life's underdogs. It was easy to identify with your fellows. The poverty and suffering of Germany during the 1920s left Ibing stunned by the sheer immensity of the misery, desperation, and degradation people experienced. Out of the fertile soil of Germany's tragic suffering grew the evil of fascism. Ibing saw the brownshirts in action and thought, "This is spawning degenerates; there can be no good in this." Ibing watched the fascists evolve into the Nazi party, saw the party begin its march to power. In 1930, sick at heart at the hopeless environment of Germany, Ibing emigrated to Canada. He unwittingly slipped in just under the wire. An order-in-council issued by Prime Minister Bennett in August stopped all further immigration into the country.

After being held in the immigration halls at Halifax for several days, during which he and his fellow passengers on the ship were grilled about their political affiliations and leanings, Ibing was released. The immigration officials said he would have been turned back had the ship not already sailed from Germany before the order-in-council was passed.

From Halifax, Ibing travelled west to Manitoba, working first on combine crews before finding the job as a Winnipeg truck driver. Since landing that job he had settled into the city's German district and come to know other German workers who had encouraged him to join the German Workers and Farmers League. From this loosely socialist organization Ibing had drifted further left in his political orientation, finally joining the Communist Party.

By the fall of 1936, Ibing was a veteran Communist who jokingly told

51

friends he had only recently stopped being "holier than the Pope" about his leftist beliefs. But his anti-fascist stance was ardently held, and his concerns about the fate of Spain increased daily.

When Ibing heard that the Committee to Aid Spanish Democracy was seeking volunteers to serve in a new pro-Republican International Brigade, he knew he had to go. The Republic "must be supported by every honest anti-fascist," he told his German friends, "and that means me too."

Decision made, Ibing went to his employer and handed over the keys to the truck, telling him tersely that he quit. At Winnipeg's Communist Party office, Ibing demanded help in getting to Spain. The office workers agreed to make the arrangements. Ibing went home and waited.

Twenty-year-old Thomas Beckett had also decided that he must go to Spain. The young chairman of the Bedford Park Unit of the Eglinton Constituency's Co-operative Commonwealth Federation Youth Movement believed that unless fascism was stomped out in Spain it would soon come to Canada. Indeed, Beckett felt that in many ways Canada was already a fascist state.

Beckett kept a small notebook in which he recorded random thoughts and impressions, which usually assumed a political shape. For all his thinking life it seemed the depression had been there, becoming more monstrous and threatening with each passing year.

In his notebook, Beckett considered the question of "how the Bourgeoisie get out of a crisis." He determined there were seven strategies bourgeois politicians historically followed. Beyond these, there was nothing the bourgeoisie could do that would resolve an economic or social crisis and still protect their privileged status. A bourgeois government's solutions entailed either destroying surplus commodities, seeking foreign markets, lowering prices, exhausting workers' savings, opening new colonies and territories to exploitation, developing new, better techniques and machinery, or starting a war. In the past all these strategies had been used, often in some form of combination, to escape an economic crisis. Beckett believed the Great War had ultimately been the last step in heading off a looming depression by plunging the world into catastrophic war.

Today, however, the crisis would not abate despite the bourgeoisie's best efforts. "This is not a cyclic crisis," he wrote, "but a general capitalist crisis." There was, then, no viable means by which the capitalist system could escape this unique depression. Except, perhaps, through war. Beckett was not convinced that the war option had been properly exploited yet.

Twenty-year-old Thomas Beckett believed there was no finer thing he could do than go to Spain and join the International Brigades.
(NAC PA194600)

True, there had been the invasion of Abyssinia and other small engagements throughout the 1920s and 1930s, but did these constitute the degree of war necessary to get the industrial engine moving again? Perhaps Spain was the required war or, just as likely, a war in Spain might be the beginning of a larger conflagration—one that would rival the Great War in its scope and ability to get the giant capitalist engine up and running again. The more Beckett considered the matter, the more this latter possibility efficaciously suited the bourgeoisie's goal of sustaining its privileged position.

The problem then was determining how to stop capitalism from triumphing behind the guise of the Spanish fascists. Demonstrations here in Canada were of little effect. After the breaking up of the On to Ottawa Trek, Beckett had joined hundreds of other young people from Ontario in going to Ottawa and demonstrating before the Parliament Buildings. They had demanded reforms, demanded the changes unsuccessfully sought earlier by the Trekkers. They had been ignored, even by the police, who had not bothered to break up the rally. In the end, the young people peacefully trailed away home like the good Canadians they mostly were.

Beckett had gone to Ottawa brimming with enthusiasm. In his notebook he had written:

The city of political babbling and startling promises is going to see something that has not been seen since 1837–38, when William Lyon Mackenzie, the progressive, exposed and fought against the parasites of that period. Instead of this there is to be the voice of vigorous, demanding youth who want not promises but action. And they are going to get it! This voice of youth is the start of the energetic youth movement that is at heart dissatisfied with what degenerate capitalism has to offer to young people and demands changes. . . . Capitalism has brought misery to the people, young and old. And against capitalism the fight will be waged, ever-growing and increasing.

With the demonstration's failure, Beckett's optimistic dreams had been dashed. He returned to his Toronto suburbs and resumed the endless process of CCF organizing. Increasingly, however, it seemed more was required of a young man who wanted to bring about real social change. Now the opportunity to do something more momentous than organizing appeared to be at hand. There was the call for volunteers to fight in Spain.

Beckett could think of no finer thing to do, so he volunteered. All across Canada volunteers were coming forward. Nobody had ever expected so many volunteers. People like Tim Buck, A. A. MacLeod, Joseph Salsberg, and the Methodist social activist Salem Bland were said to be awestruck by the enthusiastic response to their call to arms.

Since the morning of July 18, 1936, when Lionel Edwards had first read of the fascist uprising in Spain, the war had obsessed him. There was little else to occupy his mind. Edwards, an accountant by trade, was unemployed, so he had lots of time to think. It was apparent to Edwards that in the midst of this depression, training mattered far less than connections. Although born in Alberta and acquainted with many people, Edwards obviously moved in the wrong part of Calgary's social strata.

Edwards thought it ridiculous that Canada, so endowed with rich natural resources, should have 1.3 million of its 11.5 million citizens on relief. How could the fact that one out of every nine Canadians was on relief be tolerated? Why did the government allow it? Why did decent people—whether capitalists or Christians—allow this to continue? It was horrifying to see so many people in need and nobody caring. Edwards cared. He desperately wished to help bring about change.

But the On to Ottawa Trek had been smashed. Having joined the trek in Calgary, Edwards had been there in Regina when the police waded in with their clubs and guns. He believed the chance to effect peaceful change in Canada ended that day in Regina's battered Market Square. After July 1, 1935, it was obvious that the government would repress the people by every means at its disposal, including police violence.

If Edwards could do nothing to help bring about change in Canada, the same was not true for Spain. The very fate of the world hung in the balance there. As the weeks passed and the war worsened, as the fascists closed on Madrid, Edwards followed the news with horrified fascination.

Occasionally he read reports about Emil Kléber, an Austrian who claimed to be a naturalized Canadian and was being called "the defender of Madrid." Wedded to the stories of Kléber was always the claim that Madrid would be the "tomb of fascism." Kléber was in command of what had been designated the XIth International Brigade. That brigade, organized as three battalions totalling nineteen hundred men, had marched into Madrid at the moment of decision on November 8, when the city was on the verge of being overrun by the fascist juggernaut. Kléber flung the XIth Brigade—composed of German, French, Belgian, Polish, and British volunteers—into the battle. When the fighting within the buildings and gardens of Madrid's beautiful and famous University City became hand to hand, bayonet to bayonet, Kléber responded to a plea for reinforcements by sending a terse one-word order that read: "Resist—K." The XIth resisted. By the dawn of July 9, one of the companies under Kléber's command had only six men left alive, but it had held its position.

The XIth International Brigade was shredded in the fighting, nine hundred of its total complement being either killed or wounded. The adjoining XVth International Brigade was reduced from fifteen hundred to eight hundred. The Internationals had seen their first action and suffered glorious casualties. Or so it seemed to a young man in Calgary. Edwards read of the Internationals fighting in Madrid and wanted desperately to be at their side, no matter the risks. Being an accountant, he could accurately calculate the odds. Given the casualty rates suffered in the Madrid fighting, the odds of a volunteer returning to Canada in one piece were dismal.

Not that poor odds in any way dissuaded Edwards from his determination to join the anti-fascist stand that progressive people from around the world were making in Spain. His motivation for going to Spain was not entirely political. Edwards confessed to himself that the war held the promise of adventure, possibly even romance. It was ultimately a chance to act, to do something decisive, rather than linger in Calgary hoping for the depression to end and employment to come his way.

Having made his decision to go to Spain, the first thing Edwards did was secure a passport. By the fall he had that precious document in hand, but found himself stumped over how to volunteer for the Canadian force that was, according to rumour, being organized. Edwards was not a

55

Communist Party member and had little connection with the left-wing movement in Calgary. He was still trying to figure out how to establish contact with the appropriate political elements when he heard that three prominent Spaniards were touring Canada on behalf of the Republican cause. They were Isabella Palencia, a delegate to the League of Nations and ambassador-elect to Sweden, Marcelino Domingo, former minister of education and leader of the Left Republican Party of Spain, and Rev. Father Luis Sarasola, a Catholic priest, scholar, and historian. Calgary was to be one of their last stops.

The delegation had been plagued with problems during its tour of eastern Canada. At its first speaking engagement in Montreal, it had faced the full wrath of Canadian fascist fury. Originally scheduled to speak at the Mount Royal Arena, the Spanish delegation and its hosts from the Committee to Aid Spanish Democracy were blocked from entering the building by hordes of blue-shirted fascists. The members of the National Social Christian Party had been supported by students from the city's French-Canadian universities and colleges, who had responded to the virulent decrees issued by French-Canadian clerics and printed in *Le Devoir* and *L'Action Nationale*. The clerics alleged that the Republicans in Spain were committing atrocities against the Catholic Church. With the fascist and student groups thronging outside the arena, the provincial and municipal governments acted immediately by cancelling the permit allowing the Spanish delegation to speak.

The committee responded by shifting the meeting to the McGill Student Union Building on Sherbrooke Avenue, near University Street. For this meeting, the doors of the building were guarded by members of the Scarlet Key Society, a McGill University student group. The fascists, as well as the French-Canadian students they had so effectively organized, shrank away.

Edwards read later that Premier Maurice Duplessis had publicly praised the students who blocked the original address of what he termed "communists." Duplessis made no mention in his speech of the fascists who were behind the student demonstration.

The nonsense of Duplessis's statement was apparent to Edwards when he attended the delegation's Calgary meeting. What he saw were two left-leaning liberals and a Roman Catholic priest. In soft, earnest voices, the three described the suffering that the war had brought the Spanish people and appealed for help. They described a country where the people were now divided into two camps—the fascists and the anti-fascists.

Edwards, who was unsure what political stripe adorned his sleeve, found this distinction appealing. One was either a fascist or an anti-fascist. That was clear and simple. He knew that he opposed fascism, the face of which he had seen coldly revealed during the Regina riot. To call oneself an anti-fascist, Edwards thought, was to assume an honourable title, one no cleric, politician, bourgeois employer, or policeman could easily condemn.

When the Spanish delegation concluded its presentation, Edwards went to the front of the hall and told the committee organizers that he had a passport and wanted to go to Spain. They gave him a warm welcome. Edwards left the meeting that night feeling euphoric. He was going to Spain. He would be a soldier in the International Brigades.

Four

*B*LOOD OF SPAIN

OUTSIDE THE WARM LOBBY OF THE GRAN VIA HOTEL, A COLD rain pelted down on the shell- and bomb-battered streets of Madrid. Lounging in a plush chair, Henning Sorenson felt drowsy and relaxed. He had been in Madrid for better than a month and found the city, despite the considerable hazards presented by the fascist air raids and artillery bombardments, much to his liking. The thirty-six-year-old Danish-born Canadian thought nowhere could be as exciting as Madrid in November 1936.

Today promised excitement of a new kind. The previous morning a cable had arrived from the committee in Canada advising Sorenson that Dr. Norman Bethune's arrival was imminent. Sorenson was to serve as his linguist and guide.

Excitement and adventure were the spice in Sorenson's life. Born and

A lust for adventure as much as political conviction drew Henning Sorenson to travel to Spain as the advance man for Dr. Norman Bethune's blood transfusion unit.
(NAC PA172324)

59

raised in Copenhagen, Sorenson had, upon completing his schooling, entered a career in banking. After only a few months, however, he attended a senior bank accountant's retirement party. With fifty years of service behind him, the accountant looked every bit the executive banker with clipped beard, serious demeanour, and slightly stooped walk. As he came forward to accept the inevitable gold watch, Sorenson suddenly felt nauseated. "No," he all but shouted out, "I will not work here fifty years. I'm getting out somewhere else."

Sorenson resigned, leaving Denmark to explore the world. He travelled through Germany, spent time in France (where falling in love with a woman provided added incentive to learn the language), and worked as a shipping chandler in North Africa before, on a passing whim, emigrating to Canada. In Montreal, he eventually found work with the Sun Life insurance company. The company—developing him for a posting to Latin America—funded Spanish lessons. No sooner had Sorenson completed his lessons than the Spanish Civil War broke out.

Responding, as always, to immediate impulse, Sorenson decided to quit his job and rush to Spain. To his more steadily minded friends, Sorenson explained that—perceiving himself to be neither Canadian nor Danish but rather an internationalist—it was necessary for him to go where he could best contribute a "tiny bit towards making a better world." Honourable purpose aside, Sorenson was thirsting for new adventure.

Conveniently, the Committee to Aid Spanish Democracy was seeking someone with Spanish fluency who could assess the Spanish Republic's medical needs. Sorenson successfully presented himself as the perfect candidate for the job. In September 1936, Sorenson travelled to Spain.

He was attentively watching the Madrid hotel's entrance when a dapper-looking gentleman with a little moustache, straight military bearing, and a bit of a swagger sauntered into the lobby. Behind the nattily dressed individual followed two scruffily dressed militiamen carrying rifles. It was obvious to Sorenson that the man was unaware of their presence and had no idea of the dangerous situation unfolding behind him.

Sorenson hurried over and confirmed that the gentleman was Dr. Bethune. One of the militiamen interrupted the conversation to announce that the doctor was under arrest. Sorenson countered with an explanation of Bethune's identity and the purpose of his mission to Madrid. "He is a friend of Spain," Sorenson concluded.

"Well, he's very suspicious, and we've been following him," the Spaniard replied. They had heard him speaking English on the street and had recognized only one word in all he said. That word was "fascism."

"Well, that's ridiculous," Sorenson said indignantly. It was ridiculous to arrest someone for merely saying fascism. Finally the two militiamen relented and took their leave. During this entire dialogue Bethune stood by, paying only passing interest. Sorenson realized that his Spanish was so poor he had not understood any of what transpired.

After getting Bethune registered, he escorted the doctor to his room. Inside, Bethune presented Sorenson with a letter from his Montreal girlfriend. Just as Sorenson started opening the envelope, the door burst open. A policeman stomped in and snatched the envelope from Sorenson's hands. Bethune and Sorenson shot each other startled glances. The policeman unfurled the letter and then, apparently seeing the letter's opening endearment of "Darling," paused, looked about with embarrassment, gave Sorenson a curt apology, and abruptly fled the room. After these two brushes—little more than fifteen minutes apart—with Madrid's increasingly paranoid, Fifth-Column-seeking authorities, Sorenson decided he was going to be very important to Bethune's well-being.

For his part, Bethune was anxious to get started, so that very afternoon Sorenson escorted him to the state press office on the third floor of the Telefónica building, across the street from the hotel. As they received a briefing from the press attaché, the building was struck by an artillery shell. Although the entire building shook violently, the press room staff looked up at the sound for only a second and then, seemingly unconcerned by the closeness of the call, returned to work. Sorenson could see Bethune was greatly impressed by this determined calm.

For the next few days they toured hospitals and met with military and medical personnel, both in the rear areas and on the front lines. One day, at Madrid's largest military hospital, they stood outside the main entrance watching a continuous stream of wounded soldiers being unloaded from ambulances. Before being converted to its new role, the hospital had been a grand hotel. Now its great ballrooms, dining halls, and luxurious suites housed eighteen hundred beds.

Bethune and Sorenson went inside and walked among the wounded. Men, women, and children lay side by side on stretchers packed into the hallways because of the lack of beds. Periodically Bethune knelt by one of the wounded and commented to Sorenson that the person was dying of shock. The hospital had six operating theatres in which some fifteen

61

doctors worked simultaneously. In a hallway outside the surgery, a small group of blood donors waited. When a transfusion was required, a donor was put on a bed next to the patient. A direct transfusion line was then run between donor and patient. Even to Sorenson's untrained eye this system seemed slow and unreliable.

Bethune asked questions, Sorenson translated. They learned that only three Madrid hospitals had transfusion services. The rest, including the casualty clearing stations and field hospitals near the front lines, had none. There was always a critical shortage of donors.

Sorenson was unsure where Bethune's line of investigation was leading. He was also finding the doctor a difficult working partner. Sorenson was constantly having to assert himself or be relegated to serving as Bethune's personal vassal. After one incident, when Bethune imperiously started snapping orders, Sorenson said, "Don't try to push me around."

Bethune apologized only to jump on Sorenson the next day as they left a meeting. "You don't give me enough importance when you introduce me," Bethune scolded.

Sorenson fired back, "What do you mean? We're all fighting a civil war. Nobody's more important than the other guy." Bethune again apologized, but it was apparent the doctor had problems putting egalitarian philosophy into action. For the most part, however, Sorenson got along relatively well with Bethune. This was partly because the doctor's desire to relieve the suffering of Spain's Republican wounded was obviously sincere.

Bethune and Sorenson toured the front, hitching rides in trucks and ambulances. The roads were rough—often torn with shell holes. Bethune watched the ambulances crammed with wounded bouncing along and vividly described the terrible pain the wounded would be suffering because of the jostling. He told Sorenson it would deepen their state of shock and contribute to their dying. If they had been able to get a transfusion before starting that agonizing journey, he said, their survival chances would greatly improve.

At the end of Bethune's tour of Madrid, he and Sorenson met with General Emil Kléber. The general advised Bethune to go to Albacete, the headquarters of the International Brigades, and meet with their chief medical officer. The very next day the two Canadians journeyed to Albacete by truck. Dr. Erwin Kisch was a Czech who had been in Spain for about two months. In badly broken English, he suggested that Bethune's surgical expertise was the greatest asset the Canadian doctor might contribute. Out of

Sorenson's earshot the two doctors had a short, seemingly argumentative conversation. Soon Bethune gestured Sorenson outside. "I couldn't work with that bastard," Bethune said. "Let's get out of here."

They caught a train from Albacete to Valencia—to which the Spanish government had recently moved its capital, fleeing embattled Madrid. During the train ride, Bethune stared thoughtfully out the window at the passing countryside. Finally, he turned to Sorenson. "Henning, I have got an idea. Now you tell me what you think of it. I think we should organize an ambulance blood service, a blood transfusion service."

Bethune hastily sketched a preliminary plan. At a central blood depot they would collect and preserve blood in bottles. From this supply, blood could be sent in fast cars to hospitals on an as-needed basis.

In Valencia, Bethune pitched his idea to some of Spain's top officials, including two leading Spanish doctors. One of the doctors thought the plan impractical. But on the train Bethune had worked feverishly assembling figures to support his conviction that unacceptable numbers of casualties were dying for want of blood transfusions. Finally, the two doctors relented, and Bethune was authorized to form an independent Canadian Medical Unit.

Elated, Bethune fired off a cable to the committee headquarters in Toronto requesting that funds be cabled to the Paris headquarters of the International Committee to Aid Spanish Democracy. They could outfit an ambulance and purchase the necessary medical equipment in Paris and London. Bethune and Sorenson departed for France the following day.

Hazen Sise was in love. True, because Moran Scott seemed incapable of deciding her feelings for him, it was an often frustrating, perhaps one-sided affair. But he was in love all the same. Their families in Montreal were closely acquainted, and it seemed they had always known each other. Now they both lived in London—Sise working, although not very seriously, as an architect, Scott drifting, flitting back and forth between Paris, London, and Montreal. Sise's father, Paul, was president of the Montreal-based Northern Electric Company, so there was always money. Scott's parents were equally privileged. Sise and Scott were young, living on the fringes of London's bohemian culture, becoming increasingly immersed in leftist causes, and generally enjoying Europe.

On this particular day, the Sunday of November 29, 1936, Sise was puttering around his old studio at 35 Bury Walk, by the Fulham Road, on the borders of Chelsea. Outside, a cold rain fell, dripping from the leafless trees bordering the street. Sise read *The Sunday Times,* spreading it out on the big bed, sipping a cup of coffee, relishing the warm glow of heat from the Franklin stove. It seemed a good day to be indoors. The day would have been nicer if Moran could have come over, but when he had called earlier she was going off to distribute anti-war leaflets. They agreed to meet that evening at a monster rally being held at Albert Hall to support Spanish democracy.

A young woman was coming later in the day for tea, however, so the day would not prove a complete loss. That was the way he and Moran were. They dated other people and shadowboxed with words, Moran professing that she did love him, but perhaps not in *that* way. As if there were other ways. Perhaps, however, she was right and other forms of love were possible. Perhaps it was he, rather than she, who was deluded or evading the reality of their relationship. Sise hoped that was not the case.

The phone ringing stirred him from this rather futile, but common enough, circular train of thought. Sise took up the phone gratefully. The caller was a solicitor friend, Clunie Dale, who asked in his very precise, clipped voice whether Sise would like to meet a Canadian fellow by the name of Norman Bethune who had just returned from Madrid and was in London organizing some sort of ambulance work. "From Madrid?" Sise asked. "Jesus, Clunie, I certainly would like to see him." Sise proposed that Bethune and Dale both come by at 6:30 and they could go together to the Albert Hall rally. Dale said he was busy but would see if Bethune wished to go. "He's a great talker. I know you'll go at it hammer and tongs," Dale said and rang off. A few minutes later Clunie phoned to confirm that Bethune would accompany Sise.

The young woman came and went, Sise not really focussing on the conversation that passed between them. He spent the rest of the afternoon pouring over a copy of *Shepheard's Historical Atlas,* concentrating exclusively on Spanish history. Throughout the afternoon, Sise was vaguely aware of a sense that some fateful event was in the air. But when the doorbell rang he was so wrapped up in his atlas he had all but forgotten about Bethune and the rally. Glancing out the window, Sise saw a newish-looking Ford station wagon parked below. Curiously it had the spare tire tied onto the roof rather than stored inside.

When he opened the door, Sise saw a man, caught in the dim glow of a nearby streetlight, standing before him. His hands were plunged deep inside the pockets of his trench coat. Sise noted a strong, almost cruel, face that seemed very tense, an expression at odds with the rather jaunty, flat-topped fedora he wore.

Bethune snapped out "Hello," in response to Sise's greeting, and then walked past him, up the stairs, and into the studio with such a detached air that it was as if he had barely registered Sise's presence. Sise, feeling some-what flustered, hastened after Bethune. Standing in the middle of the stu-dio, still wearing his coat, the doctor explained in terse, concise sentences how he was forming a Canadian Medical Unit to provide blood transfusion treatment to wounded Spanish Republican soldiers. Barely five minutes after Bethune's arrival Sise impulsively blurted out, "My God, I wish I were going with you." Bethune smiled thinly. He told Sise he needed an ambulance driver and that Sise should give the decision careful thought before making any commitments. Then the two men left for the Albert Hall rally.

On December 1, Hazen Sise wrote in his journal:

At about 9:30 A.M. I finally decided, after about 36 hours of mental agony, to accompany Bethune and Sorenson to Madrid. . . . I wasn't able to contact Beth till about 7:00 that evening but spent all day mak-ing arrangements. . . . Mike Pearson [Lester "Mike" Bowles Pearson was first secretary to the Canadian High Commission in London from 1935 to 1941.] agreed to give me a certificate of Canadian citizenship. Also said, National Government would do nothing to imperil their precious "neutrality" [but] . . . we'll get good backing at Canada House if we get into bad trouble. Moran knew in her heart that it was right for me to go, but her apprehension kept popping out, though for the most part she hid it bravely . . . the others for the most part showed only too plainly that, although they could find no valid reason for restraining me (knowing the strength of my feelings on the subject) they thought I was going to almost certain death. This night I slept more easily; the decision having been made and a task found which could command all that I had in me—without misgivings.

Sise spent Wednesday frantically getting his affairs in order. One friend argued he had no right to cause his family so much worry. To his journal Sise confided:

That side of the business is damn hard—but I think that there can't be any greater duty in life than to put oneself right with the dictates of one's reason or one's conscience—but if both are satisfied together; then the greater is the compulsion and the higher is the sanctity of one's actions. Both Bethune and Sorenson admit the strength of this compulsion and though I think both are a little in love with death, (especially Sorensen) the essential rightness of their action seems to give them a sort of shining hallowed quality; and strength too. I think they are right.

He and Moran stayed up late that night preparing his pack. Sise was up at 5:15, suffering from nervous diarrhoea, and feeling in "a complete daze." Moran came by for a hurried good-bye and at 6:15 Bethune and Sorenson arrived. The three drove off to catch the car ferry to France.

The back of the Ford station wagon was jammed with medical supplies. Although they were worried about going through French customs, they were passed through without any questions or a vehicle search. Despite all being groggy with lack of sleep they pushed on hard for Paris. Bethune was worried that the military situation in Spain or the political

In an ambulance bulging with medical supplies, Dr. Norman Bethune (with hat), Henning Sorenson (at ambulance back), and Hazen Sise travelled from London to Paris and then on to Madrid. (NAC PA116885)

situation in France might at any time lead to a closure of the French-Spain border. Leon Blum's French government was rumoured to be considering such an action because of pressure from Britain. In Paris, Sise took a wrong turn, and they spent forty-five minutes driving in circles before arriving at their night's destination, the Hotel du Quai de Voltaire.

The next evening, still in Paris, Sise wrote the letter to his father that he had been dreading. "This is a very hard letter to write," he said in opening.

I despair of being able to explain to you the nature and strength of the inner compulsion which has driven me to this fateful decision—to go to Madrid with the Canadian Ambulance Unit. No one persuaded me; no one even asked me to go. Looking back now, it seems as if some such conviction had been brewing in me for a long time. . . . As you no doubt realize by now, I am a person who cannot compromise on the essentials of this life. Over a period of years I have slowly and painstakingly come to support certain beliefs, both political and spiritual which I have tested both with my intellect and my heart and found to be essentially right. When one feels this way it is both contemptible and stupid to stand aside and let others fight your battles.

I am not a Communist, but have been driven very close to their way of thinking, both by the logic of their beliefs and by the trend of events, which, every day, go more and more to justify their position. Now the only difference between Communists and that great mass of left opinion which hopes for Socialism is that the Communists know very well that we will never get it unless we fight for it—that indeed, we will not be able to even preserve Democracy in the face of the threat of Fascism unless we are willing to organize, to impose discipline on ourselves, and to fight.

I believe that our futures will be very largely determined by the result of the conflict in Spain and that is why you find men from all over the world rallying to fight for the Spanish government. . . . So I am going to do my little bit.

I am sick to think of the worry this is going to cause you and mum, but I cannot withdraw on that account. If I had been of age in 1915 you would not have wanted to stop me—and the issues now are much clearer than then.

To lessen your anxiety—you must understand that we will not be in the front line but in Madrid and will only be running the risks that everyone else must run when the Fascists bomb an open town. We will be in uniform and wearing the red cross. The car will be armour-plated on top, etc. The red cross will NOT be painted on top as Franco has already bombed one unit which was so conspicuously marked. I will take no foolish risks and will have no hesitation in claiming sanctuary at the British Embassy if the Fascists enter the town.

As to money. I will need very little, unless Franco wins and I have to get out of the country. . . . I should add that I will quite understand and have considered the consequences if you wish to have nothing more to do with me (as regards allowance etc.).

Being afraid of the shock to Granny I have told her that I am simply driving out to Barcelona as a relief driver and will be back in a few weeks. . . . Goodbye and please forgive me. I must live my life according to my beliefs.

All my love,
Hazen

For the next three days they drove south through France toward the Pyrenees. Along the way Sise took photos of the three of them posing by the ambulance and then sent the film off to Moran Scott for developing. This led to his first "tiff" with Bethune, who was annoyed because Sise refused to ask Scott to send prints to a raft of Bethune's friends in Canada. He "accused me of being uncomradely," Sise confided to his journal, "quite forgetting that it wasn't a question of that but of the load of work I would have to put on Moran at the other end."

On December 8, "in glorious early sunshine," the ambulance unit crossed from France into Spain with minimal delay and formality. They were passed into Spain by Catalonian militia manning the border post. Two days later they were closing on Madrid. "As we get closer and closer to the real front at Madrid," Sise wrote,

there is increasing evidence of purpose and organization underlying the apparent (to Anglo-Saxon eyes) confusion. The two great trade unions C.N.T. and U.G.T. seem to be running all the essential services under a mandate from the government and they seem to be doing it very well. . . . Everyone goes about in the most astonishingly varied and luxuriant costumes or uniforms, many of which give one the queer

On the way through Spain en route to Madrid, Sise and Bethune passed
through villages touched by the war. Sise always had his camera nearby, ready
to record his experiences.   (NAC PA172311)

illusion of being in Quebec as there are many checked mackinaws and
shirts and those leather peaked hunting caps. Nearly everyone packs a
gun, adding to the wild-west atmosphere of the costumes. It is amus-
ing to see a gun-check man at the entrance to all government offices,
factories etc.

In Valencia, while getting in touch with the medical authorities
headquartered there, Sise heard his first air-raid siren. Later that evening
he wrote that the streets were "surging with people who made no attempt
to get to the refuges. I was both scared and curious to find what it would be
like, so unreal it was to look at the gay people and the fantastic commercial
architecture of Valencia and to imagine what a shambles it might be in a
few minutes. The best place being indoors, we went and had some lunch.

And then, after a quarter hour, it seemed obvious that nothing was going to happen and it was an awful let down. We found out that three tri-motors had reconnoitered over the harbour but had dropped no bombs."

On December 12, Sise drove the ambulance into Madrid. "My first impression of the city—vast, ugly, plunked down for no apparent reason in the middle of a high desert plateau. Cold as hell. Streets teeming with people. Long food and fuel queues. Wrecked buildings here and there and frequent barricades and machine gun nests for the first half mile of suburbs. It's a vulgar, ugly, commercial, and snobbish city. Sort of Provincial Spanish Beaux Arts architecture."

In the Puerto Del Sol tram station, Sise met a British friend of his, Claude Cockburn. "He looked very dirty, unshaven, tired, but happy. In his element. Had spent the night up in the line with the International Brigades." They went for lunch together at the Gran Via Hotel, dining in the basement grill "with the foreign journalists, some with hats and all with overcoats on. Just across the street from the Telefónica, so they can easily pop over when a wire is clear to send out their stuff. A cheery crowd of scavengers."

As *The Toronto Daily Star's* veteran feature reporter, Frederick Griffin sought to make the siege of Madrid brutally palpable to his Canadian readers. Since early December he had been bearing witness to the most violent siege of a civilian population in modern history. On December 5, just before dusk, the downtown area was subjected to a heavy artillery bombardment of shrapnel rounds. Griffin was in the Telefónica building, which he described in a story wired home for the paper's Monday, December 7, edition as

the tallest and strongest sky-scraper in Spain. It consists of thirteen storeys surmounted by a tower and it is white and visible for miles. Imagine yourself in the Canadian Bank of Commerce building [in Toronto] while an enemy out in Lake Ontario tries hitting it with shrapnel shells directed at about the eighth storey. That was my experience on Saturday and I did not like it.

I had almost called it a day when the hollow boom of a distant gun just outside the city and to the north was followed by the sharp crack of an exploding shell. We all rushed to the window of the fifth floor in time to see a wisp of smoke fading.

As we watched within half a minute came the sight of another black explosion followed by a bang. Shrapnel shells were bursting within two hundred yards of us.

The corridor filled with anxious people, the telephone girls and other women and men, watching with strained faces while keeping behind the edges of windows.

Altogether 15 shells came closer and closer, each exploding at the same height over nearby roads.

None spoke much. Then as unexpectedly as it began, the shelling ceased and shortly the dark quietude of the night settled on the uneasy city which is absolutely lightless.

The veteran reporter, who had worked for the *Daily Star* for thirty-seven years—starting out as a library assistant shortly after his arrival in Canada as a young Irish immigrant—had built his reputation by writing about people rather than the grand sweep of politics and ideologies. He left that kind of work to the paper's European correspondent Matthew Halton, who was even now in London following the abdication debate surrounding King Edward's refusal to abandon plans to marry the divorced American socialite Wallis Simpson. Griffin wrote about the common person, the individuals who were the flotsam in the flood of history created by the politicians.

In 1932, he had gone to the Soviet Union and travelled its breadth to profile the dramatic changes being experienced by the country's 160 million people. His newspaper reports had been collected in a book entitled *Soviet Scene: A Newspaperman's Close-ups of New Russia*. The last sentence in the book read: "Who can ever hope to measure the effect of what is taking place in Soviet Russia to-day?"

Griffin felt much the same as he tried to measure Madrid's siege. It seemed incomprehensible that the city could hold against the fascist might. The fascists were obviously so much better equipped, becoming more so every day, while the International Non-Intervention Committee moved ever more decisively toward blocking all shipments of aid to the Republicans. Even now the flow of supplies through France to Spain had slowed to a trickle. While they choked off supplies to the Republicans, the committee was incapable of getting Germany, Italy, and Portugal to suspend either matériel aid or the deployment of military personnel into Spain. German and Italian bombers dropped high explosives on Madrid every day, while German and Italian artillery routinely hammered the city.

Yet Madrid held, serving as proof that it was the individual will, not firepower, that would decide the battle. Visiting the front-line trenches on December 7, Griffin wrote for the following day's paper: "I can't see how General Franco can take the city. He will literally have to take it foot by foot, block by block . . . the visit was remarkable proof of the defenders' morale and of the various elements joined in the fight for liberty. . . . Unless Franco receives very great foreign reinforcements he will not take Madrid, even though he may destroy it."

The situation in Madrid was worsening. Bitter, whistling winds swept off the Guadarrama mountains to increase the suffering of the people, most of whom had no means of effectively heating their homes due to fuel shortages. Tens of thousands of refugees had been driven out of the western working-class districts of the city and were crowded into abandoned shops, basements, and underground subway stations.

There was no meat or potatoes, coal was rare, anything made of wood was likely to be carried off in the night for fires. Griffin saw a group of women nearly mob a peasant who offered three cabbages for sale on the street.

"I am living in a pension," he wrote, "that is like a tomb. Guests never remove their sweaters or overcoats, eating, and I think, sleeping in them. Last evening's dinner was a soup made of garlic, red peppers and rolled oats plus a spoonful of macaroni and a trifle of fried cauliflower.

"I have taken to wearing thick ski boots and two pairs of woollen socks."

On the afternoon of December 8, Griffin was in a store on the Gran Via when "there came the ugly sound of half a dozen bomb explosions nearby." The area hit was the Arguelles neighbourhood, which was badly damaged. "It was a bombing without objective or gain," Griffin wrote for the newspaper's December 9 edition, "except to terrorize the civilian population. . . . As I write the thudding of bombs continues. Its malicious rumble rises above the clatter of journalists' typewriters."

On December 10, leaflets instead of bombs rained down from fascist planes. Signed by Franco, the leaflets "carried the usual cry that Spain is in the hands of Jews and of Soviet Russia and demanded that the people support him."

Of all the defenders of Madrid, the man who most impressed Griffin was Emil Kléber, the mysterious commander of the International Column fighting in Madrid. Kléber commanded the defensive line stretching north of Madrid to the Guadarrama mountains, which guarded the northern approaches to the city and the vital Escorial Road. For weeks Franco's forces had been trying to flank Kléber's lines.

Kléber, Griffin wrote in the December 12 edition, "is a sturdy-set man of 41, dark and handsome with a strongly etched face, suggesting the Slav, with a splendid head surmounted by a grizzled, virile pompadour. . . . He has quick intelligence and power of will written all over him. He speaks excellent English and displays a wit, a philosophy and a breadth of view."

He also easily parried Griffin's attempts to either confirm or deny the story that Kléber was a naturalized Canadian, something the Canadian government vehemently denied. Smiling at Griffin, Kléber only said, "Do you know Tim Buck? Ask him. He knows all about me." [Griffin never asked Buck, nor apparently did any other journalist. No record exists to prove Kléber was ever naturalized as a Canadian, although it seems likely he was in Canada between his service in China and his return to Europe. Kléber's real name was Emil Stern.] Kléber claimed to have been captured in 1917 while serving in the Austrian army on the Russian front. He told Griffin he managed to escape and come to Canada. In 1919, he returned to Russia, serving with the Canadian Expeditionary Force in Siberia. Disgust with the treatment of the populace by Canada's Japanese and White Russian allies prompted him to defect to the Soviet side.

From Russia, Kléber said he went to China and fought with the communist forces against Chiang Kai-Shek, successfully leading a force of fifty-six thousand men out of an encirclement by more than one million troops. From China he returned to Canada, travelling on to Europe only a year before he came to Madrid.

"Such is the background of the strong man of the defence of Madrid," Griffin wrote,

who appeared without a hat, wearing a heavy gray pullover sweater, riding breeches, golf socks and boots in a plain room, unheated except for charcoal embers in a brazier. . . . I am told that Kléber has a magnetism that needs no display and is trusted and obeyed unflinchingly.

He is no brass hat leader back in a dug-out, but frequently is in the front line and often, earlier in the defence, he took a rifle, or handled a machine-gun while he was instructing and rallying new troops.

Kléber refused to prophesy, but spoke quietly and confidently. "The defence of Madrid," he said, "is a psychological question rather than a matter of men and materials of which we now have enough."

It was the example set by the International column, Kléber said, which gave the Spanish Republicans the determination needed to resist. "A miracle quietly happened," he claimed, and a resistance akin to that put up by the French during the Great War at Verdun, which became known as the Miracle of Verdun, had occurred in Madrid.

On December 12, as the sixth week of the siege of Madrid closed, Griffin walked down the Gran Via near the Telefónica when there was a sudden "bang, like the crack of a whip overhead." Looking up, Griffin "saw the ugly white cloud of a shell bursting about 100 feet above the exact middle of the street." He ducked into a doorway for cover even as he realized the futility of the act—if you've heard the explosion it's too late to seek shelter. Nearby, a man was down, blood running from his head. As the artillery salvo continued to rain shells into the area, Griffin dodged into the relative shelter of the Telefónica building.

Most of the fighting centred on the embattled University City area—a sprawling group of buildings in the city's northeast corner, surrounded by great parks and boulevards. In mid-November, Franco's forces had penetrated this area, and heavy fighting had persisted ever since. Griffin visited the Republican entrenchments there regularly, marvelling at how tenaciously both fascist and loyalist troops held their ground. For weeks the fascists had clung to positions within the massive, unfinished hospital building throwing back repeated Republican attacks. On December 14, the fascists attempted to extend their grip on the university by launching a massive tank and machine-gun-supported assault. Soldiers in the front lines swore to Griffin that German troops led the assault, which was repelled with heavy fascist losses. The following day, Franco broadened the attack to extend along a twenty-kilometre front from University City northwest into neighbouring villages in an attempt to cut the Escorial Road.

On the evening of the fifteenth, Griffin wrote an article for the December 16 *Daily Star*.

Madrid is defended by a seemingly impregnable series of trenches and wide stone breastworks. Every street is tremendously barricaded, but the enigma is the quality of the untrained and untested, highly individualistic citizen defenders when placed under an intensive barrage. On the Spanish character, rather than on her arms, hangs the fate of Madrid and Spain during the coming days and weeks.

Madrid awaits its fate stoically, its million people existing from day to day. To-day, in the rain, I walked again from the Gran Via past the barricades into Blasco Ibanez St., through part of the terribly devastated west fringe of the city. The rain and mud made the torn up streets and ravaged homes and buildings the acme of desolation. There were wide, shattered, deserted vistas, yet washing hung to dry in sheltered spots among the ruins and scores of women might be seen carrying bundles, evidently busy at the never-ending work of retrieving things of value.

Griffin was amazed by how the citizenry pursued a normal life. Services, including water, electricity, the trams, and the subways, continued to operate, but there was no heat, gas, or trains. The major tramway junction at the Puerto Del Sol, destroyed by bombs, was repaired with surprising speed by volunteer workers. At night, refugees slept on the subway platforms, but each morning their bedding was rolled and neatly stacked against the walls to make way for the commuters.

Even the great Alcala post office, with every pane of glass blown from its windows, remained open, its clerks wearing heavy overcoats but continuing to staff their wickets. Five cinemas functioned, showing mostly Russian pictures. Every day, as Griffin passed the Capital cinema on the Gran Via making his way to the Telefónica, he could see long queues forming to see *Chapieff, the Red Guerilla Fighter.*

"Such is the unquenchable spirit of hope and defiance which animates dark Madrid," he wrote. "I never cease marvelling at the courage and fatalism of clerks and others serving in stores adjacent to buildings which have been blown to ruin as a fearful example of their possible fate." By the time Griffin left Madrid to be home for Christmas, he seldom flinched when shells exploded nearby. After three weeks, Griffin felt himself somewhat a veteran of the Madrid siege that raged on unabated.

Since arriving in Madrid on December 12, the Canadian Medical Unit had been busily setting up operation. They were stationed in a ground level, palatial, fifteen-room flat at 36 Principe de Vergara, which had previously been occupied by a German diplomat who had fled to Berlin. The rest of the building housed the headquarters of Socorro Rojo Internacional (SRI), the most powerful health organization in Spain. In a letter to Rev. Ben Spence, the Canadian chairman of the Committee to Aid Spanish Democracy, Bethune described SRI as "much superior to the International Red Cross

75

(this organization is very suspiciously Fascist between you and I) or the weak Spanish Red Cross."

The SRI had located its headquarters on this wide, tree-lined boulevard in one of Madrid's wealthiest residential sections. Its organizers reasoned that Franco would scrupulously ensure no bombs fell on the property of the rich residents who had fled from Madrid to either Franco-held parts of Spain or to sanctuaries abroad. Three of the rooms served as the Canadians' living quarters. The dozen others housed laboratories, refrigerator rooms for blood storage, and reception and transfusion rooms. Although in Canada it would most often be called the Canadian Medical Unit, Bethune gave the unit the formal name Servicio Canadiense de Transfusion de Sangre, and had that painted on the sides of the ambulances.

Within days the three Canadians, Celia Greenspan (the wife of an American journalist), and a couple of Spanish medical students, as well as several Spaniards who performed various administrative, domestic, and security services, had the blood unit running. Each day the local radio and newspapers appealed for blood donors. These appeals led to long lines of up to a thousand donors queuing each morning outside the office. All were assessed for their state of health. Those deemed sufficiently healthy were grouped by blood type and provided with a donor badge to recognize their contribution. After a few days one thousand donors had been selected.

Bethune opted to use the Moss blood group classification system, which assigned Roman numeric symbols to four blood types instead of letters. Type IV was the universal type, which would be given to patients if their own blood type was unavailable or if there was doubt as to the correct blood type.

Each day about five quarts of blood were collected from one specific group of donors. This was then stored in flasks in the refrigerators. When a hospital needed blood, it was transferred to heated vacuum bottles carried in knapsacks that were also loaded with additional bottles, warm physiological serum, and glucose solution, plus a complete sterilized tin box of all the instruments needed to carry out a transfusion.

A large map of Madrid was tacked up on the wall of the office, which had formerly housed the diplomat's eight-thousand-book library and was still decorated with gold brocade curtains and Aubusson carpets. The books were gone, though, providing space for some battered desks. On the map, Sise and Bethune had determined the most direct routes to Madrid's fifty-six hospitals.

When a hospital called for blood, the team followed a prescribed routine, which Bethune described in a letter to Spence. "On arrival we're ready to start work at once. We go to the man and decide what he needs—either blood or physiological serum, or glucose or a combination of these. If blood is needed . . . we 'group' him at once with our serum. This is done by a prick of the finger, a glass stick and serum and takes 2 minutes, then after grouping we give him the blood type needed." The whole process could be completed in minutes, including the drive from the blood centre to the hospital.

Once the service was operating smoothly in Madrid, Bethune planned to extend it over the 160 kilometres of front lines near the city. Meanwhile, Bethune was wrestling with the problem of determining how long refrigerated blood would remain usable; he hoped for several weeks.

On average, through December, the team managed three transfusions daily, in addition to the blood left at hospitals for their own distribution. It was a demanding routine as the need for blood never ceased. Often the team worked at night.

"Our night work is very eerie!" Bethune wrote Spence, ". . . with our armed guard . . . we go through the absolutely pitch dark streets and the guns and machine guns and rifle shots sound as if they were in the next block, although they are really half a mile away. Without lights we drive, stop at the hospital and with a search light in our hands find our way into the cellar principally. All the operating rooms in the hospitals have been moved into the basement to avoid falling shrapnel, bricks and stones coming through the operating room ceiling."

Of the patients, he wrote that when they received the transfusion "the change in most cases is spectacular. The pulse can now be felt and his pale lips have some color."

After providing a transfusion to a French International who had lost his arm, Bethune was deeply touched when the young man raised his remaining clenched fist. "Viva la Révolution," the man shouted. Next to the French volunteer was a young Spaniard—a medical student before the war—who had been shot through the liver and stomach. Bethune gave him a transfusion and asked how he felt. "It is nothing," the boy said, "Nada."

In his off-hours, Bethune enjoyed touring the city. He was very taken by the poster art flourishing on every street. "These posters are wonderful artistic efforts," he wrote Spence. "The whole city is covered with them. They stress . . . Anti-fascism not Anarchism, Socialism or Communism. More

77

and more every day all parties are becoming united under the realization of this war against international fascist aggression.

"You may rest assured and give our assurance to the workers of Canada that their efforts and money are saving many Spanish, French, German and English lives. We will win—the Fascists are already defeated. Madrid will be the tomb of Fascism." And soon, Bethune informed Spence, the unit would be able to commence increasing the numbers of ambulances and staff, which would require more funds to cover operational costs. As for the Canadians—himself included—none drew any salary beyond what small sums of money were needed to cover living expenses.

Since Dolores, his young Spanish militia compatriot, had fallen at Irún, Bill Williamson, the first Canadian to fight in Spain, had seen almost everyone he had marched out of Bilbao with in July either die or suffer an incapacitating wound. He had nearly been killed himself many times. During an early December Republican offensive toward Vitoria, the capital of Álava, Williamson's machine-gun squad had been blown up by either a grenade or a mortar round. Everyone in the squad but Williamson was killed. He was seriously concussed and spent several days in hospital.

The Basque front was completely isolated from the rest of the Republic. The Republican forces there were bogged down before the stiffly defended Vitoria. As darkness fell around him on Christmas Eve, Williamson's column was scattered across the gently sloping side of a mountain. The ground upon which he sat was solid granite and covered with a hard frost. Digging a foxhole was impossible. The militiamen and women huddled around small, feeble fires made out of wood cut from the region's sparse, dwarf-like trees.

Looking out across the slope of the mountain, Williamson saw hundreds of fires twinkling in the night. On the valley's opposite side, similar fires burned inside the fascist lines. Once or twice in every hour a seventy-five-millimetre fascist gun fired, its shells bursting harmlessly in the rocks on the upper ridges above them. As he watched the flickering fires, Williamson thought of the Christmas carol "While Shepherds Watched their Flocks by Night."

Earlier he had read in the military newspapers that a brigade of international volunteers was fighting near Madrid. The brigade was reported to have some "Americanos" in it. Williamson was feeling increasingly lonely here on the Basque front, for although his Spanish comrades accepted him as one of their own, there always remained the gulf of his foreignness. Thinking about this, Williamson decided he would request a transfer to this newly formed International Brigade. The prospect of soon being with men who spoke his own language and shared similar life experiences buoyed Williamson, so he was in good spirits when the clock passed twelve. It was Christmas Day, 1936.

Five

$\mathcal{F}$IRST TO FALL

AS THE BUSES ROLLED THROUGH THE BORDER GATES INTO SPAIN, the French guards standing alongside the road raised clenched fists in a salute of solidarity. On one of the buses were Thomas Beckett, Frederick Lackey, Lawrence Ryan, Clifford Budgen, and Henry Beattie. The five young Torontonians were the first volunteers recruited by the Canadian Committee to Aid Spanish Democracy to arrive in the Republic for the express purpose of bearing arms against the fascists.

The buses carried the volunteers to an old fortress at Figueras. More than seven hundred years old, the Figueras fort was an awe-inspiring sight for any North American. A wide moat surrounded six-metre-thick fortress walls. The buses trundled across the lowered drawbridge and wearily the volunteers, which, in addition to the Canadians, included some twenty-five Americans and a large group of Europeans, stepped onto Spanish earth for the first time. The men were assigned to sleeping quarters in the fortress's dark dungeons and keeps. Figueras, they learned in the morning, was merely a staging point for international volunteers coming in from France. The next day Beckett's party boarded a train bound for Albacete, headquarters of the International Brigades.

By January 17, 1937, Beckett was settled in Albacete. One of the first things he did was write Audrey, a Toronto girl he was fond of.

I don't know why I am writing you. Maybe it's because I can't forget you. Or maybe it is because the dark-eyed Spanish girls remind me of you. There are many of them that look enough like you to be your sister, and they are modest and shy, with fresh clear complexions, and soft friendly eyes, and womanly virtuous morals.

You no doubt know why I am here. It is because I am what you did not want me to be, a Communist. You also no doubt know what I am doing here. Considering what is going on in Spain at the present time, you will probably think me wrong, or foolish, or wicked, for doing such a thing. As will also Rita, Laurie, and many others. Would you please show them this letter, as a request, in case I do not come back to explain?

After describing his journey through Spain to Albacete, Beckett offered his impressions of the Spanish people for whom he had come to fight.

I see about me old people, bent and crippled from long years of heart-breaking toil. I see young people prematurely old. I see a class of people whose growth is stunted, whose bodies have, through generations of this life, become squat and unbeautiful. Their houses have no conveniences of any kind, they cook over a fire on the floor, they have no comforts, luxuries, no change from the incessant toil and struggle to exist. . . . The middle class Spaniards, who are also fighting Fascism . . . are handsome, polite, and grateful, courteous and generous, and like the rest of the Spaniards, are brave and courageous to the point of being reckless in the fight to defend their new-found freedom. . . . Even if I had no political beliefs and was not a Communist, an abhorrence of cruelty, of unnecessary suffering, brutality, greed and tyranny would lead me to do the same thing. My desire to help bring peace, happiness and freedom to the people of any and every country would demand this.

. . . I feel as though I was talking to you, and would like to go on, but it is necessary for me to close now. . . . Wish me luck?

Beckett's group was assigned to the Abraham Lincoln Battalion. This unit was formed on January 2, 1937, following the arrival of the first ninety-six volunteers from the United States. The Lincolns were one of four battalions that made up the newly reconstituted XVth International Brigade. The brigade's battalions were loosely organized around the volunteers' languages and nationalities. The XVth fielded four battalions. British vol-

By mid-February 1937, the XVth International Brigade's Lincoln Battalion
had reached a strength of about 450 men, most of whom were Canadians or
Americans. They were equipped with a hodgepodge of weapons and
uniforms that had seen service in the Great War.   (NAC PA194605)

unteers served in the British Battalion, North American volunteers, with
some Latin Americans, formed the Abraham Lincoln Battalion, French
volunteers formed the 6th of February Battalion, and the Dimitrov Battalion
provided a home for volunteers from Slavic nations. Only the Lincolns had
not seen action in 1936, during the siege of Madrid.

Beckett, Larry Ryan, and the other Canadians were plunged immediately into training. Rumour had it they could be called upon to fight in as
little as five weeks. The Lincolns training headquarters was the small village of Villanueva de la Jara, fifty-six kilometres from Albacete. The village
had a population of about four hundred families. The country around
Albacete was favoured by the presence of the Jucar River and its tributaries.
Olive groves, wheat fields, vineyards, and thick stands of pine trees presented Beckett with a beautiful, lush landscape. To his parents, Beckett
wrote, "Although it is January, gardens are in full bloom and the weather is
like an early June night in Canada. The fields and surrounding country are
a maze of colour of real beauty."

The soldiers were housed in a monastery across the street from the
village church, which served as a mess hall. Both buildings appeared an-

83

cient, especially to Canadian eyes. The steps to the church bell tower had
been worn down ten full centimetres by the abrasion of countless centuries
of sandals scuffing the stone. Mass was no longer held there. On July 16—
the day of the Nationalist rebellion—the village priest, armed with a light
machine gun, had climbed into the bell tower and opened fire on the pa-
rishioners below. The priest stopped firing only when a young villager succeeded in scaling the outside of the tower and killing him with a knife. The
village, as was true of most in Albacete, was strongly Republican, and the
villagers had neither wanted, nor received, another priest.

As the training began, Beckett and his four companions were surprised
to find themselves training with Canadian rifles. These were Ross rifles,
made during the Great War for the Canadian Expeditionary Force. Like
their forebears, Beckett and the others quickly came to loathe the rifles,
which inevitably jammed after every shot. Sometimes the bolt could only
be budged by hammering on it with a rock. Not only were the rifles of little
practical use, they were also so scarce they had to be used by turns. In
addition to the rifle training, instruction was also given in mapping, scouting, signalling, and constructing fortifications. They spent many hours learn-
ing to manoeuvre and infiltrate as a unit. There was little in the way of
training in marching or parade ground drill.

By mid-February, the Lincolns' strength was up to 450 with new volunteers arriving almost daily from the United States. From Canada an evenly
mixed handful of French- and English-speaking Canadians had arrived
with reports that greater numbers would soon be on the way.

The Lincolns' commander was Captain Robert Merriman, an economics scholar and United States Reserve Officer Training Corps graduate.
Merriman had come to Spain from Moscow, where he had been living on a
nine-hundred-dollar-a-year University of California fellowship. While in
Moscow, he had acquired a pair of heavy, steel-rimmed spectacles that gave
him an oddly bookish look that belied his tall athletic physique.

Merriman divided the battalion into two infantry companies and a
smaller machine-gun company. All the companies were commanded by
Americans.

News soon reached the Lincolns that Franco had opened a massive
offensive along the Jarama River, southeast of Madrid, in an attempt to cut
the Valencia-Madrid road. All the XVth International Brigade battalions
but the Lincolns were rushed to the Jarama front. On February 12, Merriman
was called to Brigade headquarters for a meeting. Three days later a line of

five-tonne covered trucks pulled into Villanueva de la Jara's square and the Lincolns loaded up, knowing they were starting the journey to the battlefield.

As the trucks rolled out of Villanueva de la Jara in the mid-afternoon, the villagers gathered along the roadside with fists raised. They chanted: "Muerte a Franco, Abaco Fascimo, Viva España!" [Death to Franco, Down with Fascism, Long Live Spain!]

As the untried soldiers threw together their kits, Thomas Beckett scribbled a short letter to his mother in which he expressed his own solidarity with the Spanish people. "If the brutality and hostility of fascism ever dominates the heroic, soft spoken and long suffering people of Spain then the fictitious God of this superficially civilized world is indeed more of a devil than a god," he wrote. "Time's up now, will write a longer letter as soon as I get a chance."

Squeezed into the cramped cab of the Canadian Medical Unit's new 2.5-tonne Renault ambulance, Dr. Norman Bethune, Hazen Sise, and Tom Worsley, a British volunteer, sped toward Málaga. The back of the ambulance was crammed with refrigerated blood and transfusion equipment. On February 7, a combined force of fifteen thousand Italian, Spanish, and Moorish troops had launched a massive offensive against the coastal city in Spain's southern Costa del Sol resort area. The attack had included continuous bombardment of the city by planes, naval vessels, and—as the fascist assault pushed close to the city outskirts—artillery. With a population of a hundred thousand and an additional fifty thousand refugees jammed into its streets, civilian and military casualties were reportedly piling up at a rate that overwhelmed local medical facilities.

At 5:00 P.M. on February 10, Bethune reached the balmy port city of Almería. From Almería to Málaga, a road running along the coast provided the last remaining link between Málaga and the rest of Republican Spain. At Almería, Bethune was told he could go no further. Málaga had fallen. The road was likely already cut. To proceed was too risky.

Bethune, knowing there would be many wounded between Almería and Málaga, decided to press on. A road marker just outside Almería posted the distance to Málaga as 169 kilometres. Sise asked how far they would go. Bethune replied they would go to where the blood was needed. The dirt road snaked along between steep grey cliffs and breakers rolling onto white beaches, so there would be no cover in the event of an aerial attack.

They were about ten kilometres outside Almería, rounding a corner, when they met the head of what appeared to be a procession of families with all their possessions loaded on donkeys, mules, and horses. None of the people would stop to talk, but as they marched by they told Bethune they were from Málaga. They had left the city on February 6 when the commander there ordered a general evacuation. Since then they had been covering forty kilometres a day in their desperate flight. It was an amazing feat. Bethune looked at the people passing, saw they were strong and fit. How many left the city? Sise asked one man as he passed. Everyone, the man replied. They are all coming. Bethune and Sise looked at each other. One hundred and fifty thousand people on this narrow road, with the fascists closing from behind. They would turn it into a butcher's shop. These are the strongest, the best prepared, Bethune told Sise. It would be impossible for many to do this.

They pressed on. The further they went the more the road became clogged with refugees, who were in ever poorer physical condition. There were many children. Sise tried counting them and estimated they passed about five thousand aged ten years or younger. At least a thousand of these children were barefoot. Many were slung over their mothers' shoulders or clung wearily to their hands. One man staggered by gripping the hand of one child. Another of about two years of age clung to his back, which was already burdened with a bundle full of pots and other possessions. Bethune could see that most of the refugees were out of water and food. Alongside the road, or pushed off onto the adjacent beaches, lay the bodies of burros and the crumpled forms of refugees who had collapsed from exhaustion. Some of them no longer moved; perhaps they were dead. The crowds thickened, and the Renault could barely move against its flow.

Eighty-eight kilometres out of Almería, just over halfway to Málaga, they encountered the first of the retreating Republican militia troops. They pleaded with Bethune to turn around. There was no point continuing. The resistance was finished. Everyone was just trying to get away from the advancing fascist forces.

Bethune and his two companions discussed what they should do next. They had blood nobody really needed. What the refugees required most was food, water, and transport. Bethune told Sise and Worsley to dump the blood and transfusion supplies, and to rip everything out of the truck that took up space. Soon the three men had the ambulance stripped. As people realized what they were up to a frantic mob clustered around their vehicle.

With tired outstretched arms, men and women held out children whose eyes and faces were swollen and congested from four days in the hot sun and dust.

It was overwhelming, Bethune wrote later. They came forward crying, "'Take this one.' 'See this child.' 'This one is wounded.' Children with blood-stained rags wrapped around their arms and legs, children without shoes, their feet swollen to twice their size crying helplessly from pain, hunger and fatigue." Bethune wondered how to play God, who to save? How to choose between "a child dying of dysentery or a mother silently watching . . . with great sunken eyes carrying against her open breast her child born on the road two days ago."

Bethune decided the ambulance would take only children and mothers. They jammed forty people into the ambulance for that first trip back to Almería. Worsley and Sise left with the ambulance, Bethune joined the refugee column. Many hours later Sise returned, picking up Bethune and another load of refugees for the return journey.

For the next three days, working round the clock in shifts, Sise and Worsley shunted back and forth from the rear of the column to Almería with loads of the frailest refugees. When Bethune wasn't in the ambulance he was at Almería's hospital helping provide medical attention and organize the distribution of clothing and food. Between driving shifts, Sise and Worsley would collapse on the side of the road to sleep. They could find no food to eat other than oranges and dry bread.

After the first few loads they gave up trying to carry only women and children. Bethune found witnessing "the separation between father and child, husband and wife became too cruel to bear." They finished by transporting families with the largest number of young children. They also tried to evacuate as many of the hundreds of orphans as possible.

Neither Bethune, Sise, or Worsley kept track of the number of trips made or the number of refugees carried. Sometimes they could squeeze only thirty into the truck, other times they managed forty.

One evening the nature of the column abruptly changed. There were no longer any men, only women and children. That morning the fascist tanks and armoured cars had overrun the last of the refugees. Apparently hoping to increase the Republic's food difficulties, they had let the women and children go. All the men had been forced out onto the adjacent beaches and shot in mass firing squads, usually within sight of their families.

By the late afternoon of February 12 it was over. The last of the escap-

For three days Hazen Sise (centre front) and Tom Worsley (driving) worked around the clock ferrying refugees down the road from Málaga to Almería.
(NAC PA117452)

ing refugees straggled into Almería. Corpses of thousands more—nobody knew how many—were scattered along the road, decomposing under the hot sun. Almería was clogged with humanity. Its population was swollen to double its size. The town centre, especially the main street, was crowded with families huddled together, sleeping in the open.

Bethune was in the street outside the Provincial Committee's ad hoc Evacuation of Refugees Centre when the air-raid sirens started. A long queue of women and children stood before the building, waiting for their meagre rations of a cupful of preserved milk and a handful of dried bread. Thirty seconds after the sirens began to wail the first bomb fell. One after another, ten large bombs detonated in the town's centre. The shrapnel and concussion from the succession of massive explosions lashed the helpless crowd.

Bethune later wrote in a pamphlet entitled "The Crime on the Road: Málaga-Almería" that as the planes left:

I picked up in my arms three dead children. . . . The street was a shambles of the dead and dying, lit only by the orange glare of burning buildings. In the darkness the moans of the wounded children, shrieks of agonized mothers, the curses of the men rose in a massed cry higher and higher to a pitch of intolerable intensity. One's body felt as heavy as the dead themselves, but empty and hollow, and in one's brain burned a bright flame of hate. That night were murdered fifty civilians and an additional fifty were wounded. . . . What was the crime that these unarmed civilians had committed to be murdered in this bloody manner?

A few days after Almería was bombed, Bethune, Sise, and Worsley returned to Madrid. They re-equipped the ambulance and got back to the desperate work of providing transfusion services to the Jarama and Madrid fronts. Fresh Republican forces were rushing to block the fascist advance on the Jarama River. Although weary and dispirited by what he had witnessed at Almería, Bethune drew upon inner reserves of strength and energetically threw himself into meeting the growing demands for blood.

Darkness was falling as the trucks carrying Thomas Beckett and the rest of the 450-strong Lincoln Battalion rolled into Albacete. Larry Ryan, who had quit his Toronto typesetting job to accompany Beckett to Spain, could not still his shivering. The air was cold, and a piercing wind blew. The volunteers unloaded, stretched, and lined up at a field kitchen where they wolfed down hot cabbage soup and a pan of fried beans. The rumour mill was working overtime. They were only changing base. No, they were en route to Madrid. Had Málaga truly fallen? Perhaps they were going to reinforce the southern city. "No, it's Jarama," one man said with more authority than his lack of rank justified. Ryan didn't bother speculating. He worried instead about the fact they had no rifles.

The food finished, the men trudged down shadowy streets and through the archway that led into the smooth, hard-packed circle of the bullring. In the centre of the ring high piles of equipment had been stacked. "Hey, fellows," Ryan shouted. "Look, rifles!" His heart was racing. There was no question now—they were bound for the front. Someone started singing: "We'll hang General Franco from the sour apple tree, the sour apple tree, the sour apple tree." A few took up the refrain, but the song soon petered out as the officers got them busy breaking open the boxes of rifles. The

The news flowing over the field phones into the Lincolns' command post was grim throughout most of the fighting at Jarama. (MTRL T-10210)

rifles were Remingtons, which none of the men had handled before. Most bore the double-headed eagle of the Russian czar. An American volunteer informed Ryan that the rifles had been manufactured in the United States in 1914 for the Russian Imperial Army. There were also Remington replicas that had been made in the Soviet Union. These bore a hammer and sickle stamp on the butt and had barrels about seven centimetres shorter than the American model.

In addition to a rifle, each man received cartridge belts fitted with three leather ammunition boxes, a triangular, stiletto-type bayonet, and French helmets like those worn by the French *poilus* in the Great War. The helmets lacked any kind of liner and the metal felt as thin as paper. The last item dispensed was 150 rounds of ammunition per man.

After they were outfitted, André Marty, the political commissar of all the International Brigades, gave a rousing speech. Then, discovering that there were a half-dozen French-Canadians in the ranks—including one with the unlikely name of Joe Campbell—he sought out each individually and offered him a French embrace.

Feeling awkward under the weight of all his new equipment, Ryan joined his section and they marched from the bullring into the darkness of the streets. Soon they came to a fleet of trucks waiting with their motors running and their lights turned off. Guides with flashlights helped each section load.

Nobody in Ryan's truck had the slightest idea where they were going. The trucks were canvas covered, so the men could barely see out. Ryan estimated the truck offered three metres by two metres of floor space into which twenty-five men and all their equipment somehow had to fit. After much shifting about, they managed to attain some degree of comfort, often overlapping legs and arms.

For hours the trucks, travelling without headlights, crawled in a long, weaving chain through the night. Finally, in the early morning, they pulled into the village of Chinchón and learned they were about ten kilometres from the front lines. After passing through the town the trucks parked in a wide valley. Dismounting, Ryan and the others lined up for a serving of cold rations. Then, lounging next to their vehicles, they struggled to clean the Cosmoline protective coating off their rifles. As there were no cloths available for this, they had to tear pieces of fabric off their shirts.

In the early afternoon the men were taken in sections, lined up, and ordered to fire five shots into a nearby hillside. Many of the men had obviously never fired a rifle before. A man standing alongside Ryan held his rifle too loosely and was badly shaken by the recoil. "Squeeze it, dummy," Ryan told him. "Imagine you're with the girlfriend on the chesterfield. Hug it tight." The novice's next shot was better.

When rifle practice was over, they loaded up and the convoy followed the Valencia-Madrid road. Their destination was a front-line position thirty-three kilometres from Madrid and a couple of kilometres north of Morata de la Tajuña.

It was early evening as the trucks ground down a hill into Morata. Leaning out of the truck to catch a glimpse of the village, Ryan saw great geysers of earth spouting up near the village and then heard the dull thump of explosions. Glancing upward, he saw a small line of enemy bombers streak away toward their own lines. The bombing raid had caused no damage that Ryan could see other than turning up the soil of the fields

91

next to the town. As the convoy rumbled through the village, however, he saw that it had been partially destroyed by previous raids and artillery bombardments.

On the outskirts, the men clambered gratefully out of the trucks and lined up at a field kitchen for some hot stew. From a nearby hilltop the spattering crackle of rifle fire could be heard, punctuated occasionally by the dull rumbling thud of artillery shells.

At 4:00 P.M. the Lincolns were ordered back into the trucks. As they were getting on board, Ryan saw his friend Thomas Beckett climbing into a nearby truck. Although Beckett held no rank, Ryan thought the young man's khaki shirt, identically coloured breeches, and high boots gave him a commanding presence. Twilight was setting in as the trucks began moving cautiously uphill toward the front-line positions.

Crouching near the back of the truck, Ryan peered into the darkness. Suddenly there was a blinding flash, followed by a deafening explosion. Ryan felt as if the roof of his mouth had been jerked upward and his eyes driven deep into their sockets. It took a moment to realize he was witnessing a battery of Republican artillery opening a barrage. The guns were positioned under heavy camouflage amid the olive groves adjacent to the highway. Each salvo's concussion was deafening and set his ears ringing.

Just past the artillery emplacement was a white building they had been earlier told was where the trucks would stop. A whistle sounded softly. Ryan gathered his gear and scrambled out into the darkness.

It was a cold night, the ground ice-hard beneath his feet. The soldiers moved up the side of the hill. Near the top, a railroad track wound around in a half-loop to brush against the Madrid-Valencia road before cutting off across the rolling plateaus that crowned the hill and stretched almost to the outskirts of Madrid. The battalion crossed the tracks and moved up to the hill's crest. Beyond, a long billow of rough ground stretched all the way to the enemy lines. In the darkness, Ryan and the others were guided by the officers into their positions and ordered to dig in.

Ryan was tired. They had been on the go for more than thirty hours with no rest other than hastily snatched catnaps in the back of the trucks. Overhead bullets whistled, making a "zweet, zweet" sound that seemed to Ryan strangely musical and consequently unthreatening. But some Great War veterans started shouting, "Damn it, get your heads down!" Ryan followed their advice. Suddenly he felt less tired and more eager to get a hole dug.

The men worked through the night with picks and shovels to grub fortifications out of the earth. The top layer was stubborn hardpan, but the soil underneath was softer and more easily moved. It was still backbreaking, sweaty labour.

Ryan had been working away for several hours when one of the Canadians came over and told him that Thomas Beckett was missing. The truck carrying Beckett and twenty other Lincolns had apparently driven past the white building that had served as the stop point marker and crossed into the nearby enemy lines. The fascists were reported to be executing captured Internationals, so it had to be assumed that Beckett was dead. Too numbed by the news to speak, Ryan turned his back on the man and returned to digging. By morning the Lincolns had constructed a serviceable defensive trench line. It was February 17, 1937, and Canada had lost her first son in Spain—twenty-year-old Thomas Beckett.

On February 17, unemployed Calgary accountant Lionel Edwards was just preparing to leave Paris for southern France. This time, there would be no buses crossing the frontier. The French government had just closed the French-Spanish border. From now on the volunteers would have to illegally cross the Pyrenees on foot.

Edwards had left Calgary with two other volunteers in early January, arriving in France two weeks later. They had shipped out from New York City to Le Havre. With about one hundred American and Canadian Internationals on the ship they had virtually outnumbered the other passengers.

At Le Havre an American consulate official had boarded and tried convincing the Americans to go home. The official said the Americans were violating U.S. law, which forbade their serving in foreign armies. All the men refused to turn back and, despite their purpose in coming to France, the customs officials quickly processed the group's entry.

They were billeted for ten days at the Paris trade union headquarters building while arrangements were made for their clandestine passage into Spain. Edwards made the best of his time in Paris, sightseeing by day and enjoying wine and food in the cafés by night.

Finally the entire group of one hundred left Paris by train for a small village near Perpignan, close to the Spanish border. Each man was taken before the municipal clerk, who gave the volunteer a small amount of money, counting out French francs while the local chief of police looked on. Considering the French government was supposedly trying to thwart the volunteers' mission to Spain, this seemed a curious show of bureaucratic fraternization.

The volunteers were in the village for only one day. In the late afternoon, they were loaded onto a bus painted a vivid crimson that Edwards figured was probably visible to anyone within thirty kilometres. The bus followed the setting sun into the foothills. When the bus stopped, the men, as earlier instructed, tumbled out and ran like fugitives through the fields and irrigation ditches to a thicket of olive trees. They hid beneath the trees until evening.

It was approaching dark when two men dressed in rough, heavy clothes appeared. The men were professional smugglers, members of a government-recognized smugglers' labour union organized by the French Communist Party. To show their international solidarity, the men said, they escorted volunteers into Spain over the ancient smuggling routes. With one smuggler leading and the other bringing up the rear, the men set off in a long line through the gathering gloom. Soon they were climbing steep mountain paths. The pace was relentless. If anyone showed the slightest sign of flagging, one of the guides would appear at his elbow and urge him to keep up. When a couple of older men, who had fought in the Great War, said they could not go on they were left behind. The guides said they would pick the men up on their way back and another route would be found to get them into Spain. At about 4:00 A.M.. the column halted. The men were given permission to talk and smoke. One of the guides said they were now in Spain. Edwards was too worn out to care.

With the dawn, pretty towns could be seen strung along the coastline. About 275 metres beyond the summit the group came to a white house, where a filthy-looking, bearded guard armed with a submachine gun halted them. The guard was an anarchist. Inside the house he had a tub of warm coffee waiting. It was the most welcome cup of coffee Edwards ever remembered drinking. He stood outside the house, gazing down at the Catalonian countryside, letting the sun warm his aching body. Everyone was laughing and joking; spirits were high. After a short rest they set off down the slopes. After the night's bitter climbing it was surprisingly easy going.

Soon they were met by trucks and taken to Figueras. After a few days there they boarded trains for Albacete. At Albacete they were gathered together in the bullring and processed into units, each man being issued a pay book and uniform. Some of the men were given rifles and sent immediately to Jarama to reinforce the Lincolns.

Edwards was not among this group. Because of his accounting experience, he was posted to brigade headquarters. There he was given a job in
the personnel office doing routine clerical and administrative work. Back
in Calgary, this was the last fate Edwards had ever imagined befalling him
in Spain. But he was also a soldier now and that meant obeying orders, so
he filed no protest. Still, he envied his compatriots who were doing what a
soldier was meant to do.

For Larry Ryan, February 27 marked the end of his war. Wounded in the
day's butchery and showing the first symptoms of tuberculosis contracted
during his ten days in the Jarama trenches, Ryan was beginning a journey
homeward to Canada. His future, he knew, was grim—years spent in
sanitariums fighting a terrible disease. Despite how his Spanish service had
unfolded, Ryan did not regret his decision to volunteer.

Ryan believed the other Canadians who had fallen on the Jarama front
would share this sentiment. Between February 17, when the Lincolns went
into the lines, and their withdrawal as a shattered unit following the bitter
engagement of February 27, seven Canadians had died. Thomas Beckett
also remained missing and was presumed dead. Frederick Lackey, one of
the other members of the group of Torontonians who had been the first
soldiers to arrive from Canada, had also been killed. So, too, had the French-
Canadian Joe Campbell. At forty-one, he had been the oldest Canadian
serving with the Lincolns.

Ryan was frankly amazed to be alive. So many had fallen during those
ten bitter days. The casualties on February 21 and 27 had been particularly
dreadful, the fighting like something out of the Great War. On the afternoon of February 21, the officers had come down the line, telling the men
to get ready to go over the top. They were to take their rifles, ammunition, gas masks, and water canteens. Nothing else, nothing that would slow
them down.

The two infantry companies moved out, advancing in ranks down the
boulder-strewn slope that fronted their defensive trenches, up a ravine,
and across the Madrid-Valencia road in a mad dash. First Company took
shelter in a half-dug trench. Second Company, in which Ryan and most of
the Canadians served, found dubious shelter in an olive grove standing
behind the trench. They were only about six to seven hundred metres from
the fascist entrenchments. Enemy machine guns searched for them with
fingers of death. The bullets from the fascist guns kept clipping olive

branches off above their heads, so foliage showered constantly down upon their helmets and shoulders. The Machine-Gun Company came up and linked into Second Company's right flank. Battalion headquarters, including Merriman, slipped into the trenches next to First Company.

Ryan had no idea what overall strategy had dictated that the Lincolns should launch an attack. He only knew that they were expected to push the fascists out of their positions. There was really no need for him to know more.

Off to one side some tanks rolled by and trundled toward the enemy lines. Lying on his belly behind a tree, Ryan gnawed on a stale chunk of bread. God knew when there would be another chance to eat. A cluster of Spaniards, carrying wounded militiamen on stretchers, came through the olive grove on their way to the rear field hospital. One bearer party lowered its burden, covered the wounded soldier's face with a blanket, and trudged back toward their lines. A Lincoln next to Ryan raised a fist in silent salute, and the two Spaniards offered clenched fists in return.

"Damn it, why don't we go?" Ryan muttered. Moments later an officer came by telling the men to fix their bayonets. "Make sure your bolts are on safety," he added. "No firing until the order is given."

Company One jumped off first. Ryan watched them go—a line of men in khaki uniforms running wildly across an open field and a vineyard. Ryan's company was ordered forward next. They scrambled out of the olive grove, across a stretch of open ground, and threw themselves into the trench vacated by Company One. The trench was so shallow Ryan had to crouch so he could stay under cover and still lay his rifle over the parapet.

Darkness was falling rapidly. Ahead of him, Company One continued running forward, dropping to the ground, then jumping back up and running again. Up, run, down; up, run, down. Pushing ever forward. The rattle of gunfire from both sides swelled to an unending crescendo. The bark of tank cannon punctuated the incessant machine-gun and rifle fire.

Company Two's officers ordered them forward. Ryan ran out into the field. Artillery shells started bursting ahead of his advancing line, bullets whispered overhead in a whistling symphony he thought sounded like, *Zwei sue, Zwei sue.* What was he thinking about that for? Nearby somebody let out a smothered, "Ugh." It was a guttural sound, involuntarily released in a surprised tone. The sound came again and again from the lips of men who then toppled to the ground, some never to move again. There was no time to help them. The officers kept ordering the line forward.

A tank behind them exploded, flames spewing from its hull. The fire silhouetted the men so they presented perfect targets to the enemy. Company One suddenly, as if responding to a single thought, all dropped flat to the ground. Some of the men started shooting their rifles, others scrabbled at the earth with bare hands in a desperate attempt to dig a foxhole.

When Ryan's company reached the point where Company One had gone to ground, they also hit the dirt. After advancing about five hundred metres they were only about two hundred metres from the enemy lines. It was two hundred metres too far, however, for they could go no farther. There were enemy machine-gun nests everywhere Ryan looked. The Lincolns were caught in the trough of a V-shaped crossfire.

When the flames from the tank burned out, darkness enveloped the battlefield. Without the burning tank to provide target silhouettes, the fascists could no longer zero their fire and it started ranging high. As long as the Lincolns hugged the ground, Ryan realized, they would be safe.

An officer shouted, "Keep your heads down, comrades, and dig. You've gone as far as you're going tonight."

"Dig! What with?" a soldier snapped back.

"Your hands, your knife, your helmet. Get your body below ground," the officer responded.

Ryan dug. At first the enemy machine guns continued to blaze away over their heads. Then, as the lack of targets became apparent, the fire turned sporadic, desultory.

From all over the field came agonized cries of "First aid, first aid." Ryan could see the flitting shadows of stretcher-bearers in the gloom. Sometimes the machine guns tried to follow the bearers, the bright tracer rounds falling in a mesmerizing arc toward the running figures. All too often, as they lost the race against the enemy guns, the shadowy figures crumpled. Ryan watched these men die and vowed in the morning to offer no fascist mercy.

Directly behind the Lincolns, a Spanish labour battalion moved in and set to digging a defensive trench as quietly as possible. The Lincolns held their position, guarding the labour battalion from any counterattack. Later, a Spanish battalion slid into the trench and relieved the Lincolns. They reformed in the olive grove from which, only hours before, the attack had been launched. Ryan and the other Canadians let out small cries of relief and offered the soft pressure of shaken hands on discovering each other still alive and unwounded. Casualties proved surprisingly light. At least one Canadian, a Russian émigré from Montreal by the name of Elias Aviezer, had fallen.

Six days later the XVth International Brigade shifted to another position facing a hillside riddled with deeply entrenched fascist machine-gun and rifle pits. This time they were to attack with no support from other Republican units, tanks, or artillery. Everyone could see it was a hopeless assault. The Lincolns' commander, Robert Merriman, tried everything short of mutiny to get it cancelled. When his superiors refused to rescind the order, he reluctantly ordered the men forward.

Despite the obvious futility of it all, the men gave their best. Some Americans from the Deep South even went over the top screaming Rebel yells as they charged. Their yells gave way immediately to screams from the wounded and dying. No sooner had the Lincolns left the trenches than they were hit by a withering fire. Merriman was wounded only a few feet beyond the parapet. Ryan fell soon after. Incredibly, a handful of the Lincolns pressed to within ten metres of the enemy barbed wire before all being killed. The British Battalion was chopped to pieces when it tried rushing in to bolster the Lincoln attack. The Dimitrov Battalion started forward but hastily withdrew in the face of the terrible fire.

In an aid station, Ryan learned his wound was minor, but the doctor also suspected he had tuberculosis. This diagnosis was confirmed at the field hospital. Of the 450 Lincolns who went into battle on February 27, 127 were dead, more than 200 were wounded.

Lying in the hospital, Ryan soon heard a song that had just been written by Glasgow volunteer Alex McDade. Called "There's a Valley in Spain," it was sung to the tune of "Red River Valley." The words seemed to aptly describe Ryan's short, terrible experience of war.

There's a valley in Spain called Jarama,
That's a place that we all know so well,
For 'tis there that we wasted our manhood,
And most of our old age as well.

Six

$\mathscr{F}$OR THE CAUSE

PRESSURED BY BRITAIN AND, BIZARRELY, GERMANY TO ENFORCE the Non-Intervention Agreement, France responded in early 1937 by ordering its army to close the easiest routes through the Pyrenees to Spain. International volunteers caught in the mountain passes were detained for deportation to their home countries. News of France's new policy had Jules Päiviö deeply worried by the time his group started preparing to cross the Pyrenees from Toulouse. His journey to Spain had proved difficult, so he feared being thwarted when he was at last standing on the very threshold.

Early in January 1937, Päiviö had impulsively quit his job in Sudbury and decided, despite lacking any contacts who could set him on the right path, to join the International Brigades. His father, Aku Päiviö, edited a Finnish-Canadian literary weekly, so Päiviö's last name was well regarded in Ontario's tightly knit Finnish community, especially in Thunder Bay, where he had been born and raised. Thunder Bay's Finnish community was typical of those in other Ontario cities such as Port Arthur, Timmins, Kirkland Lake, Sudbury, and Toronto. All shared strong egalitarian beliefs. In the Finnish-Canadian press, discussion about the Spanish Civil War often revolved around the role individuals should play in resisting fascism's spread. Päiviö, like many other young Finns, found this discussion deeply compelling. In keeping with their belief in individual responsibility, a surprisingly high number of Finns were volunteering for Spanish service. [The precise number of Finnish-Canadians who served in Spain is unknown, but Päiviö and other sources estimate that about 180 of the approximately sixteen hundred Canadian volunteers were Finns.]

Before setting out on his quest, Päiviö went to bid his family farewell. To avoid alarming his mother, Päiviö pretended he was merely departing on a long vacation. After dinner, Päiviö insisted on saying good-bye to his mother and siblings inside the cabin. Although his father was so weakened by influenza he could hardly stand, Päiviö asked for a private word.

Outside, Päiviö firmly clasped Aku's hand. "Good-bye, Dad. I am on my way to Spain," he said. At this news, Aku slumped and nearly fell. Päiviö hastened to support him.

"Have you considered this serious matter?" Aku wheezed. "Look, from such wars you do not return."

"I have considered, Dad, and decided so." Päiviö kept silent about a premonition he had that he was destined to die in Spain. How could he tell his father that such a death seemed more worthwhile than to continue working at a dead-end job in depression-riddled Canada?

After giving his father's hand another firm shake, Päiviö walked away. He did not look back—knowing the sight of his father standing in the doorway would be too difficult to bear. Päiviö could well imagine the sorrow that would etch his father's face as he watched his eldest son disappear into a night that promised to swallow him for eternity.

Bidding his family farewell proved no easier than the actual task of getting to Spain. His initial plan of sailing from Montreal on a passenger liner was scuttled when he discovered no European sailings were scheduled for several months. Returning to Ontario, Päiviö spent several weeks establishing links through the Finnish community in Toronto with the Committee to Aid Spanish Democracy. The committee arranged Päiviö's passage to France via New York City. Early in February, Päiviö and about 150 American and Canadian volunteers boarded the steamer *President Roosevelt* and sailed for Le Havre.

The volunteers followed the usual route to Paris through Le Havre. After a week in Paris, Päiviö and thirty others went to Toulouse. The next morning they boarded a bus for the foothills. Outside each town they were ordered to get down on the floor to avoid being seen. Night was falling when the bus finally stopped. Outside, the air was cool. A river, swollen with melting water, rushed by close to the roadside. Out of the gloom a guide materialized and ordered them into single file. He then led off toward the mountains.

North American volunteers to the International Brigades aboard the President
Roosevelt *en route to Europe.*   (NAC C67465)

Päiviö could barely see the back of the man before him. They passed
through a completely darkened village. No sounds came from any of the
shadowy buildings.

Beyond the village, the track started climbing. The path soon narrowed
and they wound along the edge of deep gorges. When a stone fell off the
side of the trail, Päiviö was unable to hear it strike bottom. By daybreak
they had reached the snow line. Because it was late winter, the snow came
far down the mountain's flank. Päiviö looked across the great expanse of
snow and realized they were in for a hell of a long, difficult walk.

Like most of the men, Päiviö wore only a pair of ordinary leather ox-
fords and thin socks. His clothes were more suitable for lounging around
Paris cafés than climbing mountains. The smooth soles of his shoes slipped
and slid on the snow. When the surface crust broke underneath his weight,
the jagged snow on the edge of the hole into which he fell painfully scraped
his ankles. Soon his shoes were full of snow and his feet were thoroughly
soaked.

The guide set a brisk pace, refusing all pleas for rest stops. It was a long
way to the mountain summit, he said, and beyond that lay the Spanish
border, so they must press hard or fail to make it safely before nightfall.
The air thinned, breathing became difficult. An out-of-shape, overweight
American volunteer named Steve started straggling. As the air grew ever
more rarefied Steve began stumbling and weaving. Although the snow's

surface crust could usually support the other men, Steve's weight often proved too formidable. When the crust broke beneath his feet, Steve was plunged to his waist in the soft underlying snow. There, he floundered helplessly until the others pulled him free.

About 7:00 A.M. they reached an old cabin. The guide built a small, warming fire. Each man received a small chunk of bread and a sip of wine from the guide's own gourd. The meagre offering revived Päiviö. When they shortly left the cabin and started climbing a steep four-kilometre slope toward the summit, Päiviö easily kept the pace. Although the snow grew ever deeper, its crust was still too thin for the hapless Steve. Finally the guide looped a length of rope around Steve's waist and positioned two men on either side of him. When the man broke through the crust, the other four clung to the ends of the rope and used it to drag him from the hole. They would continue pulling him across the snow until the surface was hard enough to again support him.

Päiviö and an American, Fred Field, stayed by Steve's side the whole way up. The others helped by turns. Nobody complained or bitched at Steve. They all knew there was nothing the man could do and that they were all in this ordeal together.

Their collective spirits sagged, however, as hour passed into hour and the elusive summit seemingly drew no closer. Adding to their travail was the tendency of the snow to collapse not only under Steve but also under the men helping him. Then all the mired men would have to be rescued by the others. Time and again Steve broke through the crust and had to be yanked free. The effort became so exhausting for them all that they could only advance fifteen metres or so before having to rest for several minutes.

Then Steve lost consciousness. Päiviö and the others took turns rubbing his face with snow, slapping him, or forcibly dragging him to his feet. He began begging incoherently to be left behind. To do so would be to consign Steve to death from exposure, so they ignored his pleas and kept going. Tirelessly the guide ran back and forth along the column, alternately helping a man at the back of the column who was lagging and then returning to the front to show the way.

The wind rose, snow started blowing. Minutes later they were caught in a blizzard. Päiviö could hardly see, and the blowing snow made breathing almost impossible. His light hat blew away. Within minutes he could feel his ears start to freeze. Pulling up his scarf, Päiviö wrapped it like a shawl over his head and ears.

On they climbed, stumbling wearily through the snow, trying not to show their fear. Sometimes the blizzard would lift momentarily and Päiviö would glimpse the summit, still far away. Finally, after six hours of this hellish struggle to ascend only four kilometres, the men staggered over the summit. Päiviö dragged Steve, more dead than alive, onto the level shelf. Then Päiviö gratefully plunked himself down on the snow. They were allowed only a short respite before the guide ordered them forward. Päiviö was sickened to find they were still climbing, but his apprehension turned to relief when, after only a short distance, they came to another small cabin.

The guide told them they were now in Spain and the pace would be easier. After a brief rest, they started a slow descent. Steve was still too weak to walk on his own, so the men took turns supporting him. They descended carefully, stepping into the footsteps left by the previous man in the column. If anyone slipped he would slide all the way down to an evil-looking jumble of rocks lying at the bottom of the slope. Late in the afternoon, the group reached a muddy, dirty village scrunched against the foot of the mountain. Here Päiviö learned the mountain they had crossed was more than twenty-seven hundred metres high.

The villagers fed the men and tended to their raw and frostbitten feet. Then Päiviö and his compatriots marched several kilometres to another village, where they settled down to wait for transport.

With Norman Bethune at the wheel, it had taken the ambulance only an hour to drive from Madrid to Guadalajara on March 12, 1937. Henning Sorenson, photographer Geza Karpathi, and a Spanish assistant were crowded into the ambulance. The sky was brilliantly clear, the air crisp and cold.

For four days the fascists had been grinding out of the northeast toward the provincial capital of Guadalajara in yet another attempt to seize Madrid. It was a huge offensive involving more than fifty thousand troops. The left flank of the attack was composed entirely of Italian soldiers. They numbered four divisions of thirty thousand men, supported by 250 tanks, 180 pieces of mobile artillery, and special flamethrower units. Although initially successful, the offensive was now bogging down before stout Republican resistance.

All the way to Guadalajara, Bethune passed long lines of Republican tanks, artillery, supply trucks, and soldiers marching toward the front. It was obvious the Republicans—hoping to force the fascists back from their gains—were massing for a major counterattack.

A bitter wind blew off the snow that smothered the Guadarrama range. It whistled through the broken left front window of the ambulance, making Bethune grateful for the warmth of the thick brown coat he and the others had received the previous week from the Syndicate of Tailors of Madrid. That had also been the week a swinging pole attached to a mule train had shattered the ambulance window.

Bethune drove in the oncoming traffic lane, racing past the advancing Republican forces, and only ducking into gaps in the traffic when vehicles approached from the opposite direction. This way he was able to maintain speeds of eighty kilometres an hour or more.

As they roared over a bridge spanning the torrent of the river Henares and entered Guadalajara, Bethune saw the hospital overlooking the town from a hilltop. Soon they drove into the entrance to the five-hundred-bed facility. The red crosses that had previously indicated the building was a hospital had all been painted over because fascist bombers had used the crosses as aiming points during a raid the week before.

Inside, blood-drenched stretchers, waiting to be washed, were stacked against one wall. Nurses and orderlies rushed in every direction. Bethune was told to go straight to the operating room with the ten-pint bottles of blood he carried in a wire basket.

In the surgery, doctors worked at three tables. The air stank of ether. Bethune went to the white enamelled refrigerator standing against the wall. It contained seven empty blood bottles and three that were unused. Bethune put six fresh pints in and took out the empty bottles. At this rate of consumption they would have to come back tomorrow to replenish the supply. This was how it had been since the enemy offensive began. Rather giddily, Bethune imagined himself being like a travelling salesman blessed with happy customers eager to consume all the wares he could offer.

In a separate surgery, situated at the end of a long corridor filled with walking wounded, Bethune and Sorenson found Dr. Douglas W. Jolly, a New Zealander. His surgery was packed with wounded awaiting his attention. They sat on the floor with blood-stained bandages covering their head, arm, and leg wounds. With a wide smile of greeting, Jolly cheerfully reported that his assistant André was completely out of blood.

They rushed back to the ambulance and retrieved a portable refrigerator, which they plugged into an outlet in Jolly's operating room. Inside the refrigerator were the day's remaining four pints of blood. Just as they finished, André, a young French medical graduate, rushed up. His black, short-cut beard gave him a piratical appearance. In bursts of machine-gun French he said: "Can you leave me another two needles? I need another syringe. I broke one last night. Can you give me some more grouping serums?"

Bethune handed over the supplies. "I want to write my thesis for my master's degree in the University of Paris on blood transfusion at the front. Will you Canadians help me?"

Bethune said he would. Jolly, hunched over a patient, shouted for André. "I must go now," the young man said, "but there's a wounded man upstairs from the International Brigade and we can't make out what nationality he is. He can't speak English, French, Italian, Spanish, or German. He's been hit by a bomb, lost one hand. We had to amputate the other and he's blinded in one eye. He needs a blood transfusion. We have to operate but I'm afraid he can't stand the shock. Will you give him a transfusion?"

Sorenson and Bethune went looking for the wounded International. A pretty Spanish nurse shook her dark head and smiled when Bethune asked, "Where's the man you can't make understand?"

"Oh, there's lots of those."

"He's lost both hands and he's blind."

"Here, come, this ward."

On a bed lay a man with a bloody bandage covering his head. His swollen face was caked with blood, as was the torn shirt of his uniform. Shapeless, blood-stained bandages covered the stumps at his wrists.

"Sorenson, come here," Bethune said.

The man's head turned slowly at the sound of Sorenson's name. Swollen lips moved in a question that was unintelligible to Bethune. Sorenson leaned forward, speaking in a rapid, strange language. "Why, he's Swedish," Sorenson explained. "No wonder they can't understand him."

With Sorenson calming the man, Bethune set to work. The tourniquets on the man's wrists had stemmed the blood flow from both torn radial arteries, but the look of the man's face and his feeble pulse told Bethune he had lost a couple of quarts. It took five minutes to get the blood heated to body temperature and prepare the wounded soldier for the transfusion.

When the transfusion was completed, Sorenson asked the man if he felt better. A twist of bruised lips was his only reply.

Sorenson remained hunched over the man, his face bearing the anxious, distressed air of a father worried for an only child. As Bethune cleaned

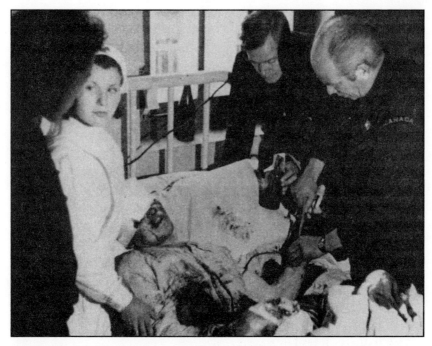

Bethune (front right) and Sorenson (next to Bethune) give a transfusion to a wounded Swedish International volunteer who had lost both his hands and been blinded after only three days in Spain. (NAC C67451, Geza Karpathi photo)

the syringe and packed his bag, Sorenson kept talking to the wounded man. When Bethune checked the pulse it was over one hundred and strong. Colour had returned to his face. "Come," Bethune said to Sorenson. Bethune watched the young Dane tear himself away with seeming reluctance. At the door he turned back to reply to something the wounded man said.

"What did he say?" Bethune asked as they walked down the corridor.

Sorenson's voice was sad. "He said, 'Ten days ago I was in Sweden. I have been in Spain three days. This was my first engagement, and now I am no more use to my comrades. I have done nothing for the cause.'"

Bethune and Sorenson looked at each other. "Done nothing!" Bethune said. What modesty, what courage, what a soul, he thought.

Not that Lionel Edwards considered his International Brigade headquarters' duties unimportant, but the Calgary accountant had not come to Spain with the ambition of serving as a clerk. Every day more Canadians passed through Albacete en route to the XVth's new training base at Madrigueras. After a brief training period, most joined the Abraham Lincoln Battalion on the Jarama front. The few held back were primarily bolstering the ranks of a new formative American unit—the George Washington Battalion.

Following the fascist offensive's collapse and the failure of the February 27 counterattack, a desultory quiet settled upon Jarama valley. Soldiers spent their days patrolling and enduring sniper and artillery fire. The resultant light casualties allowed the decimated battalions to slowly rebuild with new recruits.

Charged with processing the effects of every International who was killed in Spain, Edwards was aware of each new casualty the Lincolns suffered. Although the Jarama front was quiet, the German-Austrian Thaelmann Battalion was fighting in the bloody engagement at Guadalajara. So he never lacked for work.

Headquarters staff was composed of an amazing assortment of odd characters. They left Edwards feeling staid and, hence, very Canadian. There was Einsel, an Estonian opera star who, when given the slightest excuse, swept about the office belting out arias. An Egyptian named Salem, who had been a South Seas merchant, was oddly enough in charge of indoctrinating fascist prisoners to the glories of communism. In better times, Hans, a small, jovial German, had owned a Hamburg bar frequented by left-wingers. In the mid-1930s, with the Nazis closing such establishments and imprisoning their owners, Hans fled to Cuba and took up rum smuggling. Remembering his leftist roots upon reading of Spain's war, however, Hans abandoned his lucrative trade and volunteered as an International.

Of all of them, however, the Corsican Jacosta most amazed Edwards. He had rushed to the Republic's aid from Rio de Janeiro, where he and some friends had devised a unique scheme not only to travel to Spain but to arrive with vitally needed supplies by hijacking an ammunition-laden ship from the Argentinean port. The Popular Front government had happily accepted the offering, somehow averting an international diplomatic crisis with Argentina in subsequent negotiations.

Jacosta was fluent in seven languages and could capably, but imperfectly, manage thirteen others—including Persian. He could also read Sanskrit. His French was so adept that he understood the subtleties of most major regional dialects. In his spare time, he was writing a simplified French grammar text.

Jacosta volunteered to try sharpening Edwards's Spanish. He rousted

Edwards early every morning, plunked him down to breakfast, and then took him shopping in the markets for Jacosta's most passionately enjoyed food—luscious blood oranges. All the while, Jacosta coached Edwards through his language lessons.

Headquarters life was both interesting and immensely entertaining, but it also seemed like shirking. Every day other young Canadians laid their lives on the line, while Edwards sorted paper amid the din of operatic arias.

More than two hundred Canadians were scattered throughout the various International Brigades. By June, their numbers were likely to exceed five hundred. Within the Lincolns, they organized an unofficial Canadian section called the Mackenzie-Papineaus, in honour of William Lyon Mackenzie and Louis-Joséph Papineau, leaders of the failed 1837 Rebellion against British rule in Upper and Lower Canada. The group immediately nicknamed itself Mac-Paps. Upon forming their own unit the Canadian ringleaders cabled Prime Minister King—grandson of William Lyon Mackenzie. The cable read: "We implore you from the depths of our hearts to do everything possible to help Spanish democracy. In so doing you are serving your own interests. We are here for the duration until fascism is defeated." King never replied.

Seeing the Canadians grouping into an identifiable unit made Edwards all the more restive. Four weeks after being assigned to headquarters, he asked his brigade commander, André Marty, for a transfer to a line unit. When asked his reason, Edwards said he wanted to serve the cause in the company of other Canadians. Marty ordered Edwards to report for officer training and attached to his orders a proviso that, upon completion of his training, he should be posted to the Lincolns' Canadian contingent. As Marty was rapidly developing a reputation throughout the Internationals for possessing an erratic, sometimes dangerous, temperament, Edwards thought Marty's actions typically reflective of the man's mercurial nature.

If Bethune continued behaving as he had since Málaga, Henning Sorenson worried the doctor would share Emil Kléber's fate. In January, the Spanish government had stripped Kléber of his Madrid command. Rumours abounded that Kléber had been relieved purely because the international press had elevated him to a higher level of fame than was accorded his Spanish compatriot in Madrid's defence, General José Miaja. Kléber was reportedly languishing in a Valencia hotel, awaiting appointment to a new, lower-profile command. [Kléber would briefly command the Republican 45th Division on the Aragon front before being unjustly relieved because of further intervention by jealous Spanish generals. Retiring to the Soviet Union, he immediately fell victim to Stalin's ongoing purges. According to a February 10, 1965, article in the Soviet newspaper *Sovietskaia Bukovian*, Kléber was imprisoned and died in a labour camp. Prior to the appearance of this article—the first official Soviet acknowledgement that Kléber had indeed died as a result of Stalin's purges—it was generally believed Kléber had been shot shortly after arriving in the Soviet Union. Prior to the article's release, Kléber was posthumously cleared of the trumped-up charges that served as official pretence for his arrest and imprisonment by Stalin.]

Since Málaga, the Republican government had been trying to centralize control over the war effort. Formerly independent units, such as the militias and Bethune's Canadian medical team, were being welded to the Republican Army—now designated as the Popular Army. At Málaga the militias had suffered their first irreversible defeat. The disorganized and informal structure of the militias was being blamed for the calamity. Leading the criticism was the Spanish Communist Party, which was accusing all anarchists, and POUM particularly, of being Franco collaborationists.

Even as Sorenson and Bethune shuttled blood back and forth to the Guadalajara front, Sorenson realized the Canadian blood transfusion unit would not long be free of Spanish regimentation. Bethune, however, seemed oblivious to this emerging reality, or simply failed to care. He worked frantically to construct an ever larger, more effective blood transfusion unit. He renamed the unit the Instituto Hispano-Canadiense de Transfusion de Sangre. Staff increased to twenty-five and included a hematologist, bacteriologist, five Spanish doctors, three assistants, six nurses, four technicians, drivers, and servants. All the Madrid front's transfusion units were brought under Bethune's operational umbrella. The reorganized unit served one hundred hospitals and casualty clearing stations for one hundred kilometres around Madrid—incorporating a thousand kilometres of front-line positions. This was the first unified blood transfusion service in army and medical history, and Bethune planned to extend it to supply the entire Republican army on all fronts with preserved blood. But he was also fiercely defending his personal control over the independent unit.

It was an ambitious and noble design, but Bethune's lack of tolerance for bureaucratic delays and the frailties of human ego led to his embroilment in rancorous disputes with Spanish officials. With increasing dismay,

Sorenson and Sise watched Bethune alienate ever more people in his singular drive to expand the blood transfusion service.

Colleagues found napping by Bethune were berated for being "Franco sympathizers" and "bourgeois bastards." During one apoplectic fury Bethune smashed his fist through an office door's glass window, sending blood gushing from a deep slash to his hand.

Bethune simply could not admit human weakness, but all the volunteers in the unit were wearing down. They had been working for months, with too little rest, in a hazardous activity. Madrid's Spanish medical authorities were equally weary and prickly when harangued by some foreigner who thought he possessed all the answers on how to effectively operate transfusion services.

The fact Bethune appeared tireless in comparison to everyone around him failed to help matters. Every morning, Sorenson marvelled as Bethune emerged seemingly fresh as a daisy from his bed. While everyone else seemed to be collectively flagging with each passing week, Bethune appeared capable of a full rally after a mere hour's afternoon nap. Bethune could also sleep anywhere and anytime possible. Sorenson would enviously watch him drop into deep, untroubled sleep on a railway station platform. When the train arrived, a totally refreshed Bethune would jump up and lead the way aboard, while Sorenson grumpily and wearily trailed behind. Yet occasionally Bethune would show he was only human. In those moments, Sorenson watched fatigue wash over Bethune's features so palpably that the doctor looked as if he had aged twenty years in a moment's glimmer.

Sometimes Bethune's behaviour scared Sorenson, at other times it was merely maddening. Bethune's suave way with women especially frustrated the young Dane, who fancied himself something of a lady's man. That Bethune was attractive to women and had a personality they found magnetic was beyond question, but Sorenson thought his seduction technique lacked subtlety.

There was the case of the South African journalist who came to write about the Canadian blood transfusion unit and the siege of Madrid. Sorenson was in the hotel lounge when Bethune and she were ensconced over cocktails. Sitting at a nearby table, he could not fail to eavesdrop on the conversation. Bethune leaned forward, giving her his attentive look, which seemed to Sorenson an expression that some oily con man might adopt. "Give me your hand," Bethune said. The woman complied. "Look me in the eye." She did. "You know, you're a very nice person," Bethune continued.

That's a low line, Sorenson thought. But to his amazement the woman said, "I want to go to bed with you tonight."

All too often that bed was in the room he shared with Bethune. On such occasions, Bethune would approach Sorenson and say, "Henning, I want to go to bed with this woman tonight. Could you go and sleep in Dr. Loma's room?"

While Bethune's womanizing was, considering his success in comparison to Sorenson's own spotty luck, infuriating, it was not this part of the doctor's behaviour that was frightening. Sorenson's increasing fear came from Bethune's seemingly deliberate dance with death. Bethune could never get enough of the front lines. At every opportunity Bethune rushed toward the fighting, all too often carrying Sorenson reluctantly along in his wake.

Once Bethune drove the ambulance to a field hospital for a blood delivery. Instead of returning to Madrid along the safe road they had used on the way out, Bethune insisted on driving back via the front lines. They were still within sight of the field hospital when fascist guns opened up on the ambulance, sending them all scrambling into the ditches and crawling on their bellies back to the safety of the hospital.

A Republican infantry platoon soon cleared the hidden enemy position so Bethune and Sorenson could reclaim their ambulance. The vehicle had been hit by several bullets, including one that had gone right through the driver's windshield. Absolutely thrilled by this near contact with death, Bethune gabbled on about it endlessly for hours.

Sorenson and Sise feared Bethune's lust for danger might get them all killed. He refused to reconnoitre potentially dangerous situations, driving in as if he were leading some kind of cavalry charge instead of merely driving an unarmed ambulance. With the front lines ever shifting and vehicles from both sides constantly blundering into the other's lines, every corner turned might easily conceal an enemy machine gun. Still, Bethune, who increasingly insisted on doing most of the driving near the front, never slowed the ambulance or allowed the scouting of a suspect crossroad. It made the whole task more dangerous than necessary and greatly increased their fatigue. Unlike Bethune, who experienced an adrenalin high from danger, Sorenson and Sise derived only a rising nervous anxiety.

At times, however, it was apparent Bethune might also be feeling the strain. Like Sorenson and Sise, he drank too much. And the drinking started to affect Bethune's work. Before his hands had been rock steady. Now, when giving transfusions, they shook.

111

Despite Bethune's many faults, however, Sorenson would still follow the doctor almost anywhere he cared to lead. Sorenson especially admired and was inspired by how Bethune worked with the wounded. All the impassioned anger, the intolerance of ineptitude, the disdain for those who could not, or would not, do what Bethune considered right, melted away in the hospital wards. There, he was so very tender, so very concerned. When they entered a hospital, it was as if Bethune's whole personality changed.

Most of the patients were Spanish and could hardly understand a word Bethune spoke, but they always responded to him as if he were some beloved, caring father. With civilians his manner was especially gentle and loving. Sorenson always remembered the day Bethune was giving a transfusion to a sixteen-year-old girl in Madrid. An artillery shell had blown off both her legs. That she had been extremely beautiful before suffering such terrible wounds was obvious, and Sorenson could barely keep back his tears of anger and sorrow over all she had lost. "Who is going to marry me now?" the young girl moaned pitifully. Bethune hushed her gently. Speaking in English, he told her she was beautiful. As the doctor slowly, lovingly stroked her cheek, Sorenson saw her lips form a sad, sweet smile and her emotionally wrought state dissipated. Although the blood restored her physical ability to survive the shock of her wounds, Sorenson believed it was Bethune's gentle touch that gave her sufficient spirit to continue living.

Twenty-two-year-old Canadian POUMist William Krehm believed the Popular Front's spirit was being undermined by the Spanish Communist Party. Because of the Non-Intervention Agreement and the United States and Canada's unwavering neutrality policy, the Soviet Union had emerged as the Republic's primary source for arms, munitions, and vitally needed medical supplies. This reliance on Soviet arms had given the Communist Party ever more sway. Backing up the supplies was an influx of Soviet officers and military specialists serving as fighter pilots and tankers.

Soviet weapons and military expertise, however, failed to come without a price. The entire Spanish gold reserve had been shipped to the Soviet Union in November 1936. Ostensibly this was to safeguard the reserve from seizure by the fascists, but it also served as security for the Republic's armament purchases. [The Soviet Union subsequently confiscated the entire reserve estimated at 63 million British pounds as compensation for the "aid" it had given the Republic.] By late winter, the Spanish Communist

Party was starting to openly flex its newfound political muscle. It demanded the repression of anarchist organizations, especially those identified as being associated with Trotskyite philosophy.

The Communist Party's propaganda organs, backed by many government information outlets, publicly blamed the anarchists for every setback befalling the Republican side. POUM attracted special attention—often cited as an organization openly collaborating with the fascists. POUMists behind the lines were called Fifth Columnists. POUM soldiers were said to be playing football games with the opposing fascists in the no man's land of the Aragon and Andalusian fronts, while in the lines held by Communist units men were dying in desperate, heroic battles.

The wonderful alternative to Russian-style communism that Krehm had once believed existed in the Popular Front government was withering on the vine, nipped in the bud by a Stalinist frost. Krehm was deeply depressed by all he saw. Barcelona seemed to mirror his gloom.

By late April, a chill had settled upon Barcelona that had little to do with the threat posed by the fascists or the late breaking spring. Prominent anarchists and POUMists were disappearing without trace. Others were being arrested on trumped-up charges. The Spanish Communist Party had created its own security arm, modelled on the infamous Soviet NKVD and drawing its leadership from that security service. This unit operated independently from the Republican government's security units and the police.

Wearing the blue *mono* no longer identified one with the Popular Front. Now it signalled that the wearer was an anarchist, or more likely a potential POUM traitor. Fearful of reprisals, Barcelonians stripped off the *mono* and returned to pre-uprising clothing that denoted their station in life or their position of privilege. Perversely the Communists denounced working-class control and propagated social, political, and military distinction by rank, with those in higher positions reaping greater levels of financial benefit, status, and privilege. Luxury restaurants and stores reopened, "people of influence" were whisked about in chauffeur-driven limousines, and well-dressed and well-armed Popular Army officers and soldiers maintained a strong and intimidating presence throughout the city.

That the Communist-inspired attacks on the anarchists and POUMists were unfounded was obvious to Krehm. In early spring, when the Communists were first fielding accusations of POUMist collaboration at the front with the fascists, he had gone to visit the POUM forces deployed at Huesca on the Aragon front. He had seen no football games in no man's land.

Instead he witnessed anarchist and POUMist troops defending the Republic with little or no support from the newly formed Popular Army. The soldiers were starved for decent weapons. Their rifles were antiques, many virtually incapable of firing. There was little or no ammunition for the few machine guns. The men were ill fed, filthy, lice-ridden, and living in trenches that oozed mud from the floors and walls.

Returning to Barcelona, Krehm found himself staring at the brand-spanking new rifles and machine guns the Communist elements of the Popular Army brandished proudly on the streets of the city. Why were these guns not being sent to where they could be used to kill a fascist? Every officer sported a fine automatic pistol in his Sam Brown belt. At Huesca, the elected leaders of the anarchist and POUM units had no pistols or revolvers.

Soon after his return from the front, Krehm met George Orwell at a POUM rooming house. Orwell had just returned from the front, where he had spent three months as a POUM militiaman. He and Krehm shared the same gloomy presentiments of disaster over the developments occurring in Barcelona.

Orwell had arrived in Barcelona on April 26. Ten days earlier, the finance minister Juan Négrin had ordered the Popular Army to seize control of the Catalonian border crossings, which had been manned by anarchist units since the events of July 1936. When the authorities tried to implement the order, there were violent clashes at several border crossings between anarchist militiamen and government troops. This corresponded with raids throughout Barcelona's various anarchist strongholds by the Communist security forces. The anti-anarchist raids were launched under the guise of finding the killers of Communist official Roldán Cortada, who had been murdered on April 25 by unidentified assailants.

These various Communist-inspired actions brought about a hardening of the lines in Barcelona between anarchist and POUMist forces on one side, government and Communist Party forces on the other. On April 29, armed anarchist militiamen occupied the streets. For several days Popular Army forces attempted to disarm the militiamen without sparking open warfare. The militias refused to disperse or surrender their guns. On May 3, a Communist militia unit, accompanied by three truckloads of government assault guards, attacked the Telefónica, which was an anarchist bastion. Other military units rushed to support them when the initial attack proved successful in gaining control of the strategically vital building.

When the attack on the Telefónica started at 3:00 P.M., Krehm was at a meeting in a suburb in the city's foothills. Hearing the growing intensity of the gunfire, Krehm started running down the Passeig de Gracia toward the city centre. The closer he got to downtown, the more barricades blocked the street. A few blocks from POUM's headquarters, an unseen sniper started shooting at Krehm. He dived into a doorway and huddled there until the firing stopped. When he dodged out into the street, the sniper opened fire again and Krehm quickly sought cover in another doorway. For the rest of his journey to POUM headquarters, Krehm found himself the mouse in a cat-and-mouse game with various snipers. But he safely ran the gauntlet.

Sporadic fighting continued through to the end of the day, with neither side gaining a decisive edge over the other. Krehm took no part in the fighting but remained at headquarters writing various dispatches about the incident for POUM English-language publications. On May 7, the government and the anarchists negotiated a peace accord. That evening government assault guards dispatched from the capital of Valencia entered the city unopposed. Within days a force of twelve thousand heavily armed government troops was deployed throughout Barcelona. These troops did nothing to hinder the actions of the Communists but worked to ensure that the anarchists and POUM forces were disarmed.

With each passing day there were more reports of people going missing. An Italian anarchist Krehm knew, who had been crippled in Mussolini's prisons before escaping to Spain, was picked up by plainclothesmen driving an unmarked car. His body was discovered a few days later. A reign of terror settled over Barcelona. Krehm worried he too might be picked up by the Communists but could think of no way to protect himself from this fate. Even had it been possible, he was not yet ready to flee Spain. To do that would mean abandoning all hope that the Republican government might still yield a workers' paradise. Until it was certain that the Stalinist forces, who appeared bent on exporting their own bloodthirsty and repressive regime to Spain, had won the day he decided to stay in Barcelona and do his part.

Bethune knew that, despite the increased bureaucratic attempts to wrest control of the Instituto from him, the unit he had created was responsible for saving thousands of lives. By April, death rates among the wounded on some of the fronts had dropped by 75 percent.

The reorganized Republican army was also doing well. The fascist offensive at Guadalajara—a joint offensive undertaken by Franco's Spanish forces and Mussolini's Italian divisions—had been stopped cold and thrown back almost to its start line. Mussolini was so riled by his troops' failure to achieve the great victory the dictator had promised would shower glory on Italy that he berated them publicly to either succeed in Spain or never return to Italy. The fascists shifted their major efforts away from Madrid, concentrating on overwhelming the Basque pocket of Republican resistance among the Bay of Biscay's coastal provinces.

Meanwhile, two Spanish doctors from the Sanidad Militar (Army Medical Service) were appointed as a control committee to oversee the Instituto's operations and immediately started telling Bethune how they wanted the blood unit to be operated. Bethune was incensed by what he considered a direct attack on his credibility and organizational ability.

There were other indications that Bethune's outspoken criticisms of the Republic's bureaucracy might be endangering everyone in the unit. Bethune, Sorenson, and Sise were often followed by plainclothes policemen. One day their office was raided by police who threatened to confiscate the maps detailing the routes they used to reach hospitals. Only after Bethune carefully explained the reason for all the lines drawn on the maps did they appear grudgingly satisfied that the maps were not part of some Fifth-Column plot.

Bethune refused, however, to be cowed by this overt harassment. He continued to lambaste any official he perceived was hindering his efforts and viewed the Republic's intended integration of operations with suspicion. Bethune even suspected that unseen forces might be trying to undo the blood unit by subverting his communications with Canada.

On April 12, he fired off a cable to Ben Spence in Toronto stating that the government had assumed control of the blood unit and would allow no more independent organizations. "Our position is now nominal," he wrote. "Fortunately transfusion service is well established and can carry on without us." He requested authority to withdraw Canadian personnel serving with the unit and to hand over the equipment to Spanish control. "Remember Kléber and the International Column," he wrote. "Only future cables signed Beth Bethune are from me. Continue collection funds. Many schemes more urgent now than Blood Transfusion. Will inform you later."

The more urgent schemes Bethune had in mind had their genesis in the retreat from Málaga. Although two months had passed, images of the refugees—particularly the children—still haunted him. Thousands of young children had been orphaned at Málaga. All across Republican Spain, a horrific number of orphans had been created by the war.

Bethune envisioned the Canadian Committee to Aid Spanish Democracy mobilizing its fund-raising initiatives to finance the creation and operation of refugee centres for children. In the safe haven of Catalonia province, Bethune foresaw the creation of Children's Villages dedicated to providing decent shelter for homeless refugee children. He sent a flurry of cables to Canada laying out his ambitious plans.

The committee replied by sending A. A. MacLeod and William Kashtan to get to the bottom of what was happening with Bethune's unit and to clarify its relationship with the Spanish government. Both were impressed with Bethune's idea of the orphanages and what he had achieved with the blood unit.

The need for the former was apparent on virtually every street corner of the Republican cities. Although the Spanish government was trying hard to provide care and shelter to the millions of refugees, their needs and numbers surpassed available resources. Since the small Basque village of Guernica had been decimated by German bombers on April 26, refugee streams flowed out of villages at the first sign of war's approach. The fascist assaults on civilian populations were escalating as Franco tried to win through terror what he had so far failed to achieve militarily. Consequently, the number of orphaned children was also rising at an alarming rate.

Although fund-raising in Canada had been going well, the plight of the refugee children would, Bethune believed, serve as a catalyst to galvanize the Canadian people. When he presented these arguments to the two men, they found his reasoning convincing and compelling. MacLeod and Kashtan agreed to the change of focus for the Canadian committee's effort. Then they told Bethune he was to come home with them. His work in Spain was done, MacLeod told him, and he could achieve more by undertaking a cross-Canada tour to raise funds for the Instituto and the new orphanage scheme.

Bethune resisted, but in the end it was clear that he wasn't being asked to return—MacLeod was ordering him home. Without the funds from the committee, Bethune could accomplish nothing. Reluctantly he agreed to return to Canada. For the time being it was decided that Sise, Sorenson, and the other Canadians serving in the transfusion unit would carry on the work until the Spanish government no longer felt they were needed, which Sise predicted would be by late summer.

Across Canada, people such as these Vancouver residents strove to raise funds for the Canadian Committee to Aid Spanish Democracy. (VPL 9442)

On May 18, Bethune left for Canada. Before he left, Bethune indicated his sense of failure when he said to Sise, "I have blotted my copybook." In Le Havre, Bethune caught a ship home. He travelled steerage to save money. Throughout the journey Bethune's bitterness and resentment toward those who had clouded his achievements with bureaucratic bickering and jealousy grew.

Although the ill-equipped and poorly organized Republican forces in the Basque provinces bordering the Bay of Biscay still clung to a small pocket of mountainous terrain surrounding Bilbao, defeat now seemed inevitable. On March 31, Franco's army had launched a major offensive on the Biscayan front. Fifty thousand men, heavily supported by artillery, armour, and aircraft, had been slowly grinding down the Republican forces ever since. When the offensive started, the Republicans were able to field forty-five thousand troops. But it was an army bled virtually dry of guns and ammunition. Twenty battalions lacked any machine guns. Scarcely any artillery remained, few planes could fly, and ammunition was scarce. Isolated from the rest of the Republic, the Basque provinces could get no supplies by land. Off the coast, Franco's Spanish warships, as well as ships from Germany and Italy, ensured that practically no war matériel slipped through the net. Adding to the impossibility of naval supply to the Biscayan front was the presence of British naval ships enforcing the Non-Intervention Agreement with forced boardings and searches of vessels flying flags of neutrality.

The only ships that could elude the fascist and British ships were small, fast, patrol boats. These vessels could hug the coastline and outrun the larger enemy ships. But they were also too small to smuggle in any significant amounts of supplies.

On the night of May 1, Bill Williamson—the first Canadian to fight in Spain—boarded a patrol boat in Portugalete that was bound for St. Jean de Luz, just south of Biarritz on the French coast. Almost ten months earlier he had arrived in Bilbao to take up the cause of the Republic. Now, he was abandoning his Basque and Biscayan comrades to their fate. Williamson had seen no fighting during the latest fascist offensive. A few days before the battle broke out he had been wounded near Oviedo. Since then he had been convalescing at various hospitals, watching helplessly, and with growing dismay, as the Republican forces were slowly driven back from the mountains and ever closer to where they would eventually have their backs pressed hard against the sea.

Almost weekly, he had been shifted from one hospital to another. The reason for the constant movement was the devastating aerial bombardments by the German Condor Legion on the Republican towns and hospitals. Williamson was in Durango when it was virtually levelled by German Stukas, which bombed and machine-gun strafed the civilians there. On April 26, he was only three kilometres from Guernica when it was laid waste by Nazi bombers. Finally, the Republican command in Bilbao approved Williamson's transfer to the International Brigades on May 1 and provided him with immediate passage out of the doomed defensive pocket.

Williamson left with a heavy heart but knowing that his staying would achieve nothing for the cause. Although still suffering terrible headaches from injuries sustained when his machine-gun position had been destroyed in October 1936, Williamson's determination to continue fighting the fascists remained strong. His orders granted him two weeks' convalescence leave in Paris. On May 14, he was to report to the Communist headquarters there to arrange his return via the Pyrenees to the Republican forces. He was ordered to report by late May to Albacete for assignment to the XVth International Brigade.

As the patrol boat moved quickly out of the harbour, Williamson looked back toward the darkened cities of Portugalete and Bilbao. Throughout the afternoon and well into the evening, the fascist bombers had hammered both communities with high explosives. How different this departure was from his arrival the previous July. The length of the mole was empty, devoid of life. There were no throngs of flag-waving citizens. The cities huddled under a protective cloak of darkness to prevent offering the fascist bombers an easy target. In the streets there would be no dancing, no singing of patriotic songs. The people of Bilbao had nothing to hope for. Williamson still believed the Republicans would win this war, but he was equally certain that when the Basque provinces fell, as they inevitably must, it would be many months, perhaps even years, before they were finally liberated from the repressive fascist yoke.

Seven

*A*LLEGIANCES

ON APRIL 10, 1937, BY ORDER-IN-COUNCIL, THE CANADIAN GOVernment adopted the Foreign Enlistment Act, which made it illegal for Canadians to serve in foreign military services. The act was modelled closely on legislation passed earlier in the year by the United States government. It was designed specifically to dissuade Canadians from volunteering to fight for the Spanish Republic.

Already the U.S. government had strengthened its legislation by making it illegal for Americans to travel to Spain or its territories. Since March 4, all U.S. passports had been stamped with a notice reading: "Not Valid For Travel In Spain." This was the first time in U.S. history that such a restriction had been placed on the travel of American citizens.

In Canada, the enactment of the Foreign Enlistment Act created an immediate dilemma for the Committee to Aid Spanish Democracy and for the Canadian Communist Party, in particular, because it was the arm of the committee that was actively recruiting volunteers for the International Brigades. Communist Party general secretary Tim Buck and the party executive had to decide how far the party could go in aiding and abetting the volunteers in going to Spain before the government would be able to accuse it of conspiracy against law and order.

Shortly after the law was decreed, Buck found himself publicly addressing the party's position on the law. He was speaking at a Montreal meeting of the Junior Chamber of Commerce. The meeting was held in the Queen's Hotel, and the audience of aspiring entrepreneurs was very enthusiastic about the need to support the Spanish Republic. Several expressed interest in volunteering.

Hopeful that Buck would openly share their fervour, some of the young men started pressuring him to declare that the Communist Party would openly defy the Foreign Enlistment Act. Buck refused. He said instead, "Every man must decide for himself in light of his own conscience what he wants to do." Those who volunteered, he said, must know they were defying the law and could expect no assistance from the Canadian government should they find themselves in trouble overseas. Buck's comments failed to satisfy the crowd, many of whom accused him of hedging.

Buck *was* hedging. He believed if the Communist Party openly advocated violating the law, the government would respond with renewed repression of the party. That repression during the 1930s had forced the party to operate illegally and had resulted in leaders, such as himself, spending years in prison. The party, he and the party executive decided, would continue to organize and fund volunteers travelling overseas to join the International Brigade, but it would do so clandestinely.

As for the Committee to Aid Spanish Democracy, it would cease being openly connected with volunteer recruitment. Rather, the committee would focus attention on fund-raising for provision of philanthropic aid to the Republic. At the back of all the meetings, parade ceremonies, and rallies across the country, however, open recruitment would continue.

There was no shortage of recruits. During the meeting at Aranjuez, Spain—where the decision had been taken to form the International Brigades—Buck had tentatively suggested Canada might contribute 250 volunteers. Already twice that number had gone and Buck expected the number of recruits would eventually exceed one thousand. There was no problem recruiting volunteers, the problems came in securing passports for those selected, raising the funds to cover their transport and getting them discreetly out of the country. Equally challenging was ensuring none of those recruited were police informers or Trotskyites, the latter being as despised by the Communist Party in all countries as the former.

To avoid either of these risks, volunteers were drawn wherever possible from politically reliable groups. The veterans of the On to Ottawa Trek and the Relief Camp Workers' Union in British Columbia and the Young Communist League were preferred sources of volunteers. Ukrainian-Canadians, Finnish-Canadians, and other ethnic groups with strong linkages to workers' movements and leftist politics could also be relied upon. Jewish volunteers, even if not Communists, tended to be dedicated anti-fascists, and, given the RCMP's innate anti-Semitism, were unlikely to be penetrated by police informers. Ultimately, however, Buck knew recruitment depended on the unique attributes and apparent commitment of each prospective volunteer. The local recruitment committees were allowed a free hand in assessing and selecting recruits from their area, just as they were given complete freedom in how they approached raising funds.

The committee's fund-raising achievements never ceased to amaze Buck. Enough money had been raised to fully outfit Dr. Norman Bethune's blood transfusion unit. Tons of milk and other foodstuffs had also been purchased

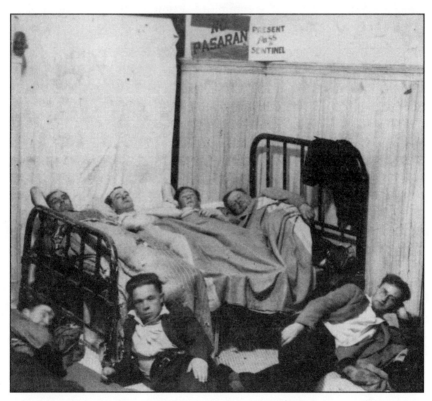

Blacklisted from the relief camps and denied regular relief because they were single, Relief Camp Workers' Union organizers, such as these Vancouver-based men, were often forced to live eight or more to a flophouse room. It was from the ranks of the poor that the strongest support for Republican Spain was found in Canada. No Pasaran—the Republican battle cry—called as strongly to these men as it did to Spanish Loyalists. (VPL 13344)

and shipped to the Republic. More money was now being raised to establish and operate shelters for refugee children.

Two centres were built with Canadian funds. One, the Residencia d'Agullent, was opened in a former eighteenth-century convent in the small village of Agullent near Barcelona. This residence provided shelter for about fifty boys and girls ranging in age from eight to fourteen. Another residence in a Barcelona mansion, known as "The Pines," would open in the fall. This facility would be called the Reverend Salem Bland Home, after the dedicated Methodist social activist and honorary chairman of the Committee to Aid Spanish Democracy. It would initially house about one hundred children, aged two to fifteen. The committee's eventual aim was to fund up to three hundred children—the maximum number the two facilities could accommodate.

The children at Residencia d'Agullent were drawn from the thousands of refugees who had escaped from captured or destroyed communities. They came from Málaga, from the charred shell of Guernica, from the ruins of Oviedo. Their parents were missing or dead. Many had memories of seeing their parents butchered by fascist firing squads along the road from Málaga to Almería.

Money raised in Canada provided these children with shelter, clothing, food, schooling, medical care, and even psychological help to recover from the trauma they had experienced. The committee sought pledges of five dollars a month to support one child. In addition to the funds raised for the direct care of the refugee children in the centres, the committee also raised large sums of money for the purchase of milk and other foodstuffs. In June 1937 alone, ten thousand dollars was raised for this purpose.

The committee's fund-raising activities were unceasing. They were also dependent on the support of the common Canadian. Buck knew that the corporations, wealthy philanthropists, federal and provincial governments, and the mainstream churches gave next to nothing. As Salem Bland wrote in one fund-raising pamphlet, the response to the committee's appeals came chiefly from "the ranks of labour and Canadians of foreign birth. We cannot but glory that these Canadians who include but few people of wealth have shown magnificent generosity, but I confess to a deep regret that in proportion to their means they have outshone those of us who have for a longer period enjoyed the advantages of this favored land."

Somewhat more cynical than the good Methodist reverend, Buck knew that most wealthy Canadians had little sympathy for the Republican cause and so could quietly ignore the plight of the refugee children. Like their prime minister, William Lyon Mackenzie King, they dismissed the Spanish conflict as being far away and of no relevance to Canada.

Prime Minister King seldom worried unduly about the international arena. Canada was a Dominion of the British Commonwealth; therefore, its policies inextricably reflected those of Great Britain. As Great Britain had opted for non-intervention, the Canadian stance must obviously be one of neutrality.

King had little sympathy for the Republican cause, which he believed was Communist-inspired and led. King considered the Communists a serious threat both at home and abroad. He fully sympathized with governments, like that of Germany, which resorted to stamping out Communism by legalized repression.

King had recently come to greatly admire Germany's Adolf Hitler. The prime minister had met Hitler in June after attending the coronation of King George VI in London.

His trip to Europe had been particularly pleasurable. In London, British prime minister Neville Chamberlain had shown an apparently genuine interest in King's opinions on European politics and how to maintain world peace. For his part, King had confidence in Chamberlain's judgement. King believed the British policy of appeasing Germany, rather than resisting its ever growing expansionist claims, both prudent and wise.

During his meeting with Chamberlain, he convinced the British prime minister that it would be useful if he, King, were to meet with Hitler. By reminding Hitler that—in the event of war—the Commonwealth would stand by Britain, King could surely influence Hitler to moderate his territorial ambitions so as not to abuse Britain's lenient approach to Germany's expansionist policies.

In Berlin, King met first with British ambassador Sir Nevile Henderson. The two got along famously, agreeing on most issues involving Germany and its relationship with Britain, Europe, and the world.

Henderson informed King that Austria was largely German, the Sudetenland in Czechoslovakia was primarily populated by Germans, Germany needed to expand its borders to fulfil its national destiny, and Britain should not try to prevent Germany's expansion into these regions. The British ambassador also argued that Nazism had many positive sides and should not be too quickly condemned.

Over the next four days King visited Hitler Youth Camps, observed the Labour Service Corps at work on farms, viewed the construction of the Autobahn highway system, and met formally and informally with Hitler, Hermann Göring, and various minor Nazi functionaries. He extensively toured Berlin, each evening pausing to record many favourable impressions in his diary.

For his meeting with King, Hitler appeared dressed in white tie, a top hat, and tails, rather than his customary military uniform. The Canadian prime minister thought the choice of outfit a deliberate attempt to set King at ease and assure him of the dictator's good will and intention. After the meeting he confided to his diary that

> I spoke of what I had seen of the constructive work of his regime and how I hoped this work might continue and that nothing would be permitted to destroy that work, that it was bound to be followed in other countries to the great advantage of mankind. Hitler said that in order to keep his control over the country he had to have the support of the people. That he was not like Stalin, who could shoot his generals and other members of his government who disagreed with him, but had to have back of him what the people themselves merely wished and the people of Germany did not want war or commitments to possible war in advance. While he was talking in this way, I confess, I thought he was using exactly the same argument that I had used in the Canadian Parliament.

King was as impressed by Hitler himself as he was by the man's words.

> He smiled very pleasantly and indeed had a sort of appealing and affectionate look in his eyes. My sizing up of the man, as I sat and talked with him, was that he is really one who truly loves his fellow man. His face is much more prepossessing than his pictures would give the impression of. It is not that of a fiery overstrained nature, but of a calm, passive man, deeply, and thoughtfully, in earnest. His skin was smooth. His face did not present lines of fatigue or weariness. His eyes impressed me most of all. There was a liquid quality about them which indicates keen perception and profound sympathy. Calm. Composed. And one could see how particularly humble folk would have come to have profound love for the man. As I talked with him, I could not help but think of Joan of Arc. He is distinctly a mystic.

Of his visit to Nazi Germany, Prime Minister King (centre with cane) wrote: "Looking back over the German visit I can honestly say that it was as enjoyable, informative, and inspiring as any visit I have had anywhere." (NAC PA119013)

At the end of the meeting, scheduled to last only a half-hour but running twice that length, Hitler presented King with an autographed picture of the Führer.

After his meeting with Hitler, King also visited German foreign minister Baron Konstantin von Neurath, who reiterated Germany's determination to avert war. Prior to the rise of Hitler, Neurath told King, Germany had been falling to pieces, mostly because of the Jews. "He said to me," King wrote after,

> that I would have loathed living in Berlin with the Jews, and the way in which they had increased their numbers in the City, and were taking possession of its more important part. He said there was no pleasure in going to a theatre which was filled with them. Many of them were very coarse and vulgar and assertive. They were getting control of all the

business, the finance, and had really taken advantage of the necessity of the people. It was necessary to get them out, to have the German people really control their own City and affairs. He told me that I would have been surprised at the extent to which life and morals had become demoralized; that Hitler had set his face against all that kind of thing, and had tried to inspire desire for a good life in the minds of young people.

King, who himself had opposed the growing Jewish presence in an Ottawa suburb and never hesitated to express his wish not to have Jews as neighbours, did not find these anti-Semitic comments objectionable. Although the Nürnberg Laws had been in existence since mid-1935, King chose not to comment in his diary about any of the measures against Jews that were clearly visible on the streets of Berlin during his visit. Jewish-owned businesses had been foreclosed. Jewish citizens were forced to wear the yellow Star of David and were barred from entering grocery stores, drugstores, bakeries, and dairies. They could not stay in hotels. More than half of all Germany's Jews were denied lawful employment because of various prescriptions against Jews working in both public and private sectors. Signs standing outside almost every business declared that Jews were neither welcome nor permitted inside.

After King left Germany, he wrote in his diary,

Looking back over the German visit I can honestly say that it was as enjoyable, informative, and inspiring as any visit I have had anywhere. The German people seem much easier to understand and more like ourselves than either the French or the English. Fear of Germany in other lands is that of ideas. That liberty and equality of the classes may spread from Germany to their own lands. One does not like regimentation, but it is apparently the one way to make views prevail. I have come away from Germany tremendously relieved.

Within weeks of his return from Europe, one of King's first acts was to order rigorous application of the Foreign Enlistment Act to what he called the "Spanish conflict." Further, all passports issued after August 10 would prohibit travel to Spain or its territories. These actions, the prime minister hoped, would make it difficult for Canadians to continue supporting the Republican cause.

The Communist Party clerk warned Joseph Salsberg that all hell was breaking loose upstairs. Dr. Norman Bethune had burst into the Toronto office
only minutes before and was insisting on an immediate return to Spain.
Not for the first time, Salsberg wished A. A. MacLeod had returned from
Europe with Bethune and could take responsibility for ensuring the doctor
bowed to the party's plans for him. Although Salsberg knew Bethune, he
did not feel adequately prepared to argue the party's position on the doctor's
future role, but he was also the only national party executive official
present.

Salsberg found Bethune striding back and forth across the party's meeting room. Salsberg felt strength literally oozing from the man's every pore.
This strength was not purely the product of the doctor's obvious natural
charisma, rather it seemed to derive from a seemingly limitless courage and
energy that made Salsberg feel somewhat shameful, as if he somehow lacked
the same vital elements.

Bethune spread a large, detailed map of Spain across a table. He quickly
sketched the various battlefronts around Madrid and the closing fascist
pincers that threatened to encircle the city. "Joe, if I don't make it now, I will
never be able to get in. And I'm needed there more than here. You're all
here. All of you can go and raise money. My blood transfusion unit is there
and I must go back."

Salsberg explained that Bethune's presence in Canada was urgently
needed to sustain the Spanish committee's fund-raising efforts. Hundreds
of Canadians were tirelessly organizing rallies across the nation. Rallies in
Toronto's Queen's Park routinely drew twenty to thirty thousand people.
The same was true in cities across Canada, particularly those with strong
labour movements, such as Vancouver, Hamilton, Oshawa, Toronto, and
Halifax. The Canadian working class clearly understood the historic significance of what was happening in Spain, Salsberg told Bethune. His
presence at those rallies was vital for reinforcing this popular commitment.
After a long deliberation, Bethune reluctantly accepted Salsberg's argument.

Neither man raised the other compelling reason for Bethune not returning to Spain—the obvious fact that the Spanish government no longer
would approve his presence because of the disputes over the role of the
Canadian blood unit that had made his last months there so controversial.

To twenty-five-year-old Ross Russell it seemed impossible that the thin,
frail-looking man could so mesmerize the thousands gathered in Montreal's

129

Mount Royal Arena. Yet here was the Canadian who had made medical history in Spain describing his experiences among the refugees fleeing from Málaga to Almería, and Russell was as enthralled as all the others in the arena. Dr. Norman Bethune graphically related how the fascist planes heartlessly swept down to strafe helpless women and children. He recalled the details of individual transfusions given to wounded soldiers on the battlefield, transfusions that granted the men a chance to live and fight again.

Bethune's words were like the cherry topping the sundae of logical reasons he had been creating to justify his volunteering for Spanish service. The possibility of going to Spain had contributed to a recent decision to quit his job as assistant manager of the Woolworth's department store at McGill College and St. Catherine's. The other reason he had quit the department store chain's second largest outlet had been the anti-Semitism embedded in the company's operations. Although Russell was a nonpractising Jew, his appearance—dark, small, and wiry—clearly indicated his Jewish roots.

As assistant manager, Russell had trained many other young, non-Jewish men and proceeded to watch them go on to assume managerial positions at other Woolworth stores. Russell's career had plateaued; obviously he had gone as high as Jews were allowed. His Scottish manager was lazy and inordinately fond of the bottle, but he was also kind and relatively honest. When Russell demanded to know why management continually overlooked him, the Scot said, "Well, those guys, that's just the way they are and I don't have authority to override them."

"You mean because I'm a Jew they won't advance me?"

The manager just shrugged, which was answer enough.

Angry, deciding immediately that this was no place for him, Russell quit. Everywhere he looked anti-Semitics strutted boldly about Montreal. Virtually every Saturday night the bully boys of Adrian Arcand's National Social Christian Party took to the St. Lawrence district streets to smash up the Jewish stores. In the morning, broken glass littered the streets and any unbroken windows were soaped with swastikas. Russell had watched Arcand's thugs do their work while the police stood by and refused to intervene.

Spain and the anti-Semitism in Canada seemed intertwined. In Germany, the Nürnberg Laws legitimized every kind of imaginable abuse of Jews. The Canadian government, like all the democracies, turned a blind eye to the growing German atrocities. Their only response was to deny desperate Jewish refugees, who fled Germany, from immigrating.

Russell was infuriated by how the world's democracies catered to the fascist nations, coddling them like they might misunderstood children who were incapable of properly demonstrating their truly good nature and intentions. Meanwhile, these same governments smashed labour unions, imprisoned or harassed left-wing advocates and politicians, did nothing to end the plight of the millions who suffered because of the world depression, and turned a blind eye to anti-Semitic attacks.

About the same time Russell quit his job, he happened across a Baha'i-operated library. Montreal had few libraries, so it was always difficult to find good books. At the Baha'i library, Russell discovered book-crammed shelves.

He also found a new friend, Louie Kahn. A Russian, Kahn had originally come to Canada on a posting to buy grain for the new Soviet government. He had also formed an organization called the Friends of the Soviet Union. Evening after evening, Kahn sang the Soviet Union's glories to a rapt Russell. The Soviet system seemed so much fairer than Canada's own.

At the library, Russell soaked up newspapers and books on world affairs. From all he read, it seemed obvious that Germany was developing its tactics in Spain, testing its equipment, marshalling its resources, preparing, in short, for another world war. And when that happened the Jews of Europe would be persecuted as they had not been in centuries. What amazed Russell was that the politicians in Canada, in the United States, and in Europe persisted in burying their heads so deeply in the sand of ignorance that they remained blind to this inevitability.

Considering the crisis point upon which Russell believed the world was poised, it was essential that anyone opposing fascism volunteer for the International Brigades. This was even true for a newlywed such as himself, who had been married only nine months. Luckily, his wife was also a progressive person and supported his decision, although she wished it were not necessary.

During the Bethune meeting, Russell tried to enlist as a volunteer, but the people who were obviously volunteer recruiters all pretended to know nothing of any formal organization. Russell knew they were lying, probably because he held no Communist Party card. They were wary, afraid of informers. On reflection, Russell could hardly blame them for their caution.

He proceeded to seek out every left-wing contact he knew. "Where? How?" he would demand. Nobody confessed to knowing. Finally he confronted Frank Rose, reputedly one of Montreal's primary Communist leaders. Rose applauded Russell's intentions but tried to dissuade him from volunteering. Going to Spain was illegal, Russell was married, he had responsibilities at home, when the war was over the federal government might prosecute the Canadian volunteers or refuse their readmisson to Canada. When Russell refused to be swayed, Rose agreed to put him in contact with the recruiters.

First he was sent to a doctor for a thorough medical examination. "Can't send you over there just to have you become sick," the doctor said. When the doctor gave him a clean bill of health, the Communist Party organizers handed Russell a train ticket to Quebec City. He departed Montreal so quickly there was barely time to bid good-bye to his new wife. They had a tearful parting in the train station. In Quebec City, he took passage on a French liner bound for Europe.

Everywhere in Canada and the United States that Dr. Norman Bethune went, crowds showered praise and honour upon him. But Bethune spurned their offerings. With each passing day, he shrank further into himself. On the podiums he was superb, speaking eloquently of Spain's plight and the need for democratic nations to provide the Republic with financial support. Inside, however, he felt a breeze of spiritual desolation blowing over his seemingly barren soul. Bethune had been relegated to the starring role in a travelling sideshow. The world stage on which Bethune felt fated to perform seemed to have no role to offer him.

The fascists were everywhere on the march. In Spain, Germany, Italy, and Japan they paraded. The Japanese had invaded China, bringing war to a land of countless millions. As he had with Spain, Bethune read everything available on the war in China. Even as the Committee to Aid Spanish Democracy shuttled him from one Canadian city to another, an idea was starting to crystallize in Bethune's mind.

At the same time he became bolder and more outspoken at every engagement. Bethune no longer cared what the government or anyone else thought of him.

In Kirkland Lake he said of the prime minister, "I asked Ottawa for permission to recommend the use of a Canadian ambulance and I was refused by Mackenzie King, the same man who a little later was photo-

graphed shaking hands with the biggest murderer in the world today—
Hitler."

On July 19, during a banquet at the St. Charles Hotel in Winnipeg, he
said, "I have the honour to be a Communist. . . . They call me a Red. Then
if Christianity is Red, I am also a Red. They call me a Red because I have
saved 500 lives." In Saskatoon, he added, "You can't talk about humanity
without speaking of the class struggle. I'm preaching it and the sooner the
people realize it, the better. The old form of individualism is gone. The day
when a person could open the world like an oyster and eat it has passed.

*Bethune's tour of North America after his return from Spain was a fund-raising
and propaganda success for the pro-Republican Spain forces, but with each
passing week the doctor felt he was starring in a meaningless sideshow while
the epic events of history were passing him by.* (NAC PA116900)

The tentacles of the octopus of monopolistic capitalism are stretching out and the aggression of Japan in China is just one more instance of it."

Bethune was speaking everywhere—in towns big and small. There would soon be nowhere of the slightest importance where he had not trotted out his dog and pony show. When the tour finally drew to its inevitable close, Bethune could hardly see returning to a comfortable medical practice in Montreal. The social stature and commitments that accompanied such a position would suffocate him. There was, Bethune realized, no going back. In Spain, he had set himself on an irrevocable course that demanded his personal involvement in the struggles facing progressive mankind.

The war in China worsened daily. Japan was winning ever more ground, leaving thousands of dead in its bloody wake. The war in Spain dragged on, the fascists nibbling away at the Republican flanks like hungry wolves. But the bureaucracy of the Republicans left a bitter taste in Bethune's mouth. Earlier he had begged Joseph Salsberg to send him back to Spain. Now, recalling how the Republican officials had tried to curtail his independence, he found himself nearly ill at the thought of returning.

The future, both for himself and the world, he decided, lay in China. That was where the ultimate showdown between fascism and communism would be fought. In August, after speaking to a small rally in Salmon Arm, B.C., Bethune told local Committee to Aid Spanish Democracy representatives he would not return to Madrid, but rather wanted to leave as soon as possible for China. The following month, at the end of the latest round of speaking engagements, Bethune asked Tim Buck to support his request.

Buck called Earl Browder, chairman of the American Communist Party. Neither party leader could figure out how to finance or arrange Bethune's request—all their attention and resources were focussed on Spain. A few days later Browder called back. He had consulted with Philip R. Jaffe, publisher of the left-wing American publication Asia Today. Jaffe had just returned from China and was bullish on the need to support the Communists, who, led by Mao Tse-tung, were fighting the Japanese. Through his newly formed organization, the China Aid Council, Jaffe pledged to support Bethune's mission to China. Various other U.S. leftist organizations anted up the necessary cash.

Bethune withdrew from his Spanish-aid tour and prepared to enter his life's next phase. He was forty-seven, divorced, childless, and had turned his back on friends and associates in Montreal. But there was a new cause for which to fight, a cause where his true potential could be realized. And that, in the end, was all that mattered.

Spain was Ronald Liversedge's obsession. Liversedge was no starry-eyed idealist. He knew all about war. Born in 1899 to working-class parents in Keighley, Yorkshire, Liversedge had enlisted in 1916 and served on the Somme, in the Ypres salient, and at the Marne before being badly wounded. Some years after the Great War ended, Liversedge wrote that upon entering the Somme trenches he realized "I had landed myself into something that I could hardly bear." In the same note he said it was during the slaughter-house of the Ypres salient that he "started to take a good look at life and death and to realize that it was all a big sham, a big dirty lying rotten obscenity run in the most glaring inefficiency by Oxford and Cambridge grads who should have known better."

Right after the war, Liversedge joined the British Communist Party. He read everything written by Marx, Engels, and Lenin and proudly declared his political stripe. In 1926, Liversedge emigrated to Canada, bringing along his unflinching beliefs. Everything that had happened in Canada since had served only to harden his ideals. Liversedge had been a leader of the On to Ottawa Trek, had organized for the Relief Camp Workers' Union, unionized miners in Atlin, B.C., and fought stoutly for workers' rights on more battle-fronts than he had seen in Flanders. The fascists, he believed, were the evil progeny of capitalism and its ultimate manifestation. In Spain, that evil threatened an infant workers' democracy, so it was in Spain Liversedge must fight again for what was right and just.

On May 1, 1937, Liversedge learned that he would finally get his chance. Early that morning a local organizer, Jim McEwan, dropped by and told him to bring a suitcase along to that afternoon's May Day Parade. Liversedge's travel arrangements were in place and he should be ready for an immediate departure.

It was a wonderful parade under a bright, sunny sky that came as a welcome relief after a long, dank April and a bleak, cold winter. Dozens of labour organizations paraded down Vancouver's main city streets toward a massive gathering in Stanley Park. Many of the banners they carried called for an end to Spanish fascism and supported the Republican cause. Liversedge, toting his suitcase, joined the march. By the time the parade reached Stanley Park the crowd numbered at least ten thousand.

On May 1, 1937, thousands of Vancouverites marched in the May Day Parade. Among those who joined the march was the Girls Brigade to Aid Spanish Democracy. (VPL 9446)

On a large podium, a band played workers' songs and dignitaries delivered speeches. Liversedge paid them little attention. He was looking around for McEwan, constantly checking his coat pocket to ensure the hard-won passport remained safe.

It had taken bloody months to get that passport, which was why Liversedge was still in Vancouver and not in Spain. Thinking of the passport application process always made Liversedge smile, though, for his mind turned inevitably to the day he asked Dr. Lyle Telford to witness the application. The witness was supposed to be someone of community standing, who had known the applicant for five years and could vouch for his good character.

Liversedge, of course, knew nobody who might be construed to be of good community standing. He knew workers, communists, and union organizers. They had standing in the left-wing community, but if some bureaucrat saw their names on a passport application the document would become just so much shredded paper. One of the recruiting organizers told Liversedge that most of the volunteers faced the same problem and that he should go see Dr. Telford, a Vancouver physician known to be sympathetic to Spain's Republic. Liversedge had never met the doctor, but he went in with his application. "My God," the doctor groaned, "not another. I've signed enough already to get me locked up."

Laughing, Liversedge handed him the form. "Oh come on, doc, in for a penny." With a shake of his head, Telford took the form and signed it.

In for a penny. That was about all Liversedge had in his pockets right then. He was going to Spain completely on the bum. It was a good thing the recruitment committee could afford to pay his passage.

Liversedge's thoughts were interrupted by the arrival of two women friends. They had a couple of thermoses of tea and some sandwiches. He gratefully agreed to share their lunch. They had just started toward a shady spot on the crowd's edge when someone tapped Liversedge on the shoulder. He turned to face Jim McEwan.

"Can I have a word with you?" After Liversedge excused himself from the women, the two men walked a few paces away. "You ready to blow?" Liversedge nodded. "Come on then." McEwan led the way over to the speaker's platform and exchanged some words with his father, Tom, who was the chief organizer of Vancouver's volunteer recruitment committee. He then signalled Liversedge to follow him uptown. As they passed out of the park, Liversedge heard Tom McEwan's voice booming over the loud-speaker. "Right at this moment," he said, "a man is leaving this rally on his way to Spain. Let's give him a cheer and send him with our greetings to the Canadian boys over there." A tremendous roar washed over the entire park and up the streets. "Probably the only guy going to Spain ever gets a send-off like that," McEwan joked.

They reached the streetcar platform and McEwan paused, obviously waiting for a car to come. Liversedge told him he lacked money for the fare. McEwan checked his pockets but discovered he could only afford one pass. They walked to the train station, where McEwan gave Liversedge his five-dollar ticket to Toronto.

As Liversedge headed down the ramp to meet the train, it occurred to him that he should feel a bit lonely setting out on such a long and momentous journey by himself. But he could still hear the supportive roar of ten thousand people drifting about inside his mind. "The Canadian government," he thought, "may not want us to go to Spain, but the Canadian people are sure behind us."

Eight

$\mathscr{A}$T THE DOOR OF
THE ANGELS

THE SHIP WAS CRAMMED WITH INTERNATIONAL VOLUNTEERS AND desperately needed food supplies. Ronald Liversedge and Jurai Sarvas—an Eastern European immigrant from Ontario's tobacco country who went by George—were jammed into a tiny cabin that was hard up against two bulkheads. Two days earlier, he and Liversedge had been smuggled aboard the *Ciudad de Barcelona,* a small Republican freighter preparing to sail from Marseilles to Barcelona. Liversedge and Sarvas were lucky. Some of the volunteers had already been hidden on board for five days. Their presence was illegal, a violation of the Non-Intervention Agreement. The ship was only approved to carry a food shipment to Republican Spain.

When the vessel sailed out of Marseilles harbour on May 28, 1937, it carried 245 volunteers in addition to its approved food cargo. On board were Bulgarians, Hungarians, Czechs, Poles, Italians, a few Australians, at least one New Zealander, and about thirty Canadians.

All went well at first, the ship entering Spanish territorial waters about noon the following day and following a southward course toward Barcelona. Arrival in Barcelona harbour was scheduled for 5:00 P.M. Wanting to be fresh and alert for the landing, Liversedge went below at 2:00 P.M. for a short nap. No sooner had he stripped off his shoes, socks, and shirt, stretched out on the bed, and closed his eyes, than a terrific explosion lifted the ship out of the water. As the vessel settled back into the sea, its entire hull shuddered strangely, like a dying animal might. "Jesus Christ," Liversedge thought, "is this thing hit?" Figuring he knew the answer, Liversedge hastily tied on one of the cabin's two life jackets and bolted for the door without pausing to dress. Sarvas, looking frightened, arrived just as he opened the cabin door. Liversedge thrust the spare life jacket into his arms and the two men rushed for the deck.

The wide stairway leading toward the deck was choked with men desperately trying to escape. Stalled next to a porthole, Liversedge looked out and saw that the shoreline, about six kilometres distant, was perpendicular. "Jesus Christ, there's something wrong with that there," he muttered. "It shouldn't be like that."

Topside, Liversedge was horrified to see the ship's bow thrust high in the air and the ship sliding rapidly into a dark, watery hole. Barrels, crates, bits of canvas, broken planking, and even wooden bedsteads floated in a wide arc about the sinking vessel. Mixed in with the flotsam were the bobbing heads of survivors and the splayed forms of all too many dead. The water around most of the corpses was stained a deep crimson.

On the starboard side, fifty men had piled into a lifeboat, but the combined effect of the ship rolling to port as it sank and the men's weight had solidly jammed the lifeboat in its davits. One man was hacking away at the lifeboat's restraining ropes with a fire axe. Suddenly, he severed a critical line and the boat crashed into the water, went under the surface, and sank. Most of the men escaped this calamity and started swimming away from the doomed freighter.

Liversedge hastened down to where the ship was sliding under the surface, crawled over the rail, and splashed into the water. Remembering stories of how a sinking ship will pull down those close to it, he frantically started swimming away. The cork life jacket held him up, allowing him to make good progress. All around him men were screaming in terror and crying for help. Liversedge heard others bravely singing "The Internationale" as they slowly sank to their deaths.

After each stroke, Liversedge glanced back in dreadful fascination at the sinking ship. On one over-the-shoulder glance, Liversedge recognized a Canadian named Karl Francis standing on the foredeck. The man pulled himself hand over hand up the rail to the very top of the bow, where he grasped hold of the little jack mast. Liversedge and other men in the sea started yelling at Francis to jump and swim clear. But he refused to budge, clinging desperately to the mast. In one smooth, sucking motion the *Ciudad de Barcelona* and Francis disappeared.

A Republican seaplane roared overhead and started dropping a line of depth charges, trying to destroy the submarine that had torpedoed the freighter. With each exploding depth charge, however, Liversedge felt his legs being nearly torn off by the underwater concussion. When its explosives were exhausted, the plane set down and started taking on survivors. Liversedge saw big Ivor Anderson, who everyone called Tiny, dragging fellow Canadian Joe Schoen to the plane. He bundled Schoen aboard and then clung to the plane's frame as it slowly taxied along toward the shore with its brimming load of survivors.

Even though he knew it was beyond reach, Liversedge swam landward. Long before any of them reached it, they would all perish from hypothermia or exhaustion. Their only chance lay in being rescued.

Soon he heard someone calling his name. Looking about, Liversedge saw a small Jewish lad from New York called Syd Shostick supporting a big Finn who weighed about two hundred pounds and couldn't swim. Liversedge estimated that the Finn outweighed Shostick by at least eighty pounds and was amazed the two were still afloat. He joined Shostick in supporting the larger man.

Several fishing boats came and started plucking survivors from the sea, but the rescue vessels were working on the other side of a large, wreckage-strewn patch of water, and Liversedge thought they were unable to see his party. The three men tried working their way through the debris, but because of the trouble they had keeping the Finn afloat, it was a hopeless task. When they came to some planking and chunks of canvas, Liversedge and Shostick used the materials to fashion a crude raft upon which they loaded the Finn. The raft proved, however, too clumsy to paddle or push. Both the Finn and Shostick lacked life jackets and were completely exhausted, so they urged Liversedge to try reaching the boats alone.

Liversedge set off. Swimming through the wreckage, he came up behind another man who clung to a wooden bedstead. "How are you making out?" Liversedge called.

"Not so good," the man said weakly. Then he turned his head and seeing Liversedge said, "Good Lord, are you here too?" The man was Ellis Fromberg from Vancouver. Neither had realized the other was on the ship. Ellis was in rough shape. He couldn't swim, had no life jacket, and was suffering leg and arm cramps.

Liversedge gathered together some bits of lumber for Fromberg to cling to, but lacking any kind of binding material was, this time, unable to fashion even the crudest raft. If he left, the man would surely drown. For two

141

hours they floated, slowly, inevitably weakening. It took all Liversedge's concentration to prevent the semi-conscious Fromberg from sliding off the scraps of lumber and sinking into the black depths. Liversedge's eyes burned from the salt, and the bright sunshine, which seemed to hold no warmth, blinded him. He was on the edge of giving up hope when a fishing boat started nosing through the wreckage, heading roughly in their direction.

Mustering his last reserves of strength, Liversedge waved frantically and nearly wept with joy when one of the fishermen returned the motion. Soon the little boat was alongside and the fishermen dragged Liversedge and Fromberg from the sea. Although the boat trolled back and forth through the wreckage, there appeared to be no remaining survivors amid the debris.

The fishing boat landed on the beach before the village of Malgrat. Liversedge was trembling so badly with shock and cold that he could barely stand. One of the men lowered him to the ground and cut away his sodden pants with a knife. The daughter of another fisherman brought over a bottle of cognac. She thrust a big tumblerful of the liquor into Liversedge's hands. Although he downed the fiery drink in one swallow it failed to warm him or still the uncontrollable chattering of his teeth. Some clothes were brought and Liversedge thankfully pulled them on. The pants were baggy and far too short for his five-foot-ten-inch frame. The old shirt barely met at the front. For his feet there was a pair of rope-soled sandals, known as *alpargatas,* which laced up to the ankle.

The survivors were gathered in the village's central plaza and the dead placed in the church basement. Liversedge was asked to try identifying the fifty corpses recovered by the fishermen. He carefully examined each body but found no Canadians. Liversedge soon learned, however, that five of his countrymen had been among the sixty men who either drowned or were killed when the torpedo fired by an Italian submarine ripped the ship's hull open and sent it to a watery grave.

At 7:00 A.M. on June 16, 1937, William Krehm heard a fist hammering loudly on the door of the POUM house in Barcelona. When one of the other foreign POUM loyalists unlocked and opened the door, he was sent sprawling, and the foyer immediately filled with heavily built plainclothesmen. Half of these were obviously Russians from the dreaded NKVD secret police. The rest were Spanish. All of the men were yelling orders.

Krehm and the other POUMists were given no time to gather personal belongings. They were shoved out the door and into waiting trucks. Armed men stood guard next to the drop gate and threatened to shoot anyone who tried to escape.

Somebody asked why they were being arrested. "Spies, Trotskyists," shouted one of the guards. Where were they being taken? A brutal laugh was the only answer.

When the truck stopped, the men were herded out into a small courtyard. There were about eighty or ninety of them bunched together—all foreigners associated with POUM. Krehm learned from one of the others that Andrés Nin, the party secretary, had been grabbed. So, too, had most of the party executive. Others were on the run. George Orwell had reportedly slipped the dragnet, as had the twenty-three-year-old German refugee Willy Brandt. [The future West German chancellor, working in Spain as a correspondent for several Norwegian newspapers, was closely aligned with POUM. He escaped to Oslo. Orwell, posing as a somewhat seedy bourgeois tourist, escaped by train that night to France and returned to Britain, where he quickly chronicled his experiences in *Homage to Catalonia*.]

The NKVD men escorted the arrested POUMists into a newly constructed prison. The walls of the cells glistened with fresh paint. Krehm was put into a cramped cell with three other men. Krehm's cellmates included a young Albanian and an older Greek. As they were pushed into the cell, someone asked, "What is this place?"

With a lopsided grin one of the guards said, "The Door of the Angels," and clanged the locks into place.

Whatever it was, The Door of the Angels was no government prison. Since the arrest, Krehm had seen no government uniforms. There had been rumours that the NKVD was operating clandestine prisons on behalf of the Spanish Communist Party. Krehm had no doubt they were in such a prison. People picked up by the NKVD usually turned up dead or disappeared without a trace.

Krehm was worried about the ability of the men in his cell to survive for long. Their fear, lack of any food since the arrest, and general malnourished state due to Barcelona's food shortages promised to increase the rate of mental and physical deterioration that must come with imprisonment. The Albanian's situation was worsened by the fact that he had been in the middle of a ten-day pseudo-fast that only permitted eating dishes made solely from onions. An anarchist pamphlet extolling the diet claimed it would cure all body ailments.

The older Greek's condition was particularly cause for concern. A socialist and long-standing Trotskyite, the man had been imprisoned for years in Greece before escaping to Spain. Krehm was uncertain whether the NKVD had beaten the old man or whether some past injury from his earlier years in prison had resurfaced, but the man started spitting blood the moment the cell doors slammed shut.

The prisoners soon found themselves following a set routine that focussed on the periodic delivery of meagre meals. Except for the serving and collection of their meal utensils, the guards seemed content to allow the prisoners to rot in their cells. Periodically, the guards entertained themselves with threats that the prisoners would all soon be executed.

A week after they were imprisoned, the foreigners were unexpectedly moved to a government-run prison. Conditions were better here and there was no further talk of executions. Some of the American prisoners were visited by the U.S. consul and assured their government was working to secure their release. Krehm had a brief visit from the British consul, acting on Canada's behalf, but the man offered no assurances of an early release.

No charges were brought against any of the foreign prisoners, nor did they appear in court. Rumours circulated about the fate of various Spanish POUMists. Nin had reportedly been tortured and then murdered by the NKVD. [This was true, although the Spanish Communist Party, relying on its old propaganda line that POUM was a fascist front, tried to cover up the murder by circulating a totally fictitious story that German Gestapo agents had masterminded his escape from jail and safe flight to Germany.] Soon it was evident that the government was increasingly embarrassed about the imprisonment of the foreign POUMists. The embarrassment stemmed from the fact that the Communists had obviously arrested them without cause or authorization from the government's justice ministry.

In mid-September, after three months' imprisonment, Krehm was among a clutch of foreigners released and escorted under armed guard by train to the French border. From the train they were taken to the crossing point and unceremoniously shoved across by the armed guards. Their passports were not returned. The government guards claimed the prisoners had never had any passports. Krehm bitterly pondered just how valuable a Canadian passport might prove to Stalin's NKVD, who he was sure had confiscated all the foreign passports for its own purposes.

The loss of his passport posed no real personal problem. The French and British governments were all too happy to be rid of Krehm, so they ignored his lack of proper documents and put him on a ship for Canada. By the time he returned home, the fire of political idealism that had once burned so brightly inside his head and had made him holier than the holiest was dimmed to a flickering glow. Spain was no longer a nation standing on the threshold of a bright new future. Rather, Krehm believed, it was a nation teetering on the edge of the next world war, which, judging by the brutality of the fighting taking place in Spain, would be more terrible than any the world had hitherto seen.

From the moment Lucien Tellier tumbled out of the truck to find himself on a sun-baked ridge overlooking two villages and a sparsely vegetated, gully-riven plain, the nineteen-year-old Montrealer knew he had stepped into something far beyond his worst imaginings. Tellier was in a group of troops sent from the training base to reinforce the XVth International Brigade, currently embroiled in a major battle around the town of Brunete. On July 5, 1937, the XVth had participated in a major Republican offensive aimed at driving the Nationalists from their strongholds to the west of Madrid. Casualties were so heavy that the Albacete-area training bases were soon being scoured clean of fresh recruits who could help to bolster the XVth's ranks.

With two months of training behind him, Tellier knew how to handle a rifle, use a grenade, and carry out basic squad-level manoeuvres. All that seemed woefully inadequate, however, as he tried to make sense of the battle's confusion. Right next to the road several heavy artillery pieces were blasting away. Every time the guns fired Tellier covered his ears, but the concussion still felt like it was going to crack his eardrums. Responding to some order Tellier failed to hear, the men around him all headed off on foot. Tellier, assuming they must have some idea where they were going, rushed after them.

Holding his rifle tightly with both hands, Tellier jogged down a steep slope to a road below. Alongside the road, small clusters of soldiers were scattered. Their uniforms were torn and their faces were blackened and unshaven. Nobody smiled or offered a greeting as Tellier passed. Sprawled here and there, like forgotten bundles, blood-smeared corpses lay. Staring at the faces of the dead men, Tellier recognized a few Canadians.

The reinforcements followed the road, bypassing a small village called Villanueva de la Cañada. The town's name jarred Tellier. It seemed a bad omen for him to be fighting in a Spanish town that bore the name of his country. Villanueva de la Cañada was a smoking ruin. One of the soldiers guiding Tellier's group to the front lines said the fighting there had been terrible—the enemy had pillboxes covering the approaches and the church had been heavily fortified. A lot of Lincolns had died or been wounded cleaning that rat's nest out in house-to-house fighting.

The closer they got to the front, the more often Tellier heard the distinct tweeting sound of bullets cracking over his head. "What the hell am I doing here?" he wondered. Back in Canada—sick of the relief camps, dispirited by the smashing of the On to Ottawa Trek—going to Spain had seemed not only the right thing to do, but also something that would be romantic and adventurous. What bullshit that had been. This was all very real, and all damned terrifying.

Just past Brunete, they came to a deep gully at the foot of a high hill. Mosquito Ridge, the guide told them. Earlier that day the Lincolns and Washingtons had been cut to pieces trying to take it. The Lincolns' Mackenzie-Papineau section had gone up the slope forty-men strong. Nineteen had fallen, among them Trekker Paddy O'Neill. One of the survivors was Jules Päiviö. The Finnish-Canadian was still shaken by an incident the day before when a fascist artillery round that failed to explode bounced off the ground before his feet and—pinwheeling as it went—flew right over his head.

As the veterans told their stories to new men, Tellier noticed some officers and men gathered around a black American soldier lying on a stretcher. "It's Law," a trooper said. "He's had it." Oliver Law, thirty-four-year-old Chicago native and commander of the Washington Battalion, had been popular with everyone in the XVth. Tellier could hear him talking in a soft, weak voice.

From some hillside olive groves, enemy snipers kept banging away at anyone who showed his head above the gully's protective cover. Tellier learned the enemy facing them were Moor legionnaires, brought to Spain by Franco. Luckily they seemed to be poor shots.

An officer led Tellier's group over to a stack of metal containers holding cans of coffee, bread, and tins of marmalade. Artillery shells started falling around them. Tellier hunkered down next to the dubious shelter offered by the metal containers. After each explosion he was pelted by a rain of hard clumps of clay.

The officer ordered the scared men back on their feet and told them to take the supply containers forward to the firing line. Reluctantly, Tellier

In this barranca *below Mosquito Ridge near Brunete, Lucien Tellier and many other Canadians faced their baptism of fire.*   (NAC PA194922)

joined the other ashen-faced men in gathering up the cans and running across the open ground. The artillery barrages came in rounds of four. When the first shell fell, the men all flattened as hard as they could against the ground and counted the falling shot. Once the shrapnel stopped flying, they got up and ran like hell again until the incoming shriek of the next barrage warned them to hit the dirt. There was dust and smoke everywhere, and the stench of powder burned Tellier's nose. Finally they reached the firing line and distributed the food.

Next thing Tellier knew he was swept up in an attack, joining the mixed-together elements of the Lincolns and Washingtons in an assault up Mosquito Ridge. Before they set out, an officer announced that once the summit fell the fascist line would crumble and the road to relieving the pressure on Madrid would be open. With no further ado the men let out a cheer and rushed up the slope. Tellier joined the charge. They got a couple of hundred metres before the fire became too intense. Then an officer ordered them to dig in and hold. But there was nothing to dig with except his bayonet and the ground was too hard for it to penetrate. Some of the other

147

men were firing up the hill so Tellier emulated them by snapping off a couple of shots, but there were no visible targets.

Mostly Tellier wished he could dig a good hole. He truly wanted to get as deep inside the earth as he could because there were always bullets and shrapnel from exploding artillery shells zipping by. Not being able to dig his way to safety, Tellier tried adjusting his body to the terrain. He wriggled around like a snake, seeking the elusive fold in the ground that might provide a little cover. Soon the order came for them to retreat. The men scrambled back down the hill, dragging their wounded behind them.

As night settled in, the Lincolns and Washingtons were still in the gully, the fascists still held the ridge. Tellier thought a lot of men had died that day to no good purpose. In the darkness, lying under his thin blanket, Tellier did a lot of thinking. To survive, he was going to have to pay better attention, understand things, and do what was necessary to get the job done without getting either himself or anyone else killed. If he went on blundering around like today he would surely die. For some reason his thoughts proved calming and Tellier soon fell into a comfortable, untroubled sleep.

After the first day it was hard for Tellier to remember the order in which events unfolded. Everything interwove in one seamless tableau of smoke, fire, noise, blood, and death. They marched, countermarched; attacked, retreated. They tried pushing around either flank of Mosquito Ridge, tried exploiting every conceivable route to the summit. With the passing days the only constant was the ridge. Mosquito Ridge defied all their efforts. Adding to their torment, the fascists poured off the ridge in ever more vicious counterattacks that were thrown back only at the cost of more lives. When the Nazi bombers and fighter planes came to attack them, the planes used the ridge to muffle the sound of their approach and reduce the time available for the men to scramble for cover.

Every night, when Tellier lay down to sleep, he would feel himself gradually calming, slowing down, shaking off the terrible tension of the day. With morning—the moment he rolled out from under his blanket—the tension came back, hard and cold. It would sit there like some cancerous lump right in his throat and chest. He would be jangling with excitement, his nerves wired tight. Every day brought some new lesson in war, but the feeling of tension never eased with the experience gained. Tellier was grateful that he had been in peak condition when he got to Spain. The years of rough living in the camps and on the road served him well here.

Without that physical toughness the pressure would have broken him. Even as it was, Tellier could feel himself slowly wearing down with each passing day of continual combat.

Just when he began to think he had seen all war had to offer, something new presented itself. The bombers caught them in the open one day, marching along in a nice orderly line before Villanueva del Pardillo. Everyone scattered off the road into the bordering wheat fields when the planes came over, but there was no real cover. Tellier clawed as deeply into the dirt as he could. Each bomb blast bounced Tellier off the ground. He wanted to get up and run, to get the hell out of there, but through the dirt and smoke

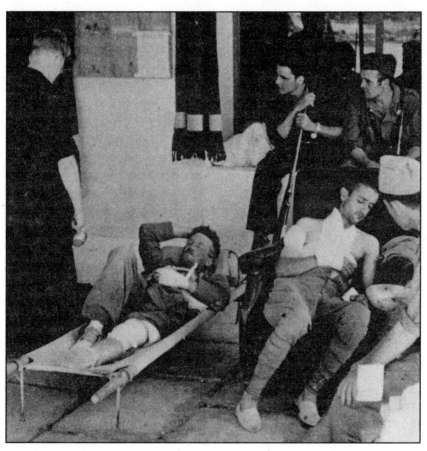

Nineteen hundred men were wounded in the fighting during the early summer of 1937 at Brunete. Among those was future Mackenzie-Papineau Battalion commander Edward Cecil Smith (on stretcher). (NAC PA172401)

149

he could see others trying to run and getting hit by shrapnel or just torn apart by the explosions. When the raid ended, Tellier got up. A couple of men stumbled past. They were glassy-eyed, their clothes blown completely off, and blood covered them.

While the medical units moved to help the wounded, the unhurt soldiers rushed forward to form a hasty defensive line to meet an oncoming Moor attack. The XVth was supported by some tanks and anti-tank guns. There were also Spanish troops in the line. Everyone was holding, unlike some other times when the Spaniards had retreated unannounced and left the Lincolns hanging in the wind.

Out of the smoke rolled Italian tanks, supporting the Moors. The Republican tanks and anti-tank guns opened up, their cannon cracking harshly and tongues of flame darting out of the gun barrels. The Italian armour was exposed, caught in the open, and the Republicans had the range perfectly. Everywhere in front of Tellier, enemy tanks were brewing up, flames and explosions tearing them apart. The fire was so intense the Moors abandoned the human wave attacks they favoured. Instead, they came on in small groups, mostly crawling. Tellier and the other Lincolns shredded them with machine-gun and rifle fire. It felt damned good to be hitting back. For three hours the fascists tried to press the attack and for three hours the Republican forces butchered them. It was a massacre, Tellier figured, but it was also just evening the score. Even after the attack petered out, the men kept firing at the crumpled corpses strewn across the killing field.

After they threw back that advance, Tellier was convinced they could hold the fascists forever. But he was wrong. The next day they started falling back, retreating toward Villanueva de la Cañada, almost back to the offensive's starting point. By July 28, the battle for Brunete was ending. The XVth International Brigade had gone into the offensive with 2,500 men. It came out with only 600 fit for duty. Tellier came through without a scratch.

On July 28, another nineteen-year-old Montrealer, Ted Allan, was trying to figure out how to keep the woman he loved from getting them both killed. Allan was on leave from his duties with the Canadian blood unit in Madrid when Gerda Taro phoned his hotel room and asked him to accompany her to the Brunete front. The young Canadian thought going anywhere near the crumbling Brunete front was a bad idea, but, masking his apprehension, he agreed to accompany her.

Allan had never announced his feelings to the twenty-five-year-old

German Jewish refugee and professional photographer. Although tortured by his love for Taro, he remained quiet about it because his best friend—the increasingly renowned combat photographer Robert Capa—was the woman's lover. Currently Capa was in Paris selling photos. Before he had left, Capa had asked Allan to keep Taro out of harm's way for him.

Taro came around to the hotel and picked him up. She was radiant as always, wearing khaki coveralls and a beret. Taro was a woman who exuded sexuality and held men in her thrall. Capa, Allan, every man Allan knew who met her, was smitten. She was small and trim. To ensure her curly auburn hair neatly framed her sculpted face, Taro plucked any hairs that deviated from a precise hairline. The young woman was not, however, merely a beauty—she was at least as good a photographer as her lover, and a more dedicated anti-fascist.

Near Brunete, Allan and Taro came across the headquarters of one of the Thaelmann Battalion commanders, who was known only as General Walter. The headquarters was between Villanueva de la Cañada and Brunete. When they entered the dugout to see General Walter, the man rounded on Allan. "Get her out of here immediately. All hell is going to break loose in a few minutes! Get out!"

Allan tried to do what the German ordered, but Taro refused to go. When he grabbed her wrist she jerked free, her two Leica cameras banging against her chest. Taro told him to go if he wanted, but she had work to do. Reluctantly, Allan tagged along.

They had barely left the command bunker when a long line of tanks and men came rushing from the direction of the front. There were hundreds of men, all running, some throwing aside weapons as they fled. Taro stopped taking pictures and swore. Dropping all pretence of being a neutral photojournalist, she ran forward and yelled at the men in good Spanish to stop retreating and to form lines. The panicked men ignored her. Fascist fighter planes and small bombers swooped down to fire machine guns and drop bombs. Allan and Taro took cover in a shallow communication trench, as wave after wave of planes swept over.

Crouching, both of her knees tucked hard into her chin, Taro asked, "Have you ever been in combat before? Are you scared?"

"I'm going to shit my pants," replied Allan, who had fought with the British Battalion before joining the Canadian Medical Unit. Taro laughed. A moment later she unwrapped a camera and started shooting pictures of the running men, of the planes, of the wounded lying on the ground screaming in their pain. Pieces of earth rose up in geysers from the bomb strikes, parts of human bodies flew through the air.

"Enough pictures! Come on!" Allan yelled. He dragged her out of the trench, forcing her to follow him toward the rear. As they retreated Taro kept shooting pictures. When not taking pictures, she held the Leica over her head as if it would protect her from the shrapnel and the blast of the bombs.

When her film was exhausted, Taro agreed to their making a hasty retreat. She, Allan, and a wounded Spanish soldier hitched a lift on a passing tank. Its armour was hot, almost scalding to the touch. They clung tightly to its body as the tank lurched down the road, its turret swinging watchfully back and forth. At Villanueva de la Cañada, Taro and Allan jumped down. Badly wounded men lay everywhere, all untended. A touring car jammed with wounded and driven by General Walter pulled up. Taro threw her cameras inside the car and jumped on the running board. Allan climbed up beside her.

Just then more strafing planes roared over the town. To the right of the car, tanks were barrelling past at high speed. One started weaving from side to side, then careened out of control and slammed into the car. Allan and Taro were tossed into the air. Allan hit the ground, tried to get up but was unable to move. Taro was screaming. Her hand stretched out toward him. Allan could not reach her.

Everything became a blur. He was dimly aware of being in movement, of eventually waking on a stretcher in a hospital. As consciousness returned, a doctor told Allan he had a crushed right foot and was at the hospital El Escorial. He asked after Taro and was assured she was fine.

Later the New Zealander, Dr. Jolly, to whom Allan had often delivered blood supplies, came by. Taro was in shock, he said. Her left hip and pelvis were mangled. There had been much bleeding and she had been given a transfusion. The surgery had gone well and she would likely be okay, but for now no visits were possible.

A nurse soon brought Allan a note. Taro wanted to know if Allan had saved her cameras. His negative response prompted another note, dropped off later by Dr. Jolly. "C'est la guerre," the slip of paper read.

The next morning Dr. Jolly came to the foot of Allan's bed. "I have terrible news," he said. "Gerda is dead." Allan refused the offered injection to help him rest. Dr. Jolly injected him anyway and then permitted Allan to be taken on a stretcher to Taro's room. He looked at her face for only a moment before asking to be taken away. She no longer looked like the woman he had known. There was none of the bright, shining light that had always been there in life.

Shortly after her death, the photos Taro had taken during the Brunete offensive appeared in *Life* under the title: "The Spanish War Kills Its First Woman Photographer." Allan could hardly bring himself to look at the pictures because the memories he experienced and the guilt he felt at not being able to prevent her death caused him almost overwhelming despair.

Nine

$\mathcal{B}$IRTH AND BAPTISM

RONALD LIVERSEDGE WAS PASSING BLOOD, DEHYDRATED, AND physically exhausted by the dysentery wringing his guts out. But he was hardly suffering alone. The disease racked virtually every Canadian at Tarazona de la Mancha, the new American-training base near Albacete.

Still, the new recruits seldom used illness to shirk a tough training regimen. In the back of every mind was the Lincolns' tragic combat debut at Jarama. Nobody wanted to replay that bloodbath. So they diligently learned the trade of warfare, hoping knowledge might prove a shield.

By early June, five hundred of Tarazona's fifteen-hundred-man complement were Canadians. The Canadian volunteers had never been so concentrated. They arrived in clutches of ten or twenty. Previously these small groupings had been scattered throughout the International Brigades, some even in Spanish units. Now, however, most were being assigned to serve together and, naturally enough, were proud of their national identity. Sufficiently so to even believe their numbers justified the formation of an all-Canadian battalion.

The Canadians' desire for a battalion of their own directly countered the intentions of the XVth International Brigade's command, which was busily creating a third American battalion. They figured the Canadians should be content to serve alongside their American comrades in a battalion named after the American labour activist Patrick Henry.

In June, when it became known that the next battalion would bear an American identity, several Canadians— including Liversedge—stormed into the XVth chief of staff's office. They demanded that Robert Merriman approve giving the new battalion a Canadian name. Merriman flatly refused. As a token gesture he offered to create a Canadian company within the American battalion and to designate it the Mackenzie-Papineau Company. Noting that Liversedge was a Great War veteran, he put the thirty-nine-year-old in command.

Liversedge was unimpressed. The Canadian company was just a patronizing pat on the head. Giving him its command was a grim joke. Ordering other men about was simply not his strong suit.

The Canadians continued demanding that the new battalion be named Mackenzie-Papineau. Merriman and his subordinates retaliated by treating them like fractious children. "Well, fellows," one American political commissar said condescendingly, "we're all in this together. We're practically one people. There are more of us Americans here. The people of Europe don't know very much about Canada. They actually think we're one nation. The people of the United States can provide more support, and, after all, the fact that there are Canadians with us is being publicized back home."

This was bunk. By summer's end about twelve hundred Canadians would be in Spain and more were expected. From a population of only eleven million, as Liversedge never tired of pointing out, Canada had raised twelve hundred volunteers. From a population of 130 million, the United States had mustered merely three thousand volunteers. This was a statistic Liversedge found very effective in disputing the American argument.

Meanwhile, the fascist naval blockade, ably supported by the British navy, which had been deployed to enforce the pro-Franco terms of the Non-Intervention Agreement, was creating serious food shortages throughout the Republic. Tea, coffee, butter, eggs, sugar, meat, and dairy products were either unavailable or scarce. Daily rations consisted of a handful of rice, a quarter cup of olive oil, and a litre of wine. Drawing from their daily salary of ten pesetas, the men sometimes bolstered the rice ration with garlic, peppers, Swiss chard, and other vegetables purchased from local peasants.

The mess hall served three meals a day. Breakfast featured burned barley coffee and a slice of bread. The mid-day and evening meals both offered rice fried in olive oil. Occasionally, garbanzo beans, also fried in olive oil, replaced the rice. If they were extremely fortunate, some chunks of burro or mule meat might serve as garnish. Then there was *bacalao*—a dried, salty codfish. The Canadians found this offering particularly foul. It was ironic that the fish came from the Grand Banks off the coast of the Atlantic provinces and the British colony of Newfoundland. Although it took the Canadian palate a little getting used too, the strong, sour wine soon became a welcome respite from the tedium of the food and the daily routine of training.

Not long after the Mackenzie-Papineau Company was formed, Merriman cottoned on to the fact that, although a proficient soldier, Liversedge lacked command presence. Liversedge refused to behave like an officer. He would not eat in the officers' mess, preferring to join his mates in the enlisted men's quarters. Instead of barking commands at his friends, he requested their co-operation. Most of the time his approach worked well enough, but it was very unsoldierly and also led to some spirited debates that were reminiscent of the anarchist approach to fighting a war—something that, since the suppression of POUM, was considered entirely unacceptable.

Finally Merriman's patience snapped. He ordered Liversedge to either act like an officer or be broken back to the ranks. Liversedge denied ever wanting to be an officer, so Merriman made him a *soldato*—the Republican Army's lowest rank.

A few days later, A.A. MacLeod—who had come to Spain to arrange Dr. Norman Bethune's return to Canada and the reorganization of the Canadian Medical Unit—visited Tarazona. Before reporting to the XVth Brigade's headquarters, the vice-president of the Canadian Committee to Aid Spanish Democracy met his national compatriots. He quickly agreed that a Canadian battalion should be formed.

MacLeod argued their case before Merriman and the headquarters' staff. He also explained that an officially formed Canadian battalion would help generate increased Canadian support for the Republican cause. Merriman remained unconvinced that the idea had merit. He agreed, however, to MacLeod presenting the Canadian position at a mass meeting that evening. Following his address, the new unit's name would be put to a vote of the fifteen hundred men. Given the American majority, MacLeod faced a tough sell.

He spoke for two electrifying hours. During his unrehearsed talk, MacLeod recounted Canada's history. He wove in the American Revolution and America's War of 1812 defeat. Finally, he spoke of the 1837 rebellions against the British in Upper and Lower Canada, describing the roles played by William Lyon Mackenzie and Joseph Papineau. When MacLeod fin-

157

ished, he humbly asked for a vote in favour of designating the new battalion the Mackenzie-Papineau. All present unanimously supported the motion. Some of the Americans approached Liversedge afterward to say that MacLeod's speech was one of the most moving they had ever heard.

The new battalion was not an all-Canadian unit. It was a mongrel of American, Canadian, and Spanish troops. Many of the platoons within the Mackenzie-Papineau's companies did, however, bear a distinctly Canadian identity. A platoon in Company Two was composed entirely of Ukrainian-Canadians. The Machine-Gun Company consisted primarily of Finnish-Canadians led by Niilo Makela. British Columbian loggers dominated a section of Company Three. Makela was, for reasons that were alternatively explained as either American chauvinism or the fact that Americans had been on the scene some months before the arrival of most Canadians and therefore had a higher level of expertise and recognition within the Internationals, the only Canadian at company or battalion command level. Total battalion strength was 625. The new battalion proudly adopted the sobriquet of Mac-Paps.

No sooner was the issue of the new battalion's designation resolved than the survivors of the Brunete offensive returned to Tarazona. The Lin-

In June 1937, the Mackenzie-Papineau Battalion was officially formed as part of the XVth International Brigade after months of lobbying by the Canadian volunteers. (NAC C74967)

coln and Washington battalions had taken such heavy casualties they had to be merged into a single unit. Liversedge was shocked by the survivors' appearance. They were emaciated, so thin their facial bones prominently protruded. Their eyes were bloodshot and streamed pus. Questions about their experiences were brusquely and rudely rebuffed. Even during the Great War, he had never seen men so drained of vitality.

The return of the Brunete veterans coincided with the grain harvest. As most of the peasants were serving in the Republican Army, Liversedge and the other soldiers helped bring in the crop. Although the hammer and sickle figured in various badges adorning their uniforms, most of the Canadians had never previously encountered a real sickle. Along with wheat stalks, many fingers, hands, and even legs were cut.

After the harvest, the pace of training quickened. The Mac-Paps became the first battalion in the XVth to learn proper marching and parade drill. They even had a bugler to sound morning reveille. While the new battalion honed its skills, the XVth's other battalions departed for the front.

To ease the tedium of the seemingly endless drill, the men learned dozens of marching songs drawn from the martial traditions of Canada's diverse national mosaic. The Ukrainian platoon indisputably had the best singers and most rousing songs. But every unit sang, each trying to outdo the others. Liversedge had never heard so much singing. He figured the Internationals must be the singingest army in the singingest war ever fought.

As a soldier in the Lincoln Battalion, Thomas Bailey also found singing broke the tedium of days spent marching on the Aragon front. After being wounded at Brunete, the former Moose Jaw Fuller Brush salesman and one-time British trade unionist had rejoined the battalion at Azaila, the assembly point for the XVth International's entry into the huge Republican offensive that had started on August 23, 1937. The offensive's objective was to capture Zaragoza, a major city straddling Aragon province's central rail and road system. From Zaragoza the fascists had repeatedly attempted to launch a drive to the sea that would cut the Republic in half, with Barcelona isolated in the north from Madrid and Valencia to the south.

The Republican government had decided to counter the fascist threat by driving Franco's army out of Zaragoza. Realizing the strategic importance of Zaragoza to his own plans, Franco had bolstered its defences, as well as those of the villages and towns on the roads approaching it from the east. Huesca, Quinto, Belchite, and Fuentes de Ebro had all been transformed into fortresses bristling with machine guns, artillery, and thousands of troops.

Aragon province was a country of barren hills and wide, desertlike valleys. It was a hard land, known to have two seasons—six months of winter, six months of hell. The Ebro River ran out of Aragon to the sea at Tortosa in southern Catalonia. The course followed by the river broke through the hostile mountain ranges on either side, providing a narrow front of valley and plain in which infantry and armour could effectively manoeuvre. The Republic's plan was for one arm of its army to drive up either flank of the Ebro, overwhelm the defences surrounding Belchite, Quinto, and Fuentes de Ebro, and invest Zaragoza from the southwest, while another arm drove out of the mountains to approach the city from the north and catch the fascists in a classic pincer.

The regrouped XVth International Brigade was to play a key role in the offensive, clearing the way through Quinto and Belchite. Thirty-six-year-old Thomas Bailey, having only just returned from a hospital near Madrid, knew from bitter experience that the infantrymen's role in an offensive paid scant resemblance to anything as ordered and purposeful as the bold, black arrows sketched on his commanders' maps. What he had learned at Brunete was the confusing and capricious nature of war.

One moonlit night he and another soldier had been on a hill, digging in a light machine-gun position. He had heard a buzzing sound, like a bee trying to fly into his ear, and then it seemed as if someone hit him on the head with a club. Bailey sprawled to the ground. A few seconds later he reached up dazedly to his face and discovered blood running from a precise groove in his scalp. Peering around, he saw the other soldier lying nearby. A bullet hole was visible in the man's steel helmet. It was obvious the soldier was dead.

Bailey was convinced the man's helmet had got him killed. Both men had been working on the skyline and a helmet formed a distinctive outline, even glistening in the moonlight. By now he realized they had both been shot by a sniper. The helmeted soldier, however, had presented the better target. Bailey, who seldom wore his helmet, had been wearing his khaki beret, which blended with its surroundings and presented a poor profile for a sniper. So Bailey was alive and the other poor fellow dead. It was small details like this that determined who survived and who died. Bailey made it a point to learn the details. He had every intention of surviving this war.

When Bailey stumbled into a first-aid post to get his head wound

Thirty-six-year-old Thomas Bailey preferred a beret to a helmet and believed this choice of headgear saved him from being killed by sniper fire on a moonlit night near Quinto.
(MTRL T34776)

patched up, the doctors were more concerned about his bleeding and swollen feet. They cursorily bandaged his head, but sent him to the rear for recuperative treatment for his feet. It irked Bailey that there had been little he could do to avoid the damage. None of the men had proper boots, most wore only rope-soled sandals. Finding clean socks was virtually impossible. Often there were no socks to be had at all. Blisters burst, feet swelled, and gangrene was common.

After several weeks of hospital care, Bailey was sent north to Aragon when the XVth Brigade gathered every man who could stand from the hospitals. Bailey rejoined the Lincolns scant days before the battalion attacked Quinto.

The morning of August 24 dawned bright and cloudless. Quick, hot gusts swept across the plain, hazing the horizon with dust. A powdery film covered everything, so that men, equipment, trees, and buildings all wore the same brown and yellow patina. From his position in the trench, Bailey looked across a deadly plain that stretched for three kilometres before rising gently to the ramparts of Quinto. All Bailey could see of the village was its church steeple. Artillery shells were bursting in the fascist positions and Republican airplanes buzzed angrily overhead dropping bombs and diving down to strafe enemy concentrations.

At 6:00 A.M., the Dimitrovs launched the first assault but were stalled by heavy fire. They quickly withdrew, regrouped, and swung north of Quinto toward the village's rear. The Lincolns followed the Dimitrovs, circling the heavy fortifications straddling the village's main streets. Bailey was part of what was now called the 1st Canadian Company—to avoid it being confused with the newly formed Mackenzie-Papineau Battalion.

161

The company probed the village's cemetery, trying to worm its way through the maze of crypts to the buildings beyond. Fascist machine-gun nests, dug in behind the facing cemetery walls, forced them back. The fascist bullets chipped the gravestones and artillery shelling breached many of the crypts, so that the long-entombed bodies of the dead were exposed.

During this effort, Alick Miller, the Canadian company commander, was shot through the head. Although the wound looked terrible and everyone thought he was dying, Miller refused assistance. Alone, he struggled one kilometre over open terrain back to the first-aid post. Bailey later learned he survived to return to Canada. As Miller left the field, Charles Nusser, a veteran of Jarama and Brunete, took command. Nusser, wearing a white sleeveless shirt that made him look more tourist than soldier, told them to get the hell out. Bailey and the others retreated happily—they had no wish to die in the ghoulish environment of the cemetery.

The fascist positions were formidable. They had reinforced bunkers constructed of heavy steel rails and hardened concrete. To Bailey it seemed that breaching these defences would be impossible. Even the continual shelling from French-made 75-millimetre artillery and Russian 105-millimetre guns seemed to barely scratch them.

Apparently somebody in command recognized the need for more firepower. Eight Russian-made tanks swept up to hammer the fascist positions with their 47-millimetre cannon. Republican bombers roared overhead and dropped bombs. Other planes screamed over the town to rip at the defences with their heavy machine guns. The concentrated fire kept the fascists' heads down long enough for the Lincolns to complete their long manoeuvring swing around the village's flanks.

At 3:00 P.M., the eight tanks suddenly fanned out and the Lincolns were ordered to form up by squads around them. The battalion machine-gun company unleashed a sustained volley of fire over the heads of the advancing infantry. A precise two hundred metres ahead and apace of the advancing Lincolns, a Republican artillery barrage walked through the fascist positions. Enemy mortar shells fell along the Lincoln line but failed to inflict many casualties or slow the attack.

The tanks ripped through the enemy barbed wire, clearing paths for the Lincolns and decimating the fascist machine-gun positions at close range. As the infantry poured into the fascist trenches, the enemy fell back in disarray, abandoning their equipment and wounded, and leaving behind piles of dead. By dusk, Lincoln patrols were pushing into the village's houses, but, lacking adequate support, were soon ordered to withdraw to the captured trenches.

In the morning, Bailey and the rest of the Lincolns fought their way back into Quinto. The fighting was house to house, bloody, and vicious. Bailey took to carrying two rifles—a Russian submachine gun and a German Mauser rifle—so that he always had one ready and loaded. A few minutes after they entered the village, Bailey knew one thing for certain. He hated street-fighting. Everything was close up and unpredictable. Turn a corner and all hell might break loose or there might be nothing but some fascists waving a white flag of surrender.

The Lincolns adeptly learned the dirty art of street-fighting. Rather than take a building by storm, they brought up a tank or anti-tank gun and hammered the fascist position down around the enemy's heads. When the building was virtually demolished, they moved up and finished off any remaining resistance and rounded up the shell-shocked survivors. If enough of the building still stood, the Lincolns erected a flag bearing the Republic's yellow, red, and blue horizontal stripes on the roof. Then they moved on to

A XVth International brigader mans a Maxim heavy machine gun during mopping-up operations in the hills near Quinto. (NAC PA 194607)

the next building and the next after that. As was often the case, the last fascist position to fall was the church, which had been heavily fortified. By late evening, Quinto was in Republican hands.

It took several more days to clear the fascists from the surrounding hills. Then, on August 31, the Lincolns marched through the night for thirty-two kilometres to the outskirts of Belchite, the next village on the road to Zaragoza.

In Belchite, the narrow streets hampered the manoeuvre of tanks and anti-tank guns, so the Lincolns fought in small groups of five or six men. They carried cans of gasoline. If resistance from a building was too severe, they set it on fire and burned the defenders out. Soon the streets boiled with smoke from raging fires. Virtually every house had to be taken in a brutal fight. Fascist snipers stayed in their positions until they were finally overwhelmed and killed. Neither side offered much quarter to the other. Finally, after six days of slaughter, Belchite fell.

In their last act of defiance, a clutch of fascist officers resorted to using captive civilians as a shield to screen their attempted escape. If the Lincolns tried to intervene, the civilians would be decimated in the crossfire, so they could only watch helplessly as the Nationalists prepared to make good their flight. While the fascist attention had been focussed on the Lincolns, however, a Spanish unit had got behind them. It jumped the Nationalist officers who, realizing the game was up, abandoned the civilians and fled into an olive grove. The enraged Spanish troops hunted them down and took no prisoners.

Bailey was detailed to take a group of prisoners captured earlier back to Codo, a village in the Republican rear. He was one of five guards overseeing about 250 Spanish prisoners and five fair-haired men wearing civilian clothes. Along the way, the guards allowed the prisoners to stop and pick grapes in a vineyard next to the road. While the prisoners harvested grapes, Bailey watched the men in civilian dress. They wore their hair in a severe martial cut and had a distinct military bearing. With their fair complexions they were obviously not Spanish. Bailey walked over to them. "No Español, Alemán?" he demanded curtly. "Si, Señor," replied the men, "Alemán." Bailey figured he was seeing his first Nazi supermen. He was not much impressed.

A week later, Bailey was delegated to represent the Lincolns in Albacete during anniversary celebrations to mark the Internationals' entry into the war a year earlier. Dolores Ibarruri and other political celebrities delivered laudatory speeches. Bailey enjoyed their words, but not as much as the bountiful banquet. It had been a long time since he had eaten meat and he made the most of it.

Bailey was concerned to find no Mackenzie-Papineau Battalion members attending the anniversary. He had planned to request a transfer to the new Canadian unit. But the Mac-Paps were gone, so his transfer would have to wait.

On September 9, 1937, the Mackenzie-Papineau Battalion quit Tarazona de la Mancha and entrained to the Aragon front. The Republican offensive had bogged down. Each side was taking a deep breath, readying for the next phase of battle.

Liversedge found the Aragon region a harsh change from the gentle country around Albacete. It was rough and hilly, deeply scoured by gullies called *barrancas*. The ground was hard, brown, and usually treeless. It seemed to be one vast, brown smudge of dry landscape sprawling beneath a steely blue and white sky. Even the villages were the same dull brown colour, blending so well into the landscape that they were only visible from close up.

The Mac-Paps' first three weeks on the front were spent nomadically. They marched from one indistinguishable ridge to another, dug in, observed the enemy doing the same across a narrow valley. Then, after a day or two, they packed up and shifted to another equally featureless ridge.

When they left Albacete, the Mac-Paps had expected to go directly into combat, but they soon realized this was only a final training phase, intended to give them a taste of front-line conditions. Although they saw no battle, they suffered casualties. Pneumonia, jaundice, and severe cases of dysentery whittled away their effective strength. Lice was also a constant problem, infesting clothing, hair, and blankets.

Eventually the Mac-Paps moved to the XVth Brigade's Azaila operational base. The Canadians found a comfortable position for themselves in a *barranca* near the base's olive groves. Clouds gathered ominously overhead. Suddenly the sky opened and rain bucketed down. Before the troops could gather up their gear and escape to higher ground, a metre-high wall of water roared down the narrow gully. While everybody managed to escape from the rushing water, much of their equipment was swept away. Liversedge and Jim Pollitt crawled up to a small cave and huddled inside. As the two men watched dinner plates, helmets, and ammunition boxes being carried off by the newly sprung torrent, they amused themselves by singing "Every Time It Rains, It Rains Pennies from Heaven."

When the storm cleared, their good humour also dissipated. Although the nearby Lincolns had comfortably weathered the storm beneath the shelter offered by heavy canvas tents, it was soon apparent to Liversedge and the other newly arrived Mac-Paps that the rest of the brigade was in a bad way. Morale was low, the men were exhausted from the fighting at Quinto and Belchite, and casualties had left the XVth's other battalions seriously understrength. Liversedge was shocked to discover that two close friends from his relief camp union days in Vancouver had fallen at Belchite—Jim Wolf and Charlie Sand. Both had died during the final moments of the battle, when the Lincolns had attacked the machine-gun position in the church tower. Liversedge was deeply troubled by the Lincolns' sullenness.

Everyone was griping and the Mac-Paps soon joined in. They bitched about their antiquated Russian rifles, cursed the Non-Intervention Pact for causing the shortages of arms and food, muttered about headquarters staff incompetence, complained about the bad food, and bemoaned the scarcity of tobacco and the irregularity of mail. Various substitutes for tobacco were developed and tested. The best proved to be dried potato plant leaves, but these were hard to find on the dry Aragon plain.

The Mac-Pap officers continued to run the battalion along stricter military lines than was the XVth Brigade norm. Each morning the bugler sounded reveille. He summoned the men to breakfast, lunch, and dinner. In the evening, bugle notes directed them to bed. After two days of this racket, the Lincolns' sense of fraternity with their junior battalion snapped. During the night they hijacked the offending bugle and flattened it beneath a truck's tire.

Even the brigade command accepted this act of vandalism goodnaturedly, as they did most breaches of discipline. But a few days later an incident occurred that even a non-authoritarian like Liversedge could not easily brush aside. In the middle of the night, a half-dozen men stole the Mackenzie-Papineau Battalion's only ambulance and made a desperate run for the French border. They were caught and returned to the brigade.

Two of the men were members of the Mac-Paps—Canadian Henry Shapiro and American Robert W. Eisenberg. Another, Richard de Witt Brown, was an American in the Lincoln Battalion. These three were quickly identified as the plot's ringleaders.

There had been earlier desertions. Canadian Hugh Garner, fearing he would miss the ultimate manly test of battle, had deserted his rear-area posting to join a unit in the battle lines. War proved a surprise to the young writer, leaving him completely unnerved by the experience. He deserted the line company, was ultimately picked up by police in Madrid, and the brigade command responded by banishing him back to Canada. There, he ably supported the Republican cause with his pen. Liversedge and everyone else in the brigade knew about Garner's desertion, but as men who had been themselves fired upon and who had seen those unable to bear up to that terrible experience, they saw no crime in a man's courage cracking during combat.

Shapiro, however, had been in Spain for only two months and during that time had seen no combat. Eisenberg had fifteen days more non-combatant service than Shapiro. Acting out of nothing but cowardice, these men had, by stealing the ambulance, proved willing to jeopardize the forthcoming battle's wounded to ensure their own safety.

But the Internationals were all volunteers. No matter the circumstances, could a volunteer be considered a deserter? In that light perhaps Shapiro and the others could be considered guilty of theft but innocent of the more serious military crime of desertion.

A military tribunal was convened to decide the men's fate. At the same time, the battalions were asked to ponder the question of what sentence would be appropriate in the event of a guilty verdict.

It was a difficult moral dilemma. After much debate, during which the political commissars said brigade command favoured a death penalty, the units voted. The majority rejected the death penalty. After the tribunal found all the deserters guilty, a few were returned to their units. The only punishment these men faced was being subjected to chastisement and shaming by their comrades. The ringleaders, Shapiro and Eisenberg among them, were never seen again. Their fate remained a matter of conjecture, but most believed they had been transferred to other units. [In an official report unearthed in Moscow by a National Archives of Canada archivist in 1996, XVth Brigade Political Commissar Dave Doran reported that Shapiro and Eisenberg were in fact executed for desertion. The report also states that de Witt Brown was sentenced to a year in prison after he gave evidence against the other two men and begged for a chance to redeem himself in combat. Doran further wrote that all units returned unanimous calls that the deserters be executed and that similar measures be taken against other deserters.

Given this evidence, it appears that Shapiro and Eisenberg were executed, but that brigade command sought to conceal their deaths from the rank-and-file, probably due to the poor state of morale. It is to be supposed that Doran then falsified the results of the vote to justify the tribunal's decision to carry out the executions.]

Although Liversedge was sympathetic to those who lost their nerve—even deserters—he never questioned his own resolve. In August 1937, while filling out a Spanish Communist Party questionnaire, he wrote that the Communist Party was "the only one capable of emancipating the human race" and pledged after this war to work for the world revolutionary movement.

With the immediate future promising the first blooding of the Mackenzie-Papineau Battalion, however, he had little time to speculate on life after the war's end. On October 10, 1937, the XVth Brigade moved by truck to Quinto. A warning order was given for the battalion to prepare for an October 13 attack on Fuentes de Ebro.

As night fell on October 12, Liversedge hunkered in a one-man slit trench dug under the sparse branches of an olive tree. Soon it started to rain. Liversedge spent the night in a cold bath, the trench filling around him with rainwater. The rain continued until early morning. All of the men were wet, shivering, sneezing, coughing, and snuffling with colds contracted during the night. Everyone had dysentery. Liversedge and many others were passing blood. It struck him that there had probably never been an army less fit for battle.

Liversedge could hardly breathe. Every time he inhaled, a sharp pain stabbed his right side. Worried, he reported to the battalion doctor and was diagnosed with pleurisy. The doctor ordered Liversedge hospitalized. Liversedge refused to go. The two men argued, but finally the doctor relented. To help ease the pain, he taped Liversedge's right side.

For the rest of the day the men loitered, waiting for the trucks to take them into action. The battalion cook, Perry Hilton, who Liversedge had known during the On to Ottawa Trek, brought up the kitchen truck and dispensed a hot meal at about midday. The stew helped warm the men and the feeble sunshine slowly dried their clothes. In late evening a line of trucks arrived. Jamming forty men and their gear into each truck, every man in the XVth Brigade was able to get aboard.

The sixteen-kilometre road between Quinto and Fuentes was so clogged with vehicles and marching men that progress was painfully slow. Dawn already dusted the hillsides when the trucks finally stopped and the men climbed out. A shallow communication trench ran for several hundred metres from the road to the front-line trenches. A wide plain stretched gradually upward from the Republican lines to Fuentes de Ebro.

The fascist position was such that it allowed them to perch like eagles, overlooking the men impatiently waiting their turn to enter the relative safety of the communication trench. As Liversedge entered the narrow trench he wondered why the fascists held their fire. The exposed line of men, both those on the road and those shuffling slowly down the shallow, dirty trench, presented a perfect target. Liversedge felt his skin tingle more feverishly with each passing minute. He could imagine the fascists looking down upon them from Fuentes, unhurriedly finishing their morning coffee, flexing their muscles, casually turning to their machine guns, working the breeches back, fitting the belts of ammunition in, slowly drawing a bead.

Half the battalion was still on the road when all hell erupted. Dozens of machine guns opened up with a shattering crescendo of fire. Men on the road started crumpling. The soldiers in the trench tried rushing forward to open space for the men on the road, but they only became entangled, slowing their steps even more. The air rang with the screams of wounded and dying men. Liversedge's section finally tumbled into the forward trench. An officer directed them to their designated position and told them to lay down covering fire. The Mac-Paps who could blazed away at the enemy line with their rifles and light machine guns.

Snapping off bursts from his light machine gun, Liversedge tried to get his bearings in relation to the enemy position. Fronted by a deep *arroyo*, Fuentes de Ebro looked remarkably like an ancient medieval castle. Although it was dry, the *arroyo* resembled a moat. On the Fuentes side the fascists had dug a trench line, linked to the village by a communications trench. Liversedge could see a line of fascist troops moving down this trench toward the main position. Previously he had been firing blind. Now, he raised the sight of the sturdy 7.62-millimetre Degtyarev DP light machine gun as far as it could go, signalled his loader to get another of the sixty-round circular ammunition pans ready, and started laying short bursts of fire into the trench. The exchange of machine-gun fire continued for about an hour until finally a heavy silence fell upon the front.

Having earlier concentrated his attention on the fascist trenches, Liversedge now took a closer look at Fuentes de Ebro itself. He saw a frighteningly perfect fortress. At the pinnacle of the town sat a huge, thick-walled church. Below that were other equally formidable buildings. While the guns had been firing, Liversedge had noticed that every window in the town seemed to be belching smoke and muzzle flashes.

Between the town and the Republican lines lay a good two kilometres of open terrain that would be constantly exposed to the fascist guns. Liversedge had seen this kind of thing as a British Tommy in the Great War. He hoped to hell the Republican generals had a few more tricks up their sleeves than the British generals had ever managed to devise. Otherwise the Mac-Paps stood before a classic butcher's ground.

There was a plan, but Lionel Edwards found no solace in knowing its details. The former unemployed Calgary accountant commanded a platoon in the Mac-Pap's Company Three. He thought attacking Fuentes de Ebro was tactically unwarranted. The Republicans could easily bypass the stronghold—leaving behind a holding force—and starve the heavily entrenched defenders into submission while accelerating their offensive push toward Zaragoza. Instead, the Republican command had settled on a direct assault that required the co-ordination of air, artillery, armour, and infantry in a manoeuvre that could only achieve success through precise timing. Such a manoeuvre would test the skill of the world's most advanced armies. Edwards could scarcely believe the Republic's fractious, ill-trained, citizen army capable of such a feat of military expertise.

His forebodings were soon confirmed. About mid-morning the scheduled artillery barrage manifested itself as a few sporadic salvos from two seventy-five-millimetre artillery batteries. After a few minutes, the guns fell silent. For two more hours the men huddled in the trenches under an increasingly sweltering sun. Their tongues swelled and their throats felt raw and sore, but they tried to limit themselves to only small swallows from their canteens in order to have some water left for the attack. Around noon they were ordered to get ready. Edwards told his platoon to dump their packs. They hooked their aluminum dinner plates to their belts, alongside their canteens, ammunition pouches, and grenades. Just down from where Edwards waited, Lauradin Roy, a young French-Canadian trapper from Rimouski, Quebec, was smearing white mud over his helmet to reduce its glare.

A straggling line of about eighteen single-engined bombers waddled clumsily over the Republican line and dropped its bombs on the fascist defences. The planes were so high up the fascists' anti-aircraft guns never bothered firing. Because of the high altitude, however, the bombs dropped by the planes exploded over such a wide front within and outside the town that the attack was largely ineffectual. The explosions did manage to obscure Fuentes behind thick wreaths of smoke and dust.

Where the hell were the tanks? Edwards wondered. According to the plan, anywhere from fifty to one hundred Russian-made tanks, mostly lightly armoured B-26s mounted with forty-seven-millimetre cannon, were supposed to support the attack. They were even supposed to carry the 24th Spanish Battalion on their hulls right into the fascist entrenchments. The tank attack should have gone forward immediately after the bombers struck, supported, of course, by the ominously silent artillery.

For one and a half more hours the men waited. Then from behind them came a roar of engines. The ground shook, and the screech and clank of armoured tracks was heard. A line of about fifty B-26s descended on the Republican trenches. Each tank had about eight Spanish infantry clinging to either side of the turret. A couple of hundred metres from the trench line the tanks jerked to an abrupt halt, nearly throwing the infantrymen off. The tanks proceeded to fire several rounds from their cannon. Then, without warning, the broad line of tanks charged.

The men of the XVth Brigade desperately scattered to get out of the way as the tanks dashed across the trench line. Whole sections of the trench's walls collapsed beneath the armour's weight. Two young Spaniards serving with the Mac-Paps were crushed. By the time the brigade was sorted out and ready to advance, the first wave of tanks was far off, racing alone toward Fuentes.

Edwards tried to sound strong and confident as he ordered his platoon forward, but he was so frightened he could hardly speak. The Mac-Paps clambered from the trenches and started after the tanks. Ahead lay the arroyo, at least a kilometre distant. They were to cross it and then climb the long upward slope leading to the fascist trenches. Edwards silently urged himself on, resisting the almost overwhelming desire to turn and run like hell. At one point he passed a young Spanish boy-soldier who was lying in a ball, hands covering a blood-soaked stomach. The boy was moaning, "Madre, madre."

Some of the tanks were burning, the bodies of the Spanish troops who had been riding them lying pell-mell across the plain. The surviving tanks, with the few soldiers who had not been shot off their hulls by the enemy machine guns, smashed through the barbed wire fronting the trenches.

They then raced across the trenches and disappeared into the streets of Fuentes de Ebro.

The largely unharmed fascist forces in the trenches turned their guns on the advancing elements of the XVth Brigade. Edwards knew the tanks and the soldiers who had been riding them were finished unless the XVth could reinforce them. Without infantry to protect their flanks, the tanks would be helpless in narrow streets. Not enough of the Spanish infantry had survived the near suicidal charge across the open plain to carry out this vital duty.

But the XVth's advance was breaking before the terrific, gut-wrenching automatic weapons barrage. Like everyone else, Edwards tried to zigzag his way forward, sporadically dropping to the earth and then jumping up and running again. A few other tanks had come up and were advancing with the men, but they were too few to offer viable support. All around him, men were grunting and falling. Company Three's commander, Lt. Joseph Dougher, fell, his foot torn apart by a bullet. Fifty yards to Edwards's right the French-Canadian Roy went down with a bullet in the head.

Edwards threw himself to the ground, hugging the earth, desperately trying to catch his breath. A tank roared up behind him. Stopping within easy reach of where he lay, it proceeded to blast away at the enemy lines. With each crack of the cannon, Edwards was sure his eardrums were going to shatter. To escape the sound of the gun, Edwards forced himself to advance. A handful of men reached the *arroyo's* edge. There they started to dig in. Edwards clawed at the soil, thinking giddily how marvellous and wonderful the earth was and wondering why he had been so long in coming to be acquainted with it.

Bill Kardash of Winnipeg was in a B-26 tank ploughing through clouds of dust raised by the tanks that had gone ahead of him. His orders were simple. Kardash was to break through the fascist lines, destroy their machine-gun and anti-tank gun nests, fire along the trenches at any infantry there, and clear the way for the Republican advance.

Earlier there had been eight to ten Spanish soldiers clinging to the hull as they roared forward at about forty kilometres an hour, but the fascists continually raked the tank with machine-gun fire, and after the first burst Kardash noticed the Spaniards had either jumped clear or been gunned down. There was no time to worry about their fate. The enemy bullets striking the armour sounded like hail falling on a tin roof.

Unable to put his head out of the commander's cupola, Kardash was trying to spot machine-gun nests through his periscope—a difficult job when the tank was bouncing along at such high speed over rough ground. Suddenly the tank slammed to a stop, causing Kardash to bump his head on the periscope.

The driver, José, yelled: "There's a steep ravine ahead."

"If you can make it, go ahead," Kardash told him. Beside him, Ruiz, the loader, was waiting with a replacement shell for the gun. The tank held only a three-man crew. Kardash was both commander and gunner.

José drove the tank into the *arroyo* and up the other side. As they came over the crest, Kardash saw the enemy trenches lying just five metres ahead. José gunned the tank forward, driving across the trench. Bullets hammered against the armoured sides. "Don't stop," Kardash snapped, but the tank suddenly lurched to a halt. "Keep on going, José." The tank didn't move. It was poised just thirty-five metres behind the trench. Suddenly the motor coughed and died. Kardash could hear the incessant tapping of bullets striking the tank. Nearby explosions rocked its hull.

"It's on fire," José shouted. Kardash looked down into the bowels of the tank. Smoke was filling the compartment. In the trench some fascists stood up, apparently to watch the flames that must have been burning the outside of the tank. He figured they had been hit by an incendiary grenade. Kardash fired a shell right into the trench where the fascist soldiers were standing. Ruiz rammed another round into the breech. Kardash fired repeatedly into the trench.

The turret, where Ruiz and Kardash were, was starting to fill with smoke. Flames were licking out of the motor section below. Kardash realized that if the gas exploded they would be immolated. But if they abandoned the tank behind enemy lines there was scant chance of their surviving.

Giving the order to abandon the tank, Kardash returned to the gun and fired into the trench to cover his men's escape. First, José leaped out of a hatch and scrambled away. Then, Ruiz jumped clear. Seconds later the cannon jammed. Kardash switched to the machine gun and started raking the trenches with it. The heat was becoming unbearable. It was time to go.

Pistol in hand, Kardash jumped out and ran toward a road leading back to the Republican lines. There was no sign of José or Ruiz. They had either got clear or been killed. Five grenades landed around him, exploding rapidly one after the other. Then a bullet tore his right leg out from under him and he fell face downward. Kardash was about five metres from the fascist trench. He raised his pistol and kept firing into it, trying to hit some fascists. Blood was streaming from his hands and face. His khaki-coloured pants were turning a dark maroon colour. When only one bullet remained he stopped shooting. Then he lay still, trying to think. As yet he felt no pain, but he knew that would come as surely as the fascists would soon find him.

Kardash slowly turned over and raised the pistol toward his head. He had three choices—either bleed to death, be killed by the fascists, or use the remaining bullet on himself. Just as the barrel of the pistol reached his head, Kardash saw a Republican tank on the road he had been running toward. Feebly he waved his hand, trying to attract its attention. The tank turned and trundled over to where he lay. Dragging his shattered leg, Kardash crawled on top of the hull and the tank started to withdraw. Enemy gunfire chipped paint off the armoured hull all around him. A grenade went off nearby and shrapnel flayed his right hand. Despite his agony, Kardash clung tenaciously, desperately, to the tank's hull through a long, rough, jolting ride to the first-aid station in the rear.

Twenty-seven-year-old Edward Komodowski of Cook's Creek, Manitoba, wished he had never started on this ill-fated foray into no man's land. He was crawling in the general direction of the *arroyo,* which seemed to be the preliminary goal of the attack. Ahead of him was a young Spaniard. The man had taken off his shoe and was holding it in front of his eyes. The shoe's heel had been shot clear away and there was a groove down the sole where a bullet had carved out a path. The man kept mumbling, "*Madre mia, Madre mia . . .*" punctuated with the calm additional comment in Spanish, "You know, they could have killed me."

Komodowski was part of a group who had advanced on their bellies for about thirty minutes but were still well short of the *arroyo* when someone ordered them to retreat. Like the others, he reversed direction. Soon he was completely disoriented. When they came across a shallow trench, the men followed it for what seemed at least two hours. The palms of Komodowski's hands were bleeding, and the knees of his pants were wet with blood. His body was plastered with dirt and the working parts of his rifle were choked with grime. Some of the men had discarded their weapons.

Behind Komodowski was a young man from New York who had neglected to leave his pack at the attack's start line. The pack rose up above the edge of the trench and was frequently torn by bullets. That served to convince Komodowski that he should stay well inside the safe haven presented by the trench.

About the time Komodowski reached this conclusion, an American lieutenant rushed up with a club in his hand and, standing on the edge of the trench, ordered everyone to get up and advance on the ridge. As far as Komodowski could see the trench they were in was heading the same direction and they would get there more safely by staying in it. But the officer was adamant that the men get up and rush forward. "Don't you know the position you are in? You're all massed up here. It would be fatal to all of you if the fascists opened up with artillery." Komodowski agreed with the officer's thoughts but figured the machine guns that would kill them if they went out into the open ground were more of an immediate threat. So far the fascists had not bothered firing any artillery.

Suddenly a tuft of cloth flew off the American officer's arm. He dropped the club, gripped his arm, and said, "Ouch." Despite this wound, the officer refused the men's entreaties that he should join them in the trench. A second later another bullet hit him. He wavered but remained on his feet, spurning their pleas that he take cover. Struck by another bullet, however, the officer toppled over backward. Komodowski decided not to take the risk of checking to see if the fool was dead, he just resumed crawling down the trench.

Eventually he came out on a road that cut across the ridge. On either side the road was bordered by embankments in which a series of foxholes had been dug. Komodowski and the others crawled into the holes and waited for the battle to sputter to its inevitable end.

From the moment they left the trenches, Company One, of which Ronald Liversedge was a part, started dying. Fifteen minutes after they had gone over the top, half the men had fallen. The survivors reeled forward under a hail of bullets coming from the church and houses of Fuentes. Commander William Neure and Company Commissar Jack Shiffman were both killed.

To Liversedge's right, battalion commissar Joseph Dallet strode forward with a walking cane in one hand and his trademark pipe in the other. Liversedge noticed that he had a little smile on his face. Just as he noted this, Liversedge heard the smack of a bullet hitting flesh. Dallet gave a small grunt and crumpled to the ground.

Then three of the ammunition carriers in Liversedge's machine-gun

squad fell. Milt Herndon, an American black, went down. Isaac Schatz,
a stretcher-bearer from Toronto,
crawled over to Herndon. But as he
turned the dying American over, a
bullet tore through Schatz's shoulder.

Liversedge and the survivors
crawled forward, trying to continue
the attack. Whenever he reached a
small hummock of earth, Liversedge
set up his machine gun and fired a
few bursts at the fascist positions.

Ahead of them, well inside the
fascist positions, Liversedge could
see Republican tanks burning. Some
of the crews escaped from the burning tanks only to be cut down by the
fascist guns. A few of the Spaniards
from the 24th Battalion were hud-
dling helplessly behind the burning
wrecks.

The enemy fire became so intense Liversedge's unit could go no
further. They tried to dig holes in the
hard Aragon soil with their dinner
plates. As evening fell, the enemy
machine-gun fire became so intense
that they were forced to move from
their shelters. Crawling to their left
they came upon part of an old trench,
into which they thankfully tumbled.

*When the Mackenzie-Papineau
Battalion first went into battle at
Fuentes de Ebro all its commanders
were Americans, such as New Yorker
Saul Wellman. Wellman rose from the
rank of company commissar to
battalion commissar following Joe
Dallet's death at Fuentes.* (NAC C67468)

To their surprise they found themselves on the rim of the *arroyo* they
had been trying all afternoon to reach. Looking at it, Liversedge realized how hopeless the entire assault had been from the very beginning. It
was much wider and deeper than they had been led to believe. Crossing
it under intensive enemy fire would have been suicidal. As if to prove the
point, two men tried to go across. They got only about one hundred metres when one took a round through the nose, the other a bullet through

the arm. Both crawled back to the trench. Jim Menzies, a sergeant from Vancouver, came up and ordered everyone to stay put until nightfall.

On the Mac-Paps' opposite flank, Lionel Edwards was also lying on the edge of the uncrossable *arroyo*. As night dropped its concealing cloak over the battlefield, a cheer rose from the fascist lines. It seemed to Edwards that the enemy was saying, "That's all for today. We'll see you again tomorrow."

Under the protection of darkness, the surviving elements of the Mackenzie-Papineau Battalion fell back a bit to regroup. They tried to drag the many dead back with them.

With almost every commander dead or wounded, it was difficult to co-ordinate anything. Stretcher-bearers kept crawling out into the field in search of casualties. Each time they returned, their stretchers bore one or more men who were either dead or wounded. There was no food or water. Everyone was exhausted. A party of Spanish sappers came up and started digging a trench on the edge of the *arroyo*, which was to be the Mac-Paps' new position.

In the pre-dawn hours the men moved into the ill-prepared position. Here they remained, enduring the concentrated fascist fire for eleven more days. More casualties were suffered for no sensible reason. On October 25, the XVth Brigade was relieved by a Spanish brigade. Initially falling back to Quinto, the brigade left the Aragon front on November 1 for the Internationals' home base of Albacete. The weary survivors of the Mac-Paps' baptism of fire settled in the nearby drafty castle of Pezuela de las Torres to recover.

Ten

$\mathcal{A}$FTERMATHS

SEVEN DAYS AFTER THE FUENTES DE EBRO DEBACLE, DOCTORS AT
a Madrid hospital amputated tanker William Kardash's right leg. On November 12, two unexpected visitors came to his hospital bedside. Peter
was an Austrian tanker who had come to Spain after serving a two-year
sentence for participating in the Vienna workers' uprising in February 1934.
He and Kardash had fought together at Jarama and Brunete. On Peter's arm
was Conchita, his girlfriend of many months. Both were happy to see
Kardash, but shocked by his appearance and the state of his wounds.

Kardash explained that the amputation had been necessitated by gase-
ous gangrene and that his other leg had been peppered with shrapnel. "The
doctor made eight cuts in the foot and still wasn't able to take all the shrapnel out," he said. Although still in great pain, Kardash was well aware how
closely he had brushed death. Losing a leg seemed fair exchange for escaping with his life.

Kardash turned the talk away from his own plight by asking about the
young couple's news. Peter had been promoted to captain and transferred
to tank training school. He was in Madrid on two weeks' leave. Not that
this meant being able to spend many hours with his twenty-two-year-old
fiancée. Conchita worked days in a munitions factory. Two evenings a week
she volunteered to teach young girls reading and writing at a local school.
Everything about Conchita amazed Kardash.

When the war had broken out in July 1936, Conchita had, like many
young Spanish women, joined the militias. She stayed at the front for two

and a half months before bowing to the government's pleas that women stop serving in combat units.

Her parents had been peasants. In her village, famine was an everyday experience, education unheard of, and the nobility and Catholic Church had ruled the villagers' lives with an iron hand. Conchita had seen the lives of her parents and older siblings slowly being ground away by their grim existence. Shortly after her fifteenth birthday, Conchita rebelled by running away to Madrid. There, she had discovered the newly formed democratic government was slowly introducing reforms. Among those reforms was the opening of schools for the poor. Conchita enrolled. A quick, enthusiastic student, she was soon sufficiently literate and schooled in arithmetic to secure a job as a clerk in a jewellery store.

Conchita also fell in love with Rodriguez, a young Basque trade unionist. The two lovers decided to marry in August 1936. On the day the army attempted to launch a coup against the Republican government, Rodriguez joined the citizens' militias manning the barricades. Three days later he was mortally wounded.

Lying in his hospital bed, looking up at this dark-haired beauty with such flashing blue eyes, Kardash wondered how anyone who had experienced so much hardship in her life could possibly retain such seemingly irrepressible joy and optimism. By the time she and Peter left, Kardash's spirits were greatly buoyed. When the Republic was victorious and Spain was again at peace, he imagined the young couple marrying. His exiled Austrian friend would find a new homeland and the happiness of loving a good woman. When a flicker of fear that Franco might win cast a shadow upon this pleasant fantasy, Kardash sharply rebuked himself. The Republic may be imperilled by fascism, he thought, but it could not possibly fall to defeat.

Even though the front lines were only seventeen blocks away, and the fascist artillery blessed it with at least one daily bombardment, the Hotel Florida remained a gay and festive establishment. Here, journalists and artists from around the world gathered. In deference to its popularity as a target for fascist gunners, however, most opted to stay in the darker, shabbier rooms at the back of the hotel. The grander suites faced not only the street but also the nearby fascist lines.

No matter which way Lionel Edwards turned in the battered hotel lobby and bar, young literary lions and lionesses lazed. *The New York Times'* Herbert

Matthews, *The Nation's* Louis Fischer, Mikhail Koltzov of *Pravda,* Claud Cockburn of London's *Daily Worker,* American author Dos Passos, *Colliers'* exciting young freelancer Martha Gellhorn. Dominating the pride was Ernest Hemingway.

Edwards, who had never before met Hemingway, was invited to use the writer's room for a welcome shower—something he learned was common for any North American volunteer who had the fortune to cross Hemingway's path.

Back in the bar, Edwards drank the night away with Hemingway and the Turkish ambassador. Both men brushed aside Edwards's offers to help pay for the continuous flow of wine bottles passing across their table.

Hemingway lectured broadly on the war, offering a seemingly informed critique of both Nationalist and Republican strategies. His sympathies obviously lay with the Republican cause. He seemed immensely fond of the Spanish people. Edwards, whose own Spanish remained merely functional, was impressed with Hemingway's fluent command of the language. It was a pleasurable evening. The next morning, however, Edwards found himself thinking that Hemingway possessed an unhealthy attraction to the psychology of violence. He seemed obsessed by war's test of individual courage. Fresh from the abattoir of Fuentes de Ebro, Edwards was little interested in this intellectual preoccupation with courage and its relation to war.

He preferred to discuss Prime Minister Neville Chamberlain's lies. The man's perfidy amazed him. Edwards had seen hundreds of Italian soldiers on the battlefield at Fuentes de Ebro. He had seen the German planes flown by the Condor Legion. Almost all of Franco's guns, ammunition, food, and fuel were supplied by Mussolini and Hitler. Italian warships openly attacked Republican freighters on the high seas. German battleships shelled Republican cities. Virtually every journalist in the Hotel Florida had reported these facts in the world press. Yet Chamberlain could, apparently without qualms of conscience, stand up in the British parliament and emphatically claim that no German or Italian military forces were supporting Franco. On the basis of this deliberate and obvious lie, the British government opted to tighten the stranglehold of Non-Intervention around Republican Spain's throat.

Edwards had heard scant news of the Canadian government's position on the Spanish war. Obviously the government was unlikely to be proud of the country's recently announced status as the second per capita contributor of volunteers to the International Brigades. In that regard, Canada lagged second only to France.

That so many Canadians had managed to elude the government's efforts to prevent them going to Spain was a source of great pride to the Canadian volunteers. But Edwards often wondered what Prime Minister King personally thought about the men who marched under a banner honouring his own paternal grandfather.

He hoped King might silently dare to approve of them, but doubted this was true. Edwards did think, however, that King was not as loathsome a human being as Chamberlain or former prime minister and now Conservative Party leader R. B. Bennett. It offended him that any Canadian, especially a former prime minister, would have the gall to do as Bennett had recently done: stand up in the House of Commons and, holding aloft a purported list of Slavic and Jewish leftists and Communists, say, "There is the scum of Canada." Edwards had served alongside many Canadian Jewish and Slavic volunteers and was incensed by this ethnic and racial slander. It reminded him of the righteousness of the cause for which he fought. Perhaps when fascism was driven from Spain, that defeat would serve to send Canada's closet fascist tyrants, like Bennett, fleeing into deserved obscurity.

Since his hospitalization, Ronald Liversedge had suffered under the tormenting hand of a very personal tyrant. Evacuated from the front at Fuentes de Ebro, Liversedge had been sent to a hospital near Barcelona to receive treatment for dysentery and pleurisy. The hospital in the village of Valls had once been devoted to providing care to the rich. Surrounded by palm trees and lush gardens, the one-storey, white-and-blue stucco buildings still gave the hospital a deceptively opulent appearance.

Inside the deception ended. Wards, which once had housed a maximum of eight to ten beds, were now clogged with fifty or more. The beds were marshalled into rows of four, each no further than a half-metre from its neighbours. Of the doctors and nuns who had cared for the rich clientele, all but the hospital's executive director had fled to Franco's side. Now, the executive director and two other doctors provided by the Republican government tried to care for hundreds of wounded and ill International and Spanish troops. They were assisted in this daunting task by young girls recruited from Valls.

Non-Intervention assured that virtually no drugs or medical supplies were available to relieve the men's pain. All day and night, the wards echoed with forlorn moans, punctuated by agonized screams.

In the bed next to Liversedge, an American from the Lincoln Battalion drifted in and out of semi-consciousness. In his more lucid moments the man loudly cursed the war, the Internationals, and the Republic in the foulest language he could muster. Liversedge, unable to sleep because of the din and his own piercing, continuous stomach cramps, had no energy to argue with the man, nor to try offering him any comforting words. In his stronger moments, he focussed on watching fearfully for the return of the young nurse who had taken it upon herself to become his torturer.

Each night she inevitably appeared. She moved slowly down the ward, an open notebook in one hand, a bottle and big spoon in the other. With a vacant stare, she studied the number card attached to the bottom of Liversedge's bed, made a great show of matching it to a column in her notebook, and then advanced on him. She spoke no English, Liversedge had only the poorest competency in Spanish. He feebly tried to protest, sought to wave her away. She forcefully pointed at the number footing his bed, stabbed a finger at the numbers in the book, and gestured that the bottle was indeed for him. The bottle was opened, the liquid poured on the spoon, the spoon thrust into Liversedge's reluctantly opened mouth.

As the castor oil burned its way into his stomach, Liversedge's bowels immediately contracted and heaved in protest. He was lucky to reach the bedpan. The young woman, seemingly oblivious to his plight, would be proceeding down the ward, distributing scraps of medicine in her wake to men who often seemed resistant to her ministrations.

By the third night of this, Liversedge was desperate. All day he had sought to find a doctor to countermand the insanity of dispensing castor oil to a man with dysentery. His search had been in vain. There were no doctors available.

Now the woman approached, bottle, spoon, and notebook in hand. In the adjacent bed the American muttered and cursed weakly. Liversedge shook his head, pleaded with the woman in his broken Spanish. She stabbed her finger at the notebook, pointed to the number on his bed, then nodded her head with grim satisfaction at their apparent agreement.

With one swift movement Liversedge snatched the book from her hand. Before she could wrest it back from him, he checked the numbers. *Aceite de ricino* (castor oil) was listed alongside the number for the American's bed, not Liversedge's. As Liversedge had come to suspect from the blank expres-

183

sion on the woman's face when she looked at the notebook, she was illiterate. Liversedge thought she had probably been too proud to admit her inability to read when the medical staff assigned her to dispensing the scant supply of available medicine. Spared the nightly dose of castor oil, Liversedge's condition rapidly improved.

An X ray revealed that his stomach had actually fallen several centimetres because of the damage the constant cramps had caused the supporting muscles. To properly reposition his stomach, the doctors fitted him with a type of corset that he was to wear during the day. When Liversedge had left Vancouver for Spain he had weighed 156 pounds. On the day he was released from hospital, he was a frail 128 pounds.

In mid-December Liversedge set out for Albacete, where he was to report for light duty. He travelled by train south to Valencia. The city was cold and miserable, entirely blacked out except for small blue lights burning at every street corner. Just days before, a large section of the railway station roof had been blown away by an Italian bomber. Eighty people had died when the roof collapsed on them. Liversedge lingered at the station for four hours, waiting for a train bound for Albacete. When the train finally departed, Liversedge was relieved to leave Valencia and escape the constant danger of air raids.

As he arrived in Albacete on December 15, he stared out the window of the passenger car at streets clogged with civilians. Although it was the middle of the night, people were everywhere marching, singing, cheering. It was like the victory parades that had filled London on the day the Great War ended.

Liversedge jumped down from the train and accosted a young man and woman who were walking arm in arm, asking them for information. The woman's voice choked with emotion. "Teruel is ours," she cried.

For months a fascist salient centred on the high-mountain city of Teruel in southern Aragon had threatened Valencia from the north. Now this key bastion of fascist strength was in Republican hands. The half-starved, ill-clad, shivering populace of Albacete had taken to the blacked-out, foggy streets to celebrate the glorious victory.

It *was* wonderful news—news that Liversedge believed reflected the new prowess and skill of the Republic's civilian army. In just seventeen months, the ragtag, hastily cobbled together militias had been transformed into an army that was not only capable of holding off fascist attacks but that could also defeat them in offensive action. Despite the shortages of equipment caused by Non-Intervention's embargoes, despite a lack of trained officers, despite the problems of trying to impose unified command on units loyal to dozens of political beliefs and leaders, the Republican army had taken the offensive against a mighty fascist stronghold and won the day.

One hundred thousand Republican troops had been thrown into the fray. Attacking during a snowfall, these troops had routed Franco's professional army. All night the people stayed in the streets discussing the news, celebrating. Liversedge, bumping into fellow Canadians Bob Kerr and Jack Lawson, spent the night on the town with them.

The next day Liversedge received orders assigning him to work with Lawson, a crusty Scot from Vancouver, in the newly formed Canadian Cadre Service office in Albacete. The cadre's job was to determine the whereabouts of all the Canadians serving in Spain. Once Lawson had that information he could ensure that the address of every volunteer was known to the Friends of the Mackenzie-Papineau Battalion. Formed on May 20, 1937—almost a month before the battalion came into existence in Spain— the Friends were primarily concerned with raising money, clothing, and foodstuffs to send to the volunteers overseas. The Friends also lobbied the government to lift the embargo of arms shipments to Spain and to sever relations with Germany because of the repression of its Jewish citizenry. With increasing numbers of ill, wounded, and disabled volunteers returning to Canada, the Friends further tried to guarantee these veterans received adequate care and had some means of support. Liversedge and Lawson had the job of notifying the Friends when veterans were returning to Canada, getting care packages to the Canadian volunteers serving in units scattered across Spain, and keeping the Friends informed of how it could best assist the cause.

Shipments of care packages from Canada arrived sporadically but steadily. In one shipment was a package containing eighteen kilograms of candy for the children of Spain. The candy had been purchased with money raised by Canadian elementary school children for the Committee to Aid Spanish Democracy. Liversedge duly helped distribute the candy to the children in a home for war orphans located in an old monastery near Albacete.

One day a woman named Jean Watts, who was working as a correspondent for Toronto's Communist publication, the *Daily Clarion*, burst into the Albacete office and demanded the right to enlist in the Mackenzie-Papineau Battalion. There were no enlisted women in the unit, she told

Liversedge, and that was just not right. Liversedge handed her a volunteer enlistment form to fill out. When Watts completed the form, she was sworn in as one of only two Canadian women serving in the International Brigades. The other was Florence Pike of Falkland, Ontario, who worked as a nurse. Liversedge heard, however, that when Watts reported for duty, the headquarters staff refused her request to serve with the Mac-Paps in the front lines. She was assigned instead to drive an ambulance.

Christmas came and went in a haze of activity. Nearly a month later a large shipment of Christmas packages arrived from Canada. By this time, the XVth International Brigade—including the Mackenzie-Papineau Battalion—had moved to the Teruel front, where a fierce winter battle raged. The shipment, consisting of sixteen large packing cases, contained individual parcels addressed to specific members of the Mackenzie-Papineau

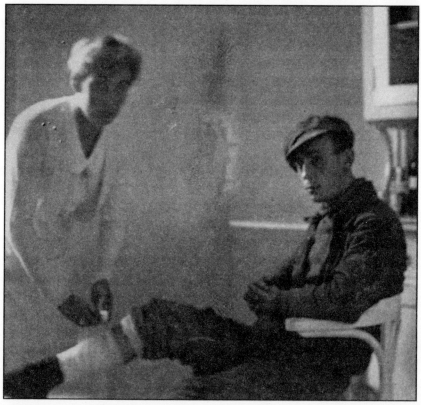

Nurse Florence Pike was one of only two Canadian women known to have served with the International Brigades. (NAC PA194599)

Battalion. Opening his own parcel, Liversedge found a pair of socks, leather kid gloves, a half pound of tobacco, and two hundred cigarettes.

To his horror, Liversedge discovered the labels would not peel off. Once word of this bounty reached the men in the lines there would be a small mutiny if each individually addressed package failed to find its owner. But half the men did not serve with the Mac-Paps. They were scattered all over Spain. What the hell was he to do?

Liversedge reluctantly set to the task of matching owners with packages. He begged and bribed passage for himself and the packages to an area just to the rear of the XVth Brigade. Working out of an old warehouse, Liversedge distributed packages to the Canadians there.

That accounted for half the packages. There was no way Liversedge could personally see that the men in all the other scattered units received their presents. He used every means he could think of to get the remaining parcels to Canadians in other units, including sending them out in the ambulances shunting back and forth from the various battlefronts.

Despite his best efforts two hundred parcels remained undeliverable. Liversedge, thoroughly sick of the task, divvied these up between the men in the other national service cadres. Then, still too underweight for the infantry, he transferred to an artillery unit, where he hoped to be of more direct use to the Republican cause than was possible shuffling papers and shunting packages from one part of Spain to another.

There was little more that William Kardash could do in Spain to further the Republican cause. In January he was finally well enough to start rebuilding his strength by hobbling about Madrid on his crutches.

Moving slowly down a busy street he chanced to meet Conchita, the young Spanish woman who had visited him in hospital. Despite her obvious delight at seeing that Kardash was somewhat recovered from his wounds and the loss of his right leg, Conchita seemed unnaturally subdued.

When Kardash asked her what was the matter, Conchita told him that Peter, her Austrian lover, had been killed in December during the great offensive that had captured Teruel. Apparently he had transferred from the training command to an active line unit so he could be in on the attack.

"We're paying such a dear price for our freedom," Conchita said. Her expression was hard, the flash of joy that had always been evident in her blue eyes gone. "But victory shall be ours," she said in a voice icy with determination.

"It must be," Kardash replied.

The two friends parted. Kardash decided that, as he could no longer fight for the cause, he would dedicate himself to generating Canadian support for Republican Spain. Too many had died, too many had been maimed, and too many faced the loss of their freedom for him to use his wounds as an excuse to retire from active participation in the struggle to defeat Franco and fascism.

Eleven

$\mathcal{A}$ Frozen Hell

ON JANUARY 14, 1938, THE XVTH INTERNATIONAL BRIGADE TOOK up position on the immediate northern flank of the city of Teruel. For almost three weeks, the fascists had been hammering the Republican lines around the mountain city with repeated attacks. Franco had decreed that Teruel must be recaptured. The Republican government ordered its army to hold. Now, the XVth stood directly in the path of the fascist juggernaut. Brigade Commander Lt. Col. Vladimir Copíc notified the battalions that they held a "post of honour."

The Mackenzie-Papineau Battalion stood on the very tip of this honourable post, with the Lincolns in reserve on the outskirts of Teruel and the British positioned in more immediate reserve on a series of hills overlooking the back of the Mac-Paps' positions. The Mac-Paps' Company One, under Niilo Makela's command, was dug in along the cliff edge of an escarpment known as La Muela. The other two companies held a trench line on the plain to the steep escarpment's right. The battalion's front covered a full two kilometres of line, far too much ground for 650 men to defend with a continuous human barrier. Instead, they deployed in a number of strong positions that had overlapping fields of fires.

Capt. Edward Cecil Smith, recently appointed the first Canadian commander of the Mackenzie-Papineaus, established his headquarters in a small railroad tunnel directly to the rear of Company Two. Company Three, under the command of newly promoted Lt. Lionel Edwards, footed its defence around three small chalk knolls. On the left lay a riverbed. There

Just before the Battle of Teruel, Edward Cecil Smith—a former Canadian Army officer—was promoted to commander of the Mackenzie-Papineau Battalion. Despite allegations of cowardice, he would retain his command to the war's end. (NAC PA117805)

were some old ruins and a small chapel astride the line and before them a large stone wall that had once served as a dam. Edwards was well aware of how vulnerable the Mac-Paps were in their new position. If the fascists were able to get around their right flank into the rear they could easily overwhelm the battalion from behind.

Everything about Teruel was grim and forbidding. The city stood almost one thousand metres above sea level in the midst of rugged mountains. Never a pretty place, in January the ancient city was frozen and stark, gripped in the fist of an unrelentingly cold winter. Half the buildings had been destroyed by fascist aerial bombardment and artillery barrages. The country surrounding the city was riven with trench lines, blackened by explosions, pocked with shell craters. A dirty snow blanketed the dark soil.

Teruel suffered Spain's coldest winters. This winter was no exception. When the Mac-Paps moved into their bleak positions, the temperature was a piercing minus eighteen degrees Celsius. A bitter wind deepened the cold and cut through the men's thin clothing. Scattered before the Republican trenches lay the frozen bodies of fascists killed in earlier fighting. In places the fascist trenches were only fifty metres away from the Republican lines. Both sides sniped constantly at each other. Not long after he entered the trenches at Teruel, Edwards was nicked on the lower lobe of his left ear by a bullet. A little while later another bullet grazed the lower curve of his right ear. This was followed by a bullet that clipped the officer's insignia off his beret. Edwards started crouching very low whenever he moved about in the trenches.

190

Ross Russell, who had been in Spain for only four months, never understood what possessed the officers who had consigned him to a machine-gun squad. The small-framed, former Woolworth's assistant manager from Montreal could barely cope with the rigours of moving the big gun from place to place. He was part of a squad manning a 7.62-millimetre Maxim M1910. The huge, antiquated weapons were designed to be dragged across the Russian steppes by horses. In Spain there were bloody few horses and the terrain was too rugged to use burros and mules as pack animals. So men played the part.

The gun could be broken into three pieces. One man carried the gun, weighing just over twenty kilograms. Another hefted the thirty-five-kilogram carriage, mounted on two steel wheels, so that one wheel rested on his shoulders with his head inside the wheel and his arms precariously balancing the load. The last gun-piece was a protective shield. Although this weighed only ten kilograms, it was extremely awkward and difficult to balance in the endless winds that rushed across the Teruel battleground. Another seven men were required just to carry the weapon's ammunition.

Russell inevitably found himself staggering under the weight of the unwieldy wheel carriage, wondering despairingly how he would possibly live to reach the next position. Teruel was a nightmare come true. He was always cold, always hungry, always hanging on the edge of exhausted collapse. An American named Thompson took the young Montrealer under his wing and helped him survive.

The night they moved into the trenches at Teruel, Russell's gun section occupied a circular trench located in a hole squat in the middle of the valley. The men had little idea which force occupied which of the surrounding hills, and in the morning they stared around them trying to figure out where the enemy was. They could see no sign of either the fascists or their own side. Worried, the men started digging the hole deeper, busting through the frozen earth. When darkness fell, Russell and several others slipped out to find their own lines. When this reconnaissance was concluded, they dug a shallow communication trench between their position and the main trench lines.

Faced with the realities of war, none of the men in Russell's section was particularly interested in long discussions about Communist dialectics, so when a directive came down that each section had to have a political commissar, they elected Thompson to the job. The American cared nothing for the political ramifications of the struggle. He had come to Spain as a fighter pilot initially, and when the government decided to stop paying mercenary wages to non-aligned volunteers who had been hired for their expertise in technical military areas he stayed on to fight as a common soldier. Thompson, Russell decided, was there to fight and that was all there was to the matter. Consequently, during hours when political discussion was encouraged, Russell's unit concentrated on catching up on sleep and scrounging for food and other necessary supplies.

Fascist snipers plied their trade. The worst times were during moonlit nights when the snow-covered plain was transformed into a pale, eerie landscape where any movement was nakedly exposed to the hidden riflemen. One night Russell and two others moved to the rear to fill water bottles and collect the cognac they had found indispensable for keeping the water-cooled machine gun functioning. Water froze in the cooling chamber, cognac did not. The cognac also warmed the continually chilled troops. One wag commented that if Franco succeeded in severing the Republic's cognac supply, the war would be lost in a week.

Returning from the rear with water and cognac, the men tried to move quietly down the knee-deep communication trench. Russell led the way Suddenly he heard a grunt behind him, followed by the bang of a shot. He spun around just in time to see the man behind him fall. The stricken soldier was so close Russell could have reached out and touched him. Russell dragged the wounded man to the gun position, but he died a few minutes later. Since coming to Teruel, Russell had seen other men die, but this was the first man killed so close to him. Russell had the uneasy feeling that the bullet had actually been fired at him but, as they had been walking fairly quickly, the other man had taken his place when the deadly slug arrived.

Russell was not the only man in the section who was uneasy after their comrade's death. There was a noticeable decrease in the men's joking, and each seemed to keep a little more to himself. The cold only further undermined their spirits.

Coming as he did from Regina, William Beeching knew a thing or two about cold winters. But Canadians understood how to dress for the cold and that made all the difference. As ill dressed as he and the rest of the brigade were, it seemed miraculous to Beeching that they managed to endure one day after another in the trenches. Beeching, who had only just completed training when the fascists counterattacked against Teruel, was assigned to a Lincoln Battalion machine-gun section. Like almost everyone else in the brigade, he wore only *alpargatas,* the rope-soled sandals that were Republican army standard-issue footwear. The Lincolns, desperately seeking clothing to warm themselves, looted the buildings within their perimeter. Often their searches unearthed bizarre rewards. One man appeared from a building with a silver fox stole encircling his shoulders and warming chilled ears.

The nights were torture. As Beeching huddled behind a machine gun on sentry duty, the cold seeped ever deeper. By the time the relief came, he was so numb the relieving soldiers had to pick him up, straighten his stiffened legs, and stand him on his feet. At times he was unable to close his hands together or even feel his feet. His body was covered with a rash of chilblains.

To sleep, the men built whatever nests of blankets and coats they could in a hole in the ground, and groups of men huddled together to share their warmth. It was then, in those moments when they were almost warm, the lice started crawling. Sleep was next to impossible as the vermin slithered through their hair and gnawed at their skin.

In the trenches of Teruel, Canadian volunteers endured piercing cold, shortages of food, and weeks of fierce fighting. (NAC C67469)

193

One morning Beeching went to relieve a gunner only to find the man had frozen to death during the night. The icy cold body sat rigidly behind the gun, eyes closed, flesh translucently pale. This was the day-to-day reality of the bitter weeks in the trenches at Teruel.

The Mackenzie-Papineau Battalion counted the Lincoln and British battalions lucky. They were to the rear, providing support. It was the Mac-Paps who hung in the wind ahead of the rest of the XVth International Brigade. Although the front was initially quiet, it was obvious the battalion would soon face a major assault. On a night patrol to the edge of the fascist lines, Lionel Edwards heard the rumble of engines. It could only be trucks dragging up artillery. In the morning, fascist reconnaissance planes circling overhead streamed smoke from flares to mark the Mac-Pap positions. Sitting helplessly below the smoke, Edwards knew how it felt to be a lamb before the slaughter.

Crawling through no man's land the following evening, Edwards and a patrol came within earshot of the enemy lines and could hear the officers giving their men pep talks. Edwards pushed in closer, risking discovery to determine what enemy they faced.

They were Requetes—Franco's most fanatical followers. Edwards could see the men huddled against the cold in their hooded coats, their red berets of Navarre visible in the firelight. The Requetes clung to the philosophical beliefs of Tomás de Torquemada, the first grand inquisitor of the Spanish Inquisition. He had been responsible for the deaths of some two thousand supposed heretics who were burned at the stake during the reigns of Queen Isabella I and King Ferdinand V. Despite his own Jewish ancestry, Torquemada had also convinced the regents to expel all of Spain's 170,000 Jews. Edwards was reminded of a host of images from a time almost six hundred years past. Descended from Huguenots, Edwards could easily have faced death by burning at the hands of the ancestors of these Requetes, had he lived then.

Edwards shuddered at the thought of facing these maniacs in battle now. Behind them, he could also see a division of Italian soldiers deploying and German artillerymen setting up an endless line of heavy guns.

It was all so unspeakably wrong, Edwards thought. Here, a ragged, ill-equipped, half-starved army braced itself to fend off the assault of a combined fascist horde and the world scarcely cared. Edwards felt his hatred rising, focussing. But should he hate these fanatics and fascists calmly preparing to slaughter his men in the morning or despise the Non-Interventionists, like Chamberlain and Canada's Mackenzie King? At some point even those self-deceiving idiots would have to fight or the fascists would conquer all. But that was in the distance, dependent on the democracies awakening from their self-induced, complacent slumber. Edwards's men would face the fight in the morning. That was certain.

With the morning, Edwards discovered a new concept of what hell must be like. It was a place of fire *and* ice. Soon after dawn the attack had begun with one squadron after another of fascist planes coming over and pounding the Republican lines with bombs. Then the artillery opened up—a solid phalanx of shrapnel and blast pouring in continuous volleys from the mouths of hundreds of guns.

Dug into one of the chalk hills, Edwards was soon blinded by smoke that hung like a shroud over the position. There was so much gunpowder floating in the air the men around him were coated with black soot and grime. When men came up to report, Edwards was unable to hear their words. Their mouths moved, sometimes they bared their teeth to laugh at what might have been a joke, but no sound was audible. Even the constant explosions seemed dull and muffled.

Wounded men were everywhere. Getting them to the rear was next to impossible because the communication trenches were being raked by rifle and machine-gun fire.

In the early afternoon the barrage suddenly ended. Edwards and his men crawled out of their holes and moved to the machine guns or stood on the firing steps dug into the side of the trenches and put the butts of their rifles to their shoulders. They could hear the attack coming before they saw it. Then the Requetes came out of the smoke in a V-shaped throng. They carried flags and banners, were shrieking at the tops of their lungs, and waving their rifles above their heads. The Mac-Paps let them come in close and then opened fire with everything they had. Caught in the open, the fascist line wavered, broke, and started to turn. But suddenly it started regrouping as fascist officers raced up and, threatening them with their revolvers, drove the Requetes forward. Again, the Mac-Paps scattered them with a fusillade of fire. At dusk, the enemy ceased the attack and returned to hammering the trenches with artillery.

For three days the fascists had kept coming on. And each attack had been thrown back. The Requetes were gone. Now, it was Moors and Italians who advanced, supported by tanks. All insisted on waving flags as they advanced. None of the Mac-Paps had seen this flag-waving stuff in previous battles. They assumed the fascists intended it to be threatening, but all it did was provide a reference point for targeting their guns. Ross Russell used the flags to determine how far the enemy was from his gun's effective range.

The machine-gun position was so well sited that its fire had contributed greatly to shattering the enemy advances. Fascist dead were strewn all over the gun's killing ground. The burning wrecks of tanks dotted the plain, knocked out by anti-tank guns dug in alongside the British Battalion overlooking the Mac-Pap positions. But still the fascists kept coming.

The circular position Russell's machine gun occupied was coming under ever increasing artillery fire. The fascist gunners were making a concerted effort to destroy the Maxim. Over and over in his head, Russell kept repeating a silly rhyming couplet: "We've become a nemesis on their premises."

Their gun was solidly entrenched in a bunker constructed of earth and scavenged telegraph poles. Enemy shells, bursting overhead, flayed the position with shrapnel. All around Russell, Mac-Pap infantry were being killed and wounded. The situation was getting desperate.

Russell watched the approach of yet another advancing line of infantry, supported by tanks. An American by the name of Rosenberg was fitting a 250-round belt of ammunition into the Maxim's breech. He suggested Russell hold his fire until they were well inside effective range. Russell, hunkered over the gunsights, asked him a question. Rosenberg didn't reply. Russell looked up from the sights, saw the man had been struck in the face with a piece of shrapnel. His face was torn apart and he was quietly dying.

There was no time to provide comfort to the dying man for the fascist tanks had opened up. Men were going down all over the trench. Russell ordered one man to scramble back to Edwards and tell him they needed reinforcements immediately. It was a good hundred metres from their position to the main trench line. He had no idea if the runner could make it because the communication trench was only knee deep. But either they got help or they were likely to be overrun.

The racket of shells exploding and guns firing was so loud that Russell felt as if he were in a boiler factory. Advancing toward them was a line of Requetes who had apparently decided to again take to the field. Russell could see their red berets and, of course, the inevitably waving flags.

Carried in three parts, the 7.62-millimetre Maxim M1910 machine gun weighed more than sixty-five kilograms. At Teruel the Mac-Paps found its water-cooling system froze unless the water was replaced with cognac. (NAC PA193628)

When they were about two kilometres off, Russell started laying down fire on them.

Suddenly Russell wasn't firing the gun anymore. Nor was he even holding the trigger grips. A huge bang deafened him. Earth and telegraph poles crashed down on him, pushing him into the dirt, burying him.

Russell drifted in and out of consciousness. He was aware of being cold, colder than ever before . . . of seeing the gun he had been manning lying twisted and wrecked amid a tangle of broken logs and burst sandbags . . . of some men setting up a Maxim next to the wreckage of the old . . . of Thompson—the American ex-mercenary pilot turned political commissar—saying, "I'll get him out."

Thompson dropped to his hands and knees next to him and some other men hefted Russell on the big man's back. Crawling, Thompson entered the shallow communication trench with Russell lying across his back. Overhead, fascist shells burst and bullets snapped. Russell remained conscious until they reached the main trench and he was placed on a stretcher. Two Spanish stretcher-bearers picked Russell up and started rushing him to the rear.

It was a hellish journey. Russell would black out, then jerk awake as the men stumbled or slipped on the ice. He felt completely frozen and could not stop trembling. He had no idea how bad his wounds were or even where he was injured.

The noise was terrific. German Stuka dive bombers pounded the Republican positions all around them—the plane's eerie sirens howling as they plummeted toward the earth. Shells exploded, throwing up huge clods of soil or crackling the air with shrapnel. The going was rough for the stretcher-bearers. Russell had no sense of time. Suddenly he awoke to find himself lying on the stretcher under the scant protection of a twisted tree. Fearing the men had put him down and fled, he twisted his head around only to find the two stretcher-bearers sitting with their backs against the tree, their faces drawn and chests pumping from exhaustion. If they leave me here I'm a goner, Russell thought. But they soon staggered to their feet, hoisted the stretcher, and stumbled on. Russell's last conscious memory was of a doctor putting a tag on him and then being loaded aboard a train. He didn't know where he was, or whether the Mac-Paps were still fighting and dying on the outskirts of Teruel.

By January 21 the situation was becoming increasingly desperate for the Mac-Paps. Lionel Edwards had extended his line to strengthen his dangling right flank by occupying a small hill. Here, he and thirty other men dug in. They had four machine guns, which enabled them to shred the fascist attempts to press around their flank and encircle them.

The Nationalists responded by hammering the position relentlessly with artillery fire and throwing wave after wave of troops in direct assaults against it. In dispatches to the rear for supplies and reinforcements, Edwards used the positional reference of Edwards Hill. Ed Komodowski, however, thought of it as Suicide Hill. It seemed to the young Ukrainian-Canadian, who had survived Fuentes de Ebro, that there had to be at least fifteen hundred fascists trying to overwhelm them from three sides. That they managed to repel each successive attack was beyond his understanding.

Half the men who had gone up the hill with Edwards were dead. Among them was a young American who had apparently been noted in the U.S. for the research he had done on light rays as a student. Also among the dead was a first-aid man from southern Alberta named David. David had worn a large cowboy buckle on his belt and had had the annoying habit of continually humming a country and western tune called, "Empty Saddles in the Old Corral."

Finally Edwards told Komodowski to go back to headquarters and inform Edward Cecil Smith that they needed reinforcements or the position would crumble. Komodowski raced to the rear through a gauntlet of machine-gun fire that followed him all the way from the hill to the bridge over the creek. He told Smith Edwards either needed support or permission to withdraw. The headquarters staff looked about desperately for spare men.

At last they found one headquarters clerk who had never been in the line and shoved a rifle in the young man's hands. Komodowski was ordered to tell Edwards that they would send more reinforcements when they were found. Outside the railroad tunnel, where the headquarters was based, Komodowski set off at a quick pace toward the front. The young clerk followed on his heels like a nervous puppy.

As they crossed the bridge, the clerk dropped to the ground and started crawling to escape the heavy enemy fire. Komodowski told him to get up, that they would have to make a dash for it or be killed. He set off running, dodging, dropping, and then jumping up to run again—moving wildly, unpredictably to avoid presenting a clear target. By the time he reached the hill, Komodowski had lost track of the young clerk. He never showed on the hill. Komodowski had no idea whether he fled or was killed. When Komodowski told Edwards what headquarters had said about reinforcements, his commander just grimaced and turned back to the fighting.

The incoming machine-gun fire was becoming so heavy it was impossible to look over the lip of the trench for more than a quick glance. Artillery shells were exploding all across the hilltop. All the machine guns were wrecked. It was a little past noon. Only six men on Edwards Hill were still alive and one of those was wounded. Edwards gave the order to retreat. One man hoisted the wounded soldier on his back and tried carrying him out. A few feet down the hillside both he and the wounded man were killed by machine-gun fire.

After that the orderly retreat was abandoned, every man fleeing for himself in a mad scramble. Komodowski ran to the creek but veered away from the bridge because he was sure the fascists would kill anyone trying to cross it. He ditched his rifle and a sack containing one hundred rounds of ammunition into the creek and then jumped down into the icy water. In places the creek was only ankle deep; elsewhere he plunged up to his waist in the freezing water. Finally he turned a bend and found himself safe from the fascist bullets.

Pulling himself from the creek, Komodowski proceeded to headquarters where he told Smith there was no need to send support to Edwards Hill. There was no longer anyone there to reinforce.

Lionel Edwards and the other three survivors had joined the rest of Company Three well to the rear of the hill. Here they dug in and waited for the fascists to sweep over the abandoned position. Hours passed and the enemy failed to show. Shells continued to hammer it. Machine-gun fire raked the hill's empty trench line. Only in the late afternoon did the fascists finally storm the hill and take up position there.

The loss of the hill was the beginning of the end for the defence of Teruel. Even with reinforcements from the British Battalion, the line was bending back on itself, and it was only a matter of time before it must break. The Mac-Paps were exhausted and had suffered heavy casualties. Neither the Lincoln nor the British battalions had sufficient resources to hold the line in their place.

On February 3, the XVth International Brigade was relieved by the 46th Division and withdrew from Teruel. It marched southeast to an assembly point at Kilometre 19 on the highway running from Teruel to Valencia. On December 31, when the Mackenzie-Papineau Battalion had gone into action, it had numbered about 650. When it regrouped at Kilometre 19, only two hundred men were counted. They had held the Teruel defensive line for twenty days.

The XVth was given orders to withdraw to Valencia for recuperation and rebuilding. No sooner had the orders been issued, however, than a massive fascist counterattack broke out seventy-five kilometres north of Teruel. The brigade hastily marched to stem the enemy advance. From February 16 to 19, the already worn units fought bitterly in sleet and snow against a vastly superior force and held. Withdrawn again from the line, they returned to Kilometre 19 hopeful that this time they would finally be allowed a welcome rest.

Edwards expected the brigade would be sent back to Albacete to rebuild, but they were instead ordered to take up positions near Belchite to the rear of the Aragon front lines. Here they would receive reinforcements while serving as a ready reserve to meet any attempted fascist offensive in this sector. With the Teruel front beginning to collapse under the continual fascist assault, the Republican command feared that Franco would extend his offensive up the length of the Aragon front.

It was obvious to Ronald Liversedge that Teruel must fall. The odds were so heavily stacked in Franco's favour he could hardly fail. All Liversedge had to do was look at the three guns that constituted the XXXVth Artillery Battery to realize how hopelessly the Republic was outgunned. True, the XXXVth's guns were huge, fierce-looking things. They were also museum pieces that had seen much service on the Russian side during the 1905 Russo-Japanese War. The guns had a long, 15.5-centimetre barrel mounted on two massive wheels. There was no recoil mechanism, and the aged breeches were so badly worn that the explosive charges packed in behind the shell threatened to destroy the gun itself with each firing.

On Liversedge's first day with the unit, one of the guns blew its breech, injuring several of the crew. Liversedge was detailed to carry shells and cordite charges from the ammunition piles to the remaining two guns. They put out a heavy fire in a futile effort to counter the fascist artillery barrages and provide support to the infantry dug in before Teruel.

From their vantage point they could see the flashes of the fascist guns. It was a long continuous line of what looked to be about six hundred artillery pieces. Liversedge could only watch helplessly as the fascist shells fell like a vicious hail on the Republican troops. Overhead, fascist planes swarmed like angry hornets, diving down to pound the trenches with bombs and machine-gun fire. The western plains before Teruel were thick with Italian tanks.

Only two days after he arrived at the battery, the fascists encircled Teruel and fought their way into the city from all sides, trapping and destroying a small Republican force that was unable to escape the closing pincers. The XXXVth hooked their guns up to trucks and fell back to a new position behind the Alfambra River, where they dug in and prepared to meet the next phase of the enemy advance. Liversedge was sure the fascist offensive would slowly, but inevitably, force the Republican army back to Valencia and the sea. Damned if they would go easily, though. Of that Liversedge was equally certain. They might be in retreat, but by no means were they on the run.

T w e l v e

*T*HE RETREATS

ON MARCH 9, 1938, FRANCO UNLEASHED A MASSIVE OFFENSIVE
on the Aragon front. Four Spanish and one Italian corps supported by
twelve German tank companies, thirty German anti-tank companies, and
fighter and bomber squadrons comprising one thousand planes struck the
Republican Army from Teruel on the southern flank to Huesca in the north.
Franco's drive to the sea was on. He threw 150,000 men against barely
35,000 Republican troops. The fascist assault was preceded by a vast artillery barrage that decimated entire sections of the Republican line.

At 2:00 A.M., the XVth International Brigade was ordered to march
from its reserve position near Belchite toward the front lines. In the distance, William Beeching could hear the crump of heavy bombing. The former
Regina weigh-scale repairman had missed the roughest of the Teruel fight.
Now he prepared for the worst. "We're going to march in battle formation,"
his officer said. "We don't know where the enemy is at the moment."

Walking through early morning light, the Lincoln Battalion moved up
a valley. Olive groves gradually gave way to barren, rocky soil and the hills
pressed ever closer. Beeching saw figures dodging about on the nearest
overlooking hill. His company commander ordered a halt and dispatched a
squad of scouts to reconnoitre the hilltops. The scouts had advanced only
a few metres when the Lincolns were hit by a volley of gunfire. The air
around his ears snapped sharply. Beeching's first thought was that a horde
of teamsters was lashing the sky with bullwhips.

A sergeant ran over and warned Beeching's cluster of inexperienced troops that they were being fired on, should take cover, and better start firing back. Beeching dived behind a small knoll and started shooting his rifle. All he had to fire at were the flashes of fascist guns. The act of firing steadied him, but he still had no idea what was going on.

New orders were passed a few minutes later. The Lincolns were to rush over an undefended hill and take up position on its opposite slope. They would be under enemy fire all the way to the hill crest. "It's very difficult," the sergeant said calmly. "But if you run and zigzag and drop down on the ground and fire back you'll get over that quite well. We'll make a stand once we're on the other side."

Beeching's squad led off. Looking down, he noticed a fog hanging about fifteen centimetres above his feet. It suddenly dawned on Beeching that the fog was actually dust thrown up by bullets tearing the ground all around him. That decided things. The sergeant's advice could go hang. Forget lying down, zigzagging, or returning fire. Beeching's feet grew wings. He soared up the hill and over the other side in one mad flight of terror.

Despite the heavy fire, Company One made it intact. Company Two followed and took light casualties. Company Three jumped off last, fleeing through air that seemed to shiver with bullets. A lot of the company's men died. Before the companies made their dash, the sergeant had told Beeching every man stood a fifty-fifty chance of getting across unscathed. Beeching realized the sergeant was wrong. Survival hinged on no mathematical chance, it pivoted instead on your place in line. When advancing, being in the rear was better; when running, the lead was preferred.

Scout platoon leader John Fowle from Calgary came by recruiting men to bolster his badly thinned ranks. He plucked Beeching and a few others up from Company One. The Lincolns desperately needed to know the enemy's strength and positioning. Things were so confused at present they had no idea even which way to face their defences. The scouts were to probe outward on all the Lincolns' flanks and map the enemy positions.

One man asked where they should look for the enemy. "I really don't know," Fowle said. "But you know there's people shooting at you from over there. So just go and find out where they are." Beeching had thought that war was conducted on sounder tactical principles than that, but so far nothing seemed to relate much to his training.

The scouts dodged across a valley being blasted by artillery fire. Creeping around on the slopes of the neighbouring hills Beeching saw an awful lot of enemy soldiers. He and the others kept low, held their fire, and tried to accurately sketch the enemy concentrations by drawing hills, trees, buildings, and other reference points on scraps of paper.

They were fired on sporadically by machine guns and rifles. The fascists were also soaking the ground forward of their positions with artillery shells and bombs. Beeching tried to be brave. He felt simultaneously as big as a house and as inconsequential as an ant. Every nearby shelter from the enemy fire beckoned, urged him to cower there. Beeching lectured himself, conducting a silent, inner dialogue with his soul: "Up to now you've been discussing things in a very high-minded way, Beeching. You've been saying how this is essential for the future. Now you've got to translate your theory into practice. This is what you've got to do," he sternly advised. But he was grimly aware that this very day he might join the legion of unknown millions that had gone before him in the so-called progress of humanity.

His own particular legion of comrades all looked quite mad. They stared out of bloodshot, haggard eyes. They laughed at the most awful moments. After a wild dash in the open, where bullets chipped the earth and stones, they fell behind the safety of boulders, leaned back against the hard stone, and succumbed to gales of laughter. Fear and laughter shook them in the same moment. After one such dash, a young New Yorker looked over at Beeching and said, "Some son of a bitch met me in Times Square, you know. And he sold me a subscription to *The Daily Worker*. Now look where I ended up." This threw the two men into a helpless giggling fit.

All through this terrible day the XVth Brigade tried to reestablish a line of defence. But it was hopeless. On either side of them the Spanish brigades, knocked senseless by artillery and overrun by fascist armour, scattered in disarray. The XVth could only join the retreat. They went slowly, though, forcing Franco to pay in blood for the ground won.

For twenty-one days the XVth maintained an orderly fighting withdrawal. One by one they abandoned Belchite and all the other villages won in the hard summer's fighting of 1937. Following an erratic path across country, moving sometimes by truck but more often by foot, they retreated to Caspe. When an attempt to hold the line here quickly crumbled, they withdrew to Maella and finally into a narrow defensive salient between Gandesa and Batea. They had retreated almost 160 kilometres. Their backs were braced against the banks of the Ebro River. Here, the Republican army prepared for a desperate stand.

A giant fascist wedge had been plunged between the Republican

Just before the start of The Retreats, members of the Mackenzie-Papineau Battalion's Machine-Gun Company proudly display a flag with the battalion's motto: "1837–1937— Fascism shall be destroyed." (NAC PA194606)

armies of the north and south. Only a thin screening force of several thousand men holding a thin strand of coastline linked the two armies. That fragile force was all that stood between Franco and his dream of wading in the waters of the Mediterranean and severing the Republic in half. Holding the southwestern shore of the Ebro, the northern army strengthened the screening force by threatening Franco's left flank. Its mere presence forced Franco to divert much of his strength to ensure the Republicans could not cut behind his forward combat divisions and attack the rear supply and support columns. Before he could drive for the coast, the Republican forces between Gandesa and Batea had to be destroyed. The XVth International Brigade knew this. They dug in and prepared to face the fascist army's full wrath.

Beeching's mind was tormented by terrible images collected during the retreat. He had seen women caught in the middle of a firefight throw themselves on their children—futilely seeking to protect them from the bullets. Beeching had seen men, who had lost their weapons or run out of ammunition, charge fascist machine guns armed with a stone wrapped in a handkerchief as their only weapon. He had seen men so exhausted and worn they refused to run farther. Beeching was haunted by the vivid memory of a former New York City stevedore who had decided his running had come to an end. The man took up a position behind a boulder overlooking a narrow *barranca* that would soon fill with fascists. "I've stood all I can stand," the man said. "I can't take it anymore. I've retreated and retreated. I'm going to stay and smoke a few cigarettes and fight all by myself." There was no time to argue, so they left him there. They had just turned away and staggered on, so weary they could barely put one foot before the other. But they had gone.

Pushed steadily southward by the oncoming torrent of Franco's mechanized army, Ronald Liversedge and the rest of the XXXVth Artillery Battery fought a long, bitter, rearguard action. As the crow flew it was only about one hundred kilometres from Teruel to the coast. But the fascists faced a stiff fight for every bit of that ground.

Liversedge had never been so exhausted. Sleep was virtually impossible. They moved by night, dug in and fired the guns during the day. As long as there was light to fly by, the waves of German and Italian bombers kept returning, saturating the country with explosives. The earth seemed to be rising in one large eruption around Liversedge. Explosions continually shivered and trembled the ground beneath his feet. The air was thick with the fumes of cordite. Falling dust, raised by the explosions, created an eerie yellow haze that reduced the sunlight to a weak glimmer. At night the flickering orange glow from countless fires combined with the flare of explosions and the flash of firing guns to create an unnatural aurora of light overhead that blotted out the moon and stars.

Food came up sporadically from field kitchens. Liversedge and the other men ate and drank automatically, hardly knowing or caring what they consumed. All their senses and perceptions were deadened. There were only the guns that had to be loaded, fired, dragged to a new position; only the endless, slow retreat. Liversedge kept hoping for a miracle, something like the great influx of volunteers that had saved Madrid in November 1936; hoping that a time would come when the Republican troops could turn and make a final, triumphant stand. It was, he realized, a completely forlorn hope.

In Napoleonic times the men who were first through a breach in a fortress's walls were dubbed The Forlorn Hope because few would live to see the sunset. Holding the line around Batea, the men of the XVth International Brigade felt they fought in the Republic's Forlorn Hope. The chance that

Jules Päiviö (standing on far right) poses with some fellow Finnish-Canadians shortly before being sent to the battlefront.   (NAC PA194604)

they could turn the tide of Franco's army was scant, yet they must try. They stood with their backs to the Ebro River, denying the fascists the defensive buffer it would naturally provide. It was a precarious salient the XVth held. The Ebro River stood like an anvil at their backs; the mighty hammer of the fascist army was readying to slam down upon them. If they were unable to withstand the hammer's blows, the presence of the anvil would make escape virtually impossible.

Since completing his treacherous crossing of the Pyrenees during a freezing blizzard, nineteen-year-old Jules Päiviö had worked as a training officer—teaching topographic map reading skills to Spanish and International recruits. With the XVth Brigade severely reduced, every available

man was rushed from rear assignments to bolster the lines near Batea. Päiviö
arrived with a draught of about eighty men. He was assigned to serve as the
adjutant of the Mackenzie-Papineau Battalion's Machine-Gun Company.

Before the reinforcements arrived, only about 250 Mac-Paps survived.
Even with the reinforcements they remained well below their intended
strength of 650 men. Half the men in the Machine-Gun Company, however, were long-term veterans. Most, like Päiviö, were Finnish-Canadians.
Päiviö felt honoured to hold the position of adjutant in a unit of such brave
men. He hoped to show the same courage in battle that they had demonstrated during countless engagements.

On March 31, the battalion received orders to march from Batea to a
position astride the Gandesa-Alcañiz road. Here, rumour held, a company
of the British Battalion had been captured the night before. Arriving around
midnight, Päiviö and the other officers groped about in the darkness but
were unable to find the promised defensive trenches on the road's edge.
Finally they took up position on a barren hill overlooking the road. Through
the remaining hours of darkness, Päiviö directed the setting up of the company's machine guns. By dawn he was pleased to see that the guns had
good overlapping fields of fire that could provide excellent support to the
infantry deployed before them.

But his hard work proved valueless as Edward Cecil Smith ordered
three of the guns moved forward to stand alongside the infantry. Päiviö
thought the order a serious blunder, but the company commander said
they must obey. The officer took two guns over to the infantry's right flank,
and Päiviö moved a gun onto a ridge that flanked Lionel Edwards's Company Three.

As he and the gunners moved into position, Päiviö saw some soldiers
about seventy-five metres farther along the ridge. He was unable to identify
their uniforms, but two of them started calling in Spanish. They said they
could see a better gun position where they were. Päiviö, almost dead on his
feet from his night's labours, innocently walked over.

When he was only a few metres away, the men suddenly raised their
rifles and shouted in Spanish, "Hands up!" Päiviö realized the uniforms
were Italian. He was unarmed—there had been no revolvers for the new
officers coming into the line. The soldiers had him dead in their sights,
making resistance futile.

One of the men—continuing to masquerade as a Republican soldier—
gestured to Päiviö's machine-gun crew to bring their weapon over. Päiviö

yelled, "They are fascists! Get back! Get back!" The other Italian shoved Päiviö in the back with the barrel of his rifle, forcing him down the hill toward the fascist lines. "Shoot! Why don't you shoot?" Päiviö yelled to his comrades. If they fired he could still make a run for it. But the men remained frozen by their gun, looking on in apparent bewilderment.

In case the gunners followed Päiviö's order, the Italians shoved him between themselves and the Mac-Paps as they hurried him down the ridge. On the other side of the crest, Päiviö looked upon a large concentration of Italian machine gunners and riflemen preparing to attack. Had his men followed his orders to fire, Päiviö realized, the gun crew would have been decimated. He hoped they had woken up to what was happening and withdrawn.

Safely out of sight of the Republican lines, the Italians subjected Päiviö to a cursory search. Päiviö realized, with a flood of relief, that he had left his officer's jacket behind and carried nothing that would identify him as anything other than a *soldato*. Knowing that the fascists usually executed Republican officers on the spot, he decided to maintain the illusion that he was only an enlisted man. Done with the search, one of the soldiers, apparently out of sheer bloody-mindedness, battered Päiviö to the ground with his rifle butt. Then they escorted him to their company headquarters, where about fifteen other captured Canadians sat sullenly under the guns of some Italian guards.

A few of the Mac-Paps offered Päiviö a strained greeting, but their smiles were grim. They all expected to be shot. Päiviö soon thought their time had come when some soldiers bustled the Canadians up against a stone wall. The soldiers formed a facing line and raised rifles to shoulders. Päiviö braced for the bullets' impact. Seconds passed. The Italians stared down the barrels but held their fire. When the tension became unbearable and all the Canadians were trembling despite trying to remain bravely at attention, the Italians lowered their guns and burst into gales of laughter at their clever joke. The men were made to sit down again under the watchful guns of their sentries.

Twice more they were ordered back to the wall and the firing squad scenario was reenacted. Each time was as frightening as the last, for there was no way of telling if joke might give way to reality.

Just as the last charade ended, a large limousine, surrounded by vehicles containing a heavily armed personal guard, drew up. An officer, draped in braid, stepped from the limousine. After a quick consultation with the officers in the command headquarters, the braid-burdened officer ordered the prisoners jumbled into a truck. The truck took them to a railway crossing, where they were locked in a cold boxcar and transported to a jail in Zaragoza. The jail was crowded with almost one hundred men of the British Battalion, who had indeed been captured the day before in the same position that the Mac-Paps had occupied. From here, the prisoners were soon transported to a concentration camp at San Pedro de Cardenna, thirteen kilometres east of Franco's capital city of Burgos in the Castile region.

Veteran Relief Camp Workers' Union and On to Ottawa Trek organizer James "Red" Walsh joined the Mac-Paps as they fell back on Batea. He became Company Two's political commissar—his job to bolster morale and remind the men of the political importance of the war they waged. Having lived and breathed class politics most of his life, he was well prepared for the job.

The situation was desperate. Hardly any food came up to the front lines. Perry Hilton, whom Walsh had known during the trek, no longer manned the Mac-Pap field kitchen. He had somehow finagled his way into a machine-gun section only to get himself captured. For more than a year the man had scrounged, stolen, and begged the means to keep the battalion fed during the most difficult times. Now he was gone and his shoes proved beyond filling.

Like food, ammunition was always in short supply, new weapons were unavailable, clothing to replace the torn rags was impossible to find, and water was scarce. The men were in a fragile state. Most were ill, all were exhausted, their feet were raw with blisters, and many had wounds covered with dirty bandages. They looked more like down-on-their-luck brigands than soldiers. But they could still fight and Walsh knew their morale was high.

To prove this they made Walsh and the other commissars the butt of their jokes. "How's the coffee?" Walsh might ask.

Looking thoughtfully at his cup and its foul coffee substitute, the section's wag would wink at his chums, chew on the sludge, and carefully consider. "It depends," he would finally reply.

"What do you mean it depends?" Walsh demanded.

"It depends whether I'm politically developed."

Walsh knew the drift but always played along. "What do you mean?"

"Well, if I'm politically developed, comrade commandante, the coffee

211

is very good. But if I'm not politically developed then it tastes like horse piss."

Nobody cared much for jokes, however, on April 1 when they became the April fools before Franco's deadly earnest assault on the Batea-Gandesa line. Outnumbering the defenders almost five to one, tank- and air-supported fascist divisions struck the entire line with the force of a tidal wave. Before the fascist flood, the thin, ill-equipped line, like a sandcastle on the beach, wavered, fractured, and then washed away as the enemy nearly succeeded in surrounding the Republican troops. Those who survived the initial assault streamed back toward the Ebro River, desperately fleeing the encircling fascist forces. Men scattered. Retreat turned to rout and survival depended on escaping across the river. The XVth International Brigade joined the flight.

Walsh fled with a handful of men commanded by Machine-Gun Company commissar Thomas Mallon. When a sniper shot Mallon the others threw together a makeshift stretcher and carried him. The man stood more than six feet tall and weighed more than two hundred pounds. They took turns carrying him, but the punishing terrain and their own deteriorated condition turned the endeavour into a torture. For twelve hours they struggled on. Finally Mallon, in agony, begged them to leave him behind and make their way to safety. Reluctantly Walsh agreed. They abandoned Mallon on a small ledge overlooking a *barranca*.

For hours they wandered lost through a maze of indistinguishable *barrancas* and barren hills. They had no compass or maps. Everyone was exhausted, their tongues swollen with thirst. Rounding a narrow corner in a *barranca*, Walsh heard a man moaning. Walsh warily climbed up to where the man lay. He found himself looking into the feverish eyes of a delirious Thomas Mallon.

Mallon was near death, but the men could not abandon him a second time. They carried Mallon with them until they chanced upon a small hut. The old Spaniard living there offered to stay with Mallon until he died.

Walsh ordered the men on. Most stuck with it and never complained. A few, however, begged Walsh to give them one of the grenades he carried so they could blow themselves up and be done with it all. Walsh refused. Every morning there were fewer men to rally. The missing had slipped away into the night and the crack of a rifle heard in darkness told the tale.

Finally Walsh's group happened upon the headquarters section of the XIIIth International Brigade's anti-fascist German Thaelmann Battalion. They had no idea where the rest of the German battalion might be, but their commander thought he knew how to reach the Ebro. Walsh's men followed the Germans, who, after weaving this way and that, managed to guide them to the town of Mora de Ebro.

A bridge ran from the town to the Republican's new defensive line on the river's eastern shore. Walsh was ordered to dig the remaining fifty Mac-Paps into a position covering the western approach to the bridge. They would hold until the engineers wiring the bridge with explosives signalled for them to withdraw to safety so the bridge could be destroyed and its capture prevented.

Walsh knew the Mac-Paps were no longer fit for battle, but he also knew they would do the job anyway. In the meantime, however, the men were starving and no food was coming up from the rear. Walsh and Lt. Joseph Kelly, also from Vancouver, set off in search of food. Fascist soldiers were already pressing in, and Walsh and Kelly ran to the town through a spray of fire.

The civilians had all fled. Inside a large house, Walsh found a cache of sugar and tinned beef. The two men each filled a bag with grub and started back. They were soon intercepted by a pair of Spaniards waving pistols and accusing them of looting. The Spaniards had the draw on them, so there was little Kelly or Walsh could do to defend themselves. Their fragmented Spanish prevented them from adequately explaining their mission. Luckily, just as the Spaniards were getting around to chambering bullets into pistol breeches, a British officer from the Internationals happened by who spoke flawless Spanish. Walsh explained the Mac-Paps' dire need and the officer translated. The Spaniards apologized and sent Walsh and Kelly on their way with their paltry supplies.

William Beeching was hungry, thirsty, and weary to the bone. His exhaustion was so pervasive that it was hard to know whether the nightmare of his daily existence was a reality or the product of slumber.

One of Beeching's most frightening moments came shortly after the rout began. Although withdrawing in an orderly manner, the Lincolns were hopelessly lost. Rounding a corner in a narrow valley, they found themselves facing a body of men. Both sides hastily deployed into a line for assault. This was the worst of all scenarios—two equally determined foes going head to head in a meeting engagement. Neither side knows the other's strength, each is determined to advance through the other, and the fighting can quickly develop into a hand-to-hand close-quarters bloodbath.

Above the other force a battle flag was raised and waved. "That's the Mac-Paps," someone yelled. Both sides hastily stood down. They soon discovered that the Mac-Paps they had encountered were but a fragment of the shattered battalion. The men who the Lincolns had nearly engaged had no idea where their comrades were, so they joined the American unit in retreating toward the Ebro.

In the confusion of a series of running battles, however, the Lincolns were soon scattered in the same way the Mac-Paps had been earlier. Beeching found himself part of a small group of men led by Johnny Gates, the Lincolns' commissar. Hearing that the bridges crossing the Ebro had all been blown, Gates decided that they should fight on as guerrillas. When the opportunity presented itself, they struck back at small pockets of fascist troops, capturing weapons, ammunition, and food. In a series of skirmishes they briefly recaptured several villages and sent various enemy units scampering, before beating hasty withdrawals themselves.

Following one such raid, Beeching was separated from the rest of the unit. While trying to find his way back to Gates's unit, Beeching entered a small valley surrounded by the hardest of Aragon desert. Here he chanced upon Mac-Pap Battalion commander Maj. Edward Cecil Smith, who was equally alone. The utterly demoralized Smith showed Beeching how to find directions with a watch before advising him that all the Internationals would soon have to fight their way over the Pyrenees to the safety of France. The cause, he said, was lost, the Republic beyond saving. The two men parted, Smith apparently using his watch to chart a course for the Pyrenees and Beeching continuing to look for Gates's unit or failing that the most direct route to the Ebro River.

Beeching's search for Gates and the others proved futile, but he soon linked up with four men from the British Battalion. One was Welsh, another a *Brighton Herald* reporter fearful of trying to explain his supposedly nonpartisan stance to Franco's men, and two anti-tank gunners with eardrums long shattered by the firing of their gun.

Both anti-tankers were terribly skittish due to battle fatigue. Every hastily grabbed attempt at sleep was disturbed when the gunners would wake up screaming. This symptom of their condition threatened everyone's safety. Fascists were sweeping the ground everywhere between Batea and the Ebro River, looking for Republican stragglers. Every day Beeching's group had to cower behind rocks or under bushes while fascist patrols trolled past.

If they happened to be catching a few minutes fitful sleep, it was necessary for the guard to alert the others. To awaken the anti-tank gunners without causing them to scream, Beeching and the Welshman took to simultaneously seizing each man by the mouth and nose so he couldn't yell. That failed, unfortunately, to stop them from thrashing about wildly as they woke. Beeching's face and body bore the bruises and cuts caused by flailing punches.

Finally the muddy waters of the Ebro were before them. The bridges had all been blown into the river by the retreating army, and the fascists controlled long sections of the river's edge. Swollen with spring melt, the Ebro was a hundred metres wide and running fast. Beeching and the others stripped their clothing off and consigned their rifles, ammunition, and personal effects to the river bottom. Then they dived in and started swimming. Somehow they missed the attention of the fascist machine gunners, escaped the dangerous undertows that plucked at their legs, and safely reached the other side.

Beeching soon learned that a good number of other XVth brigaders had drowned during the hazardous crossing. Many were dead or missing in what the world's papers were calling The Retreats. Among those missing and presumed dead were brigade commander Robert Merriman and brigade commissar Dave Doran. Beeching learned that Smith had made it out alive but had been sent to a Barcelona hospital to recuperate.

Ross Russell and several hundred other Internationals rode a train racing to escape the fascist tide's advancing wave. At best there was a slim hope they could slip past the coastal city of Vinaroz before the fascist tanks dipped their steel treads into the sea.

Russell, recovering from his Teruel wounds, had been hospitalized south of Valencia. It had been touch and go for a while because he had shrapnel in one lung and both feet were frostbitten. Russell feared they would become gangrenous and require amputation, which had been the case for Bill Tough. For several weeks Tough had occupied a bed adjacent to Russell. The Vancouver man was undisciplined, hard drinking, and Tough as tough could be. When the doctor decided his feet must come off, Tough answered, "So get the goddamned thing over with then. Cut them off."

Russell knew he could never be that tough. He pleaded for his feet. Indeed, he could barely sleep for fear of waking one dawn to find they had been taken.

Every day a nurse stuck a needle in his sole, searching for a response. Then she gave him a raw egg to eat. The egg was for his lung. The hospital lacked the surgical equipment necessary for the doctors to remove the shrapnel. The egg was supposed to build a calcium wall that would surround the shrapnel and prevent it from opening his lung. Russell was sceptical of the medical theory, but he treasured the egg—raw or not.

One day the needle went in and he yelped. It was one of the best days of his life.

Then the government decided to send all the Internationals they could find north before the fascists succeeded in cutting the Republic in two. They emptied the convalescent homes and hospitals. In a long hospital train they rolled north, racing to get past Vinaroz before the fascists reached the sea. Red crosses inside white circles adorned the roofs of the train cars. The windowpanes had been stripped of glass in case the train was bombed despite the Geneva Convention, which forbade attacks on ambulance trains and medical facilities.

Six men huddled in Russell's compartment. They pondered what to do if the train were subjected to an aerial attack. Isadora Barcena of Toronto, whose family were all famous cigar makers, agreed with a black American from the Lincoln Battalion that the best thing was to bail out of the train and find some overhead cover.

Russell demurred. He favoured climbing under a seat in the train so that when it had to race on they would not be left behind in the confusion that would surely follow any air raid. All agreed, however, that being bombed was a distinct possibility.

When the train lurched to a stop and a shot rang out from the engine at the front of the train, possibility quickly gave way to reality. Russell looked out a window. Overhead a squadron of Italian bombers was attacking the train, working from the engine toward the rear. Russell could see large bombs tumbling down from oncoming planes.

In the seconds between the train stopping and Russell getting to the window, the Lincoln leaped up and dived out the window. He obviously had known instinctively what was coming. The rest of the men in the compartment followed suit. Only Russell dithered, unsure whether to dive under a seat or take his chances outside. Then he imagined the train catching fire from the bombs. The fear of dying in fire set him plunging out the window.

Rolling down the embankment, he was aware of a bomber slowly following the line of the train. It was dropping bombs and blazing away with its machine gun. As Russell hit the ditch at the bottom of the embankment his foot took a terrific wallop. While the plane roared overhead, he staggered to his feet, sagged, and looked down to see blood streaming from one heel.

The train was wrecked. Cars burned. Others lay on their sides or roofs. Corpses blanketed the ground and hung out of windows and doors. Wounded men pleaded for mercy and aid.

Castellón lay about three kilometres to the north. Despite his wounded foot, Russell found he could walk. Thinking to get help for the wounded, Russell joined some other men in striking off for the city. They had barely started when a straggle of Spanish soldiers approached from the opposite direction. Castellón was falling, they warned; Russell and the others should retreat with them to Valencia.

Russell returned to the train. It was getting dark, and many of the wounded were in bad shape. There were virtually no medical supplies. Even bandages were in short supply. Russell helped move the wounded into the minimal shelter of a nearby orchard. He stayed there through the night, able to do little to ease the suffering of those worse off than himself.

In the morning he found a phone in a nearby village and was surprised to find the lines to Castellón still open. The operator told him, however, that Castellón was in desperate danger. Before abruptly ringing off, the operator said they should flee to Valencia. But flight was impossible. Many of the wounded were incapable of walking. So far only a couple of trucks had come to assist in evacuating the men who could not move on their own. But, by the sounds of things, the fascists might arrive at any moment. Russell reluctantly decided he could do little more for the badly wounded and should try and escape on his own.

He joined a group heading toward Valencia. For a man with a wounded heel it was terrible going, but nobody else was able to help him. At a small town Russell decided he could go no farther without treatment. The wound was starting to look infected. Luckily, the village had a small medical centre, but Russell's initial optimism at this discovery wavered when he found only an eighteen-year-old male nurse on duty.

Russell warily showed him the wound and told him there was some shrapnel in there that had to come out. The boy confidently said he could carry out such a procedure. He injected Russell with a local sedative. Then he started cutting. But the sedative failed to work and the pain was so unbearable Russell was unable to hold still. The nurse offered him a shot of gas to put him out. Fearful he would awake to find the foot chopped off, Russell refused.

The nurse instructed Russell's companions to hold him down while he treated the wound. Russell thought the wound should be opened with a crosswise cut to create a flap—similar to how an orange is peeled. But the boy just gouged his scalpel to the bone and dug the shrapnel out. When he finished, Russell could barely walk a step. The men carried him out to the side of the road and abandoned him there. Finally a truck came by and offered Russell a lift to a hospital in Valencia.

Several days after Franco's army blasted its way to the coast at Vinaroz, the XXXVth Artillery Battery marched north of Castellón to help contain the fascists in their narrow corridor. Despite all the rumours, Castellón had not fallen, and Franco's hold on the coast was narrow and vulnerable. But the Internationals trapped in the south felt even more vulnerable. If the Republic fell, they would be captured and would face imprisonment—possibly even death—at the hands of a triumphant Franco.

Luigi Longo, inspector-general of the International Brigades, flew down from Barcelona and toured the isolated International units. Longo would hear no talk of defeatism. With his head still swathed in bandages from a wound suffered during The Retreats, he told Ronald Liversedge's unit, "We fight on. We are not divided. Although the enemy is between us, we will always maintain contact. The war is not finished yet." Liversedge could see how he came by his nickname El Gallo—Fighting Cock. His words raised their spirits, and the men returned to the lines with renewed determination to continue the resistance.

The Republic faced one of the blackest of many a dark hour, but Liversedge could not yet imagine that the war was lost and the fascists on the road to victory. Surely the world would come to its senses and the democracies would send the desperately needed aid that even now could turn back the fascist tide.

Thirteen

$\mathcal{B}$ETRAYALS

THE RETREATS DEVASTATED THE INTERNATIONAL BRIGADES. Former Calgary accountant Lt. Lionel Edwards was dismayed to discover more than half the Mackenzie-Papineau Battalion members were dead, missing, or badly wounded. The Lincoln Battalion had lost more than four hundred. On April 12, the Lincolns' new commander, Milton Wolfe, could field only forty Internationals and thirty-five Spaniards.

Without reinforcements the battalions were finished. But few replacements would be coming from outside of Spain. The previously steady flow of Canadian volunteers was now a mere trickle. Vigorous enforcement of the Foreign Enlistment Act's prohibition of travel to Spain made it virtually impossible for volunteers to secure passports and travel documents.

It was the same for volunteers from other countries. The naval blockade of Republican ports made direct travel to Spain difficult and dangerous. France was tightening its patrols of the Spanish border, closing the door on many of the clandestine routes over the Pyrenees.

Nor was Spain's Republican government actively encouraging the influx of international volunteers. With the Republic now physically divided and its army desperately outnumbered and outgunned by Franco's forces, Prime Minister Juan Négrin was seeking an acceptable peace through negotiation—a peace that would preserve Spain's democracy while somehow also appeasing Franco.

On May 1, 1938, Négrin issued a thirteen-point declaration that listed the Republic's war aims. One of the points called for expulsion of all foreign military forces. Although about forty-two thousand men and women had so far served in the International Brigades, the actual number of volunteers in Spain at any given time never numbered more than about seventeen thousand. No more than six thousand volunteers ever saw battle during a single engagement.

This contrasted sharply with the Nationalists' level of foreign involvement. In the spring of 1938 it was as clear to Lionel Edwards as it was to anybody else closely following the war's development that Franco's military success was only possible due to massive support by German, Italian, and Portuguese regular army, air, and naval forces.

Italy had committed at least fifty thousand soldiers. The Italian press boasted that its air force had launched in excess of five thousand air raids and the navy had deployed about ninety warships against the Republic. For its part, Germany was showering Franco with war matériel—estimated to be worth 500-million reichsmarks or 43-million British pounds. Enhancing Germany's fraternal fascist contribution was the commitment of sixteen thousand German soldiers and airmen serving as specialists in Spain. Portugal had some twenty thousand soldiers fighting on Franco's side. There was also a motley assortment of about six hundred Irishmen, a contingent of right-wing and pro-monarchist French volunteers, a company of White Russians, and a smattering of other volunteers fighting for the Nationalists.

Edwards was well aware of just how much Franco's army depended on the Germans and Italians for its success. In repeated battles, it had been the supporting elements of German armour, artillery, and air power backing attacks by Italian mechanized infantry that had overwhelmed the Republican forces. Without the Germans and Italians, Franco would have lost many critical engagements. Certainly Republican Spain would not now be divided.

The Republic's chances of winning the war by force of arms was now slight. Its army was too weakened by casualties and shortages of supply. The Internationals themselves would only be returned to their former numerical strength through a mass infusion of Spanish conscripts. Never again would they be able to function as effectively in their designated role as shock troops—units that were first into the fight against heavily defended objectives.

The stranglehold locked on the Republic's throat by Non-Intervention was also tightening. In late April, Edwards had been shocked to see Barcelona's newspapers reporting that British prime minister Neville Chamberlain had signed the Anglo-Italian Mediterranean Pact on April 16. The pact committed Italy only to withdrawing its troops from Spain at the war's end. This pact effectively removed from Italy any obligation to comply with the Non-Intervention Agreement, of which both Italy and Germany were signatories.

It also made a mockery of the recently formed League of Nations committee, charged with supervising withdrawal of all foreign nationals from the Spanish armies for repatriation. Négrin had committed the Republic to working with the League of Nations committee; Franco was giving only lip-service support to the plan.

For the Canadian volunteers serving in the XVth International Brigade, it was difficult to measure the personal implications of this diplomatic manoeuvring. Would they be called upon to fight again? Would they soon be going home?

In the face of such uncertainty it was sensible to respond with increased caution. Nobody wanted to be the last Canadian to die on Spanish soil. Where before the Mac-Paps had been chomping at the bit to fight the

By late summer of 1938, the flow of volunteers to the International Brigades had largely come to an end. Those who remained were now all battle-hardened veterans. (MTRL T10190)

221

fascists, many now considered that it would be no bad thing if they sat out the rest of the war away from the front.

All too many were also no longer fit for combat. Months of service in front-line roles had left many a XVth International brigader with such shattered nerves and deteriorated physical health that he had to be detailed to rear area work or chronically hospitalized. Some, like former Moose Jaw Fuller Brush salesman Thomas Bailey, were in evacuation hospitals waiting to be sent to France. Others, like On to Ottawa Trek veteran Lucien Tellier, were fit only for noncombat duties. After Fuentes de Ebro, Tellier's nerves were so shot he had been detailed to work in the brigade post office.

Despite the loss of many veterans to health problems and combat fatigue, the Mac-Pap commanders worked hard to sustain both morale and combat readiness. Elsewhere, the Lincolns and the other battalions did the same. In June, the last draft of volunteers from North America arrived. Its numbers included twenty-five Canadians. They brought word that the Canadian Communist Party had ceased recruiting volunteers. Nevertheless, the Canadian Committee to Aid Spanish Democracy continued donating humanitarian aid to Spain.

Négrin, who was also serving as the Republic's war minister, had decreed that the Internationals' new role was to train Spanish recruits to replace them. The brigades were bolstered to full strength by a massive infusion of Spanish recruits. Soon four out of five soldiers in the International Brigades were Spanish. Many were teenagers, who were lacking in political awareness and widely varied in their commitment to the Republic's cause. The International veterans did what they could to motivate and train the young men in the ways of war. Edwards and the other officers tried to spur this process on because as June gave way to July it was apparent that the XVth would soon face one last battle.

In the southern half of Republican Spain an assortment of Internationals—separated from their northern comrades—were cobbled together into the CXXIXth International Brigade. Most had served in the Dimitrov Battalion and were of Slavic origins. Ronald Liversedge's XXXVth Artillery Battery was also attached to the CXXIXth. When the XXXVth's surviving ancient cannons had finally blown their breeches, the unit was reequipped with three brand-new Bofors anti-tank guns. These low, squat, long-barrelled weapons were a massive technological improvement over their previous armament. But there was a drawback that pleased nobody. Anti-tank guns, as the name implied, were intended to destroy tanks. To do that you had to get close to the enemy armour. Consequently, anti-tank gunners had low life expectancies.

Liversedge's new commander was a Serbian named Laso Latinovic. His second-in-command, a Montenegrin, was also named Laso. Six Yugoslavians armed with two machine guns arrived to form an anti-aircraft squad, bolstering the battery's strength to about seventy men. Because he was still physically weakened by his stomach problems, Liversedge was detailed to serve in the unit's kitchen. More than a few of his comrades envied his relative safety.

The anti-tank battery joined the CXXIXth in a position fronting the town of Mosquereales, situated at the end of a long plain between two lines of mountains. Here, the Republican army was trying to stem the continuing fascist attempt to widen the breach between the southern and northern parts of Republican Spain. Liversedge helped set up the guns in the trenches and then returned to the kitchen, which was located just behind the town.

From the kitchen, Liversedge had a good view of the battle. Fascist infantry and tanks poured down several roads leading out of the mountains onto the plains before the trenches. A group of seven tanks charged out of an olive grove across the open ground toward the Republican position. The anti-tank guns started pumping out a furious rate of fire. Within seconds three of the tanks were burning. The other four scuttled to safety.

In the wake of this stalled attack, the fascists spent several days pounding the out-gunned Republicans with aerial and artillery bombardments. It was the heaviest, most continual barrage Liversedge had ever experienced. Being in the kitchens seemed no safer than the front trenches. Smoke boiled over the plain so heavily that dusk seemed always near. The night sky glowed a hot red. In the trenches, men were buried alive when walls collapsed. Entire sections of the trench were clogged with dead that nobody had time to remove. To the rear, men caught in the open were ripped to pieces by shrapnel. Ammunition dumps, destroyed by direct hits, burned fiercely, and, as the burning shells cooked off and exploded, shrapnel was spewed over the surrounding area. Virtually all the communication lines were knocked out. Liversedge and the other kitchen staff were unable to get food or even water to the men in the trenches. When it seemed nobody in the Republican line could still live, the fascists flooded the plain with a vast force of tanks, troop carriers, and dismounted infantry.

The Republicans could offer little opposition against the armoured divisions of Franco's fascist army marching determinedly toward the sea. Their armour was largely antiquated tanks and armoured cars. (NAC PA194597)

Tanks rolled over the trenches and infantry dashed through gaps in the line held only by the silent dead. Liversedge's anti-tank battery barely escaped with its precious guns to a new position being established by reserve units several kilometres east of Mosquereales.

There the previous bombardment and battle were replayed. Another retreat was forced, another line drawn, another battle fought and lost. Slowly, inevitably, the Republicans surrendered ground. On June 14, Castellón fell.

Early in July, the CXXIXth took up a position on a low range of hills between two towns named respectively Mora de Rubialos and Rubialos de Mora. Liversedge could never remember which was which. Here, they threw back repeated fascist attacks, and the battering by artillery and bombers proved incapable of dislodging them from their trenches. Eventually, Liversedge knew, the Republican line would be breached but for now it miraculously held. And holding was all anyone could imagine being possible. He lost track of time, each day becoming indistinguishable from any other.

Jules Päiviö's days were indistinguishable in terms of suffering and hardship. Along with seven hundred other Internationals, he was imprisoned in an old fortress outside Franco's capital of Burgos. The Internationals were held in two long rooms. Three hundred and fifty men shared a room. The floor was their bed. At first they lacked even a single blanket or straw pallet to lie upon. Eventually these two small comforts were provided.

The fascists relished seeing the Internationals living in filth. There were only two toilets and one cold water tap for 350 men. At night mice came out of hiding to scamper over their heads as they tried to sleep. Their clothes were thick with lice. Päiviö spent two hours every morning and two hours each afternoon meticulously picking the vermin off his clothes and crushing them. He would always start tallying the lice killed, but inevitably somewhere past five hundred he lost count.

There was no hospital or clinic. The sick were confined to one end of the room to avoid the spread of contagion. When a man seemed near death he was taken to an infirmary located conveniently next to the prison mortuary.

One day Päiviö and some others were locked for hours in an outside courtyard. There was no shade to shelter them from the unrelenting summer sun. From beneath the protective cover sheltering their guard towers, the fascists laughed as the men suffered. Finally, Päiviö collapsed into semi-consciousness from sunstroke.

He eventually awakened, only to find himself in the prison room's sick zone. Later still, he awoke in the dying room. Here he hovered for three weeks on the edge of death. There were no pallets or blankets. Päiviö and the other near-death prisoners lay on the dusty, filthy floor. A couple of times a day other prisoners came to hold a cupful of water to their lips and give them a few spoonfuls of the gruel that was the regular prison fare. Päiviö somehow managed to find the strength to cheat death, but ever after when the sun touched his head he experienced immediate, piercingly painful headaches.

Each day the fascist sergeants selected some men for beatings. The guards had all been wounded fighting against International brigades and their reward was to oversee the International prisoners. They vented their thirst for revenge against the men's collective hides with whips, belts, clubs, and even fists. One Moorish sergeant took a particular dislike to Päiviö and regularly singled him out for special attention. He would beat the Finnish-Canadian on the back with a club until Päiviö collapsed in a helpless, battered ball.

Six German prisoners, aware that they could either die in Franco's prison or be repatriated to a certain death in Hitler's concentration camps, decided to escape. They somehow stole a hacksaw blade and cut away the bars covering a window. In the middle of the night they fled the prison and successfully managed to cross the Pyrenees into France.

The escape threw the guards into a paroxysm of rage. One German prisoner who had been sleeping near where the escape had taken place was accused of being an accomplice. The guards ignored his pleas of innocence and subjected him to such a brutal beating that his face was left horribly disfigured.

Nor did the rest of the men go unpunished. Päiviö, like all the others, was forced down a flight of stairs past soldiers who butted him with their rifles and tried to trip him. Finally he tumbled helplessly down the hard stone steps. The waiting guards dragged him upright and shoved Päiviö through a narrow door. In the room beyond, the sergeants were lined up in two long facing rows. Each sergeant held a whip made of leather wrapped around buckshot. As Päiviö staggered between them, the sergeants lashed his flesh with their whips. For several days the guards kept this gauntlet operating, forcing every prisoner to run it several times daily.

German Gestapo officers came regularly to the prison to conduct individual interrogations. The routine for their interrogations followed a set protocol. When Päiviö's turn came he was stripped and photographed. His body was minutely measured and described in detailed notes. He was asked endless questions about his ancestry and sexual life.

While the Germans sought scientific solutions to explain why these men would become communists and fight fascism, the Spanish Nationalists turned to religion to cure them of their atheist ways. Every Sunday, the prisoners were forced to attend a Catholic mass. Päiviö was Protestant and, because he respected all religions, was quite willing to stand quietly during the alien ceremony. But the guards demanded more than passive participation; they demanded the men kneel throughout the long ceremony. When two men refused, they were cruelly beaten for showing insufficient humility before God.

The whips and clubs used by the guards were kept locked in racks along one prison wall. When someone came to tour the prison, the prisoners could tell whether they were sympathetic to Franco by the status of the locked racks. If the whips and clubs were removed, the visitors were neutral or hostile to Franco's cause. If the whips and clubs were left on view, the visitors were pro-fascist.

During the tour by Lady Austen Chamberlain, the wife of British prime minister Neville Chamberlain, the whips and clubs were left on view. She was accompanied by a host of Franco's generals and colonels. The woman insisted on pointedly asking each man why he had come to Spain. Each in turn said he had come to fight fascism. Finally, seemingly out of frustration, she asked the captain of the guard to pick out for her one prisoner who evidenced intelligence. He replied that there was no such thing as an intelligent International. The officer and Chamberlain's wife thought this a fine repartee. From her questions the prisoners deduced that she sought someone who would confess to being a mercenary rather than acting out of political motivation.

But political conviction was the prisoners' saving grace, so they would not yield this point. Regardless of the terror, filth, and poor and insufficient food, the men retained a high level of morale. Informants were few, collaborators equally rare. They organized clandestine activities. Chess sets were carved from pieces of bread, soap, or wood and closely guarded from discovery. Scores of men participated in lengthy chess tournaments. Bridge was also popular—the cards made from scraps of paper or cloth.

A small library was built out of the few books occasionally allowed into the jail. Demand was such that a librarian had to be appointed to coordinate use of the tattered volumes.

Some of the prisoners were former university professors, teachers, or others with specialized skills or education. They developed an educational curriculum. The prisoners could study more than a dozen languages, including Spanish, French, German, Finnish, English, Russian, and Esperanto. There were also classes on Spanish history and geography, lessons in arithmetic and mathematics, telegraphy, shorthand, journalism, philosophy, zoology, and palmistry. Päiviö concentrated on language study, becoming quite proficient in Spanish, French, and Russian.

Rumours were always rife about the possibility of the Internationals being released, but time and again they proved false. Even though the International Red Cross had the names, nationalities, and home addresses of most of the prisoners, there was great anxiety that they might all still be executed or languish forever in Spanish jails. They heard little news of the war, but occasionally some news reached them that contained some truth.

In July, not long after Päiviö recovered from his bout of sunstroke, it was reported that the Republic had launched a massive surprise offensive along the Ebro River and the fascists were in retreat. At first the prisoners were sceptical, but the rumour persisted. Gradually pessimism blossomed into hope. Perhaps the Republic could still force Franco to negotiate an honourable peace.

F o u r t e e n

*T*HE LAST GAMBLE

AS A NEWLY MINTED CAPTAIN AND COMMANDER OF THE MAC-
kenzie-Papineau Battalion's Company One, Lionel Edwards knew that it
was a last desperate gamble that set the XVth International Brigade marching again to battle. At stake was Republican Spain's survival. Time was the
prize—time for the Republic to convince the world's democracies that supporting democratic Spain protected their own freedom.

In early summer, Prime Minister Juan Négrin's peace overtures had
been icily rebuffed by Franco's demand for unconditional surrender. Even
Franco's generals expressed dismay at the dictator's intransigence. A few
hesitantly acknowledged that the Nationalists were winning only because
of German and Italian support. That support came with a price of lost
national independence. Some of Franco's generals also lamented that the
war had progressed for so long, caused so many deaths, and destroyed so
much of Spain's cultural and economic structure that any victory would
prove pyrrhic, the wounds inflicted never to heal.

Beyond Spain's growing fascist borders, there was increasing outrage at
the reign of terror unleashed in the captured provinces against the civilian
population. The bomb-devastated village of Guernica, immortalized by Pablo
Picasso's massive allegorical mural unveiled at the Paris World Fair in June
1937, symbolized Franco's brutality. It was also public record that the Nationalists had arrested and executed two hundred thousand civilians. Countless others rotted in cruel prisons. Thousands of refugees had fled from
Nationalist-controlled territory into France, where they were confined to

concentration camps. Interviews with refugees revealed one thing clearly— they feared being butchered if returned to a Franco-controlled Spain.

Négrin, in a speech widely reported in the Spanish Republican press where Edwards read of it, warned the League of Nations that a victorious Franco would drown Spain in blood. Given the current rate of executions, said Négrin, at least four hundred thousand Spaniards would face death, perhaps as many as a million. Did the League wish this blood on its hands?

Spain's fate would, Négrin continued, be merely a precursor of what awaited the western democracies if they failed to rally to the Republic's cause. Hitler was escalating militarization of Teutonic Germany. The neighbouring states, even France, quavered in fear. In April, the Third Reich had forcibly annexed Austria and the League had done nothing. Germany's armies were presently massing on the Czechoslovakian border, threatening armed invasion, while the League remained silent. Mussolini was demanding the "historical right" to annex Albania and was strengthening his grip on Ethiopia, but the League cared not.

Only by making a concerted stand against the fascists would a world war be prevented, Négrin said. That stand should be made in Spain, where a people had been defending democracy for two long years. Cancel the embargo, he pleaded. Allow weapons and vitally needed supplies to flow into Republican Spain. If the democracies did this simple thing, Republican Spain would have a fighting chance.

Négrin believed that every day the Republic resisted improved the odds of the democracies coming to their collective senses and revoking the embargo. If the Republic dramatically demonstrated its military prowess, the democratic nations might be shaken from Chamberlain's appeasement policy lassitude.

Such a hope was not entirely illusory. Already Sir Winston Churchill and other British politicians had loudly and bitterly condemned Chamberlain's Anglo-Italian Mediterranean Pact and expressed support for Republican Spain. U.S. president Franklin Roosevelt was muttering misgivings about America's neutrality decision. Canada, of course, remained mum, but the Canadian volunteers had long since given up on Prime Minister King. He would dance to Chamberlain's tune.

Négrin decided the cause's last chance lay in a massive summer offensive. If the gamble failed, little would remain to hold Franco back. Most of the Republic's reserves of arms, ammunition, medical supplies, field rations, and soldiers would be gone. But as Dolores Ibarruri—La Pasionaria—

had said at the war's beginning: "It is better to die on your feet than to live on your knees!" Republican Spain took these words to heart and prepared for a last desperate battle.

Lionel Edwards never doubted the truth of La Pasionaria's rallying cry. He countenanced no defeatist talk. As the summer sun grew hotter, he drove his men hard, preparing them for the offensive. They assaulted across countless *barrancas*, stormed barren hilltops, practised launching and landing boats in river streams running with nothing more than Aragon dust.

The nature of the training told Edwards all he needed to know about their forthcoming objective. They would fight in stark, sun-baked Aragon province. They would carry the fight to the fascist side of the Ebro River.

It came, then, as no surprise when the XVth International was transferred to positions just behind the ridges overlooking the Ebro River and

Dolores Ibarruri (centre) was especially fond of the International Brigades and never hesitated to visit them at the battlefront. By the time of the Ebro River offensive many of those serving in the XVth International Brigade were Spanish teenage conscripts, such as those visible in the background. (NAC PA194921)

the fascist trenches beyond. It was a land the XVth knew well. On the other side lay Gandesa and Batea, Fuentes de Ebro was to the northwest, with Teruel and its surrounding rugged mountains to the south. All were in enemy hands. The XVth would attack across the same ground it had fled during the terrible spring retreats.

The XVth was not alone. Eighty thousand men stood ready. On July 24, the last of the newly formed army of the Ebro deployed along forty kilometres of Ebro River shoreline. Less than three thousand were Internationals. Three International Brigades—the XIth, the XIIIth, and the XVth—comprised the 35th Division. Its full strength was twelve thousand, mostly Spanish recruits. Total armaments numbered six thousand rifles, 162 light and 69 heavy machine guns, 38 mortars, and four anti-tank guns. Because the Republic had too few guns to equip them, every second man would enter battle unarmed.

Despite the terrible losses suffered during The Retreats, the men were keen to once again go into battle. There was a tremendous sense of purpose. Every man Edwards spoke with enthusiastically believed the offensive could succeed.

It would help, though, if they could snatch a few hours badly needed sleep. Summer heat had set legions of lice on the campaign road. The men tossed and turned, scratched and dug at their filthy uniforms. The lice kept marching, unstoppable and voracious. The Mac-Paps nicknamed the vermin Trimotors—after the three-engined Italian bombers that often tormented their waking hours.

There was, in any case, precious little time for sleep. At 1:00 A.M. on July 25, 1938, the Republicans struck the fascist lines. Boatmen frantically ferried advance units across the swiftly flowing Ebro in one hundred small boats. Ten preconstructed, terribly fragile bridges were thrown over the water by specially trained engineering teams. By dawn, stronger bridges were under construction. When completed, they would support the weight of tanks and supply trucks.

The XVth International joined the second wave. Ahead of them, Catalan divisions had routed the fascist army of Morocco. Surprise was total. For once no Fifth Columnists had alerted the fascists. They had been caught snoring in their beds. Thousands surrendered.

Konstantin Olynyk was elated. The Ukrainian-Canadian from South Porcupine, near Timmins, Ontario, was a machine gunner in the Taras

Shevchenko Company of the Palafoks Battalion. The battalion was part of the XIIIth (Dombrowski) Brigade—composed primarily of Internationals of Slavic origin. At 4:00 A.M., just as dawn's first glimmer touched the eastern horizon, the Dombrowskis crossed the Ebro and advanced inland as fast as their feet could carry them.

In twelve hours they travelled twenty-five kilometres, overwhelming a completely surprised fascist garrison at Corbera. Along the way, they overran and captured an entire battery of fascist artillery and rounded up hundreds of infantry. For once things were going the Republican army's way. Since coming to Spain in the late summer of 1937, Olynyk had seen some bitter fighting at Teruel and during The Retreats.

Olynyk was proud to serve in the Dombrowskis' Shevchenko Company. Named after the Ukrainian national poet who had predicted the coming of a Ukrainian revolution against czarist Russia, the company had a great sense of Ukrainian solidarity. Olynyk also felt more comfortable there than he would have in the Canadian Mackenzie-Papineau Battalion because he was embarrassed by his poor grasp of English and thought it might prove an impediment to his being accepted by his fellow Canadians.

Although Olynyk had emigrated to Canada from Romania on April 7, 1929, he had found an insular home within the Ukrainian-Canadian community. He was a dedicated Ukrainian nationalist who described himself as "born in Austria, Romanian by citizenship, Ukrainian by nationality." Born on April 1, 1904, in the village of Karaptsiv in the province of Bukovina—then part of the Austro-Hungarian Empire—he was sixteen when the Treaty of Versailles handed Bukovina over to Romania as part of the Austro-Hungarian Empire's dismemberment after the Great War. Olynyk had been conscripted into the Romanian army and served several years as a machine gunner. He had also suffered discrimination because he was Ukrainian.

The province of Bukovina was severely oppressed by the Romanians. From 1918 to 1928 it was effectively under martial law. The teaching of Ukrainian in schools was strictly forbidden. Orthodox Church services were offered exclusively in Romanian. As the firstborn son, Olynyk was the only one of eight children allowed an education. Anyone opposing the repressive anti-Ukrainian laws was labelled a communist and faced imprisonment or exile.

Finally, seeking a better life, Olynyk emigrated to Canada. He was already married and had two children, but his family had to remain in Romania. Olynyk's plan was to secure employment to finance their joining him.

The depression shattered that dream. Work was rare, saving money impossible. Olynyk had never been political, but as the depression hardened he drifted toward Ukrainian leftist politics. Soon he joined the Communist Party of Canada and also became a founding member of the Association for the Defence of Bukovina and Bessarabia—the two provinces under Romanian subjugation.

Olynyk thought the Dombrowski Brigade's motto, "For Your Freedom and for Ours," aptly described his reasons for being in Spain. Here, he fought not only for Spanish democracy but also for a free Ukraine and for worker freedom from oppression everywhere—including his adopted Canada. These struggles were intertwined and inseparable. Victory in Spain would only hasten the triumph of all oppressed peoples. And for now—with Franco's soldiers in retreat, with enemy artillery falling into the Dombrowskis' hands, and with fascist infantry flocking forward to surrender—it appeared a stunning victory was at hand.

No matter how much fascist artillery had been captured, there seemed no shortage of guns fixing the Republic's narrow beachhead in their sights. By the time the XVth International started across in boats jammed to the gunnels with men and equipment, a heavy barrage bracketed the river. Huge geysers of water were thrown up by exploding shells. German and Italian bombers hammered the bridgehead with bombs. Columns of smoke and flame rose from stacks of destroyed equipment piled on either shore. The din of explosions was deafening, but the men were still defiantly grinning and laughing as they clambered into the boats. Despite the heavy bombardment, hardly any casualties were incurred during the crossing.

Edwards's company was the first Mac-Pap unit to reach the other side. His orders were simple: "Go as fast and far toward Gandesa as possible." Edwards first concern was to secure the ridge overlooking the river, so the rest of the battalion could cross without fear of facing enemy machine-gun fire. His company tumbled out of the boats, shouldered their heavy packs, and followed a narrow *barranca* up toward the ridge. Every man's pack was crammed with all the ammunition, food, and water he could carry. Until the major bridges were assembled, allowing trucks to bring up supplies, the invading force would live and fight from its packs.

Just before Edwards crested the ridge, a massive blast immediately to his right sent him flying. Gagging on sulphur fumes, dazed by the concussion, and experiencing intense pain, Edwards rolled over to see that his

Mackenzie-Papineau brigaders cross the Ebro on the first day of the last desperate offensive launched by the Republicans. There were hopes this would force the fascists to negotiate a cease-fire and peace agreement. (NAC PA194601)

runner and one sergeant were dead, and several other men had been badly wounded. Struggling free of his pack, Edwards noticed it had been riddled by shrapnel. The heavy burden had saved his life. Edwards was, however, badly wounded. His right shoulder was ripped open and his left arm had almost been torn off. Blood gushing from his wounds had already so weakened him that he was unable to unroll a bandage or fashion a tourniquet to stem the flow.

Some troopers carried Edwards and the other wounded men to the riverside, where they were put on a boat. As they were rowed to the other side, Edwards's mind swirled with conflicting emotions. He was relieved that his soldiering days were obviously through and he was escaping with his life. But he also felt that he was deserting his men during a time of critical need.

James "Red" Walsh commanded one of the boats shunting back and forth across the Ebro. It was harrowing work. Fascist bombers and enemy artillery worked tirelessly to kill the boatmen and destroy the few bridges. Yet the actual damage to bridges and boats was slight. Walsh was amazed by how ineffective the enemy fire proved.

The river's current was his worst enemy. A lot of hard rowing was required to keep the boat on course, and it was his job to make sure they reached their designated landing point. They loaded and unloaded, working in a mad rush, frantically trying to get all the supplies needed to sustain the offensive across. Soon the men were reeling with exhaustion, but there was no chance to rest.

Landing on the eastern side, Walsh heard some coffee was ready at a nearby field kitchen. He sent a man off for a vat, while he set to loading the boat. No sooner had he turned to the task than a dive bomber shrieked down toward his boat. The next thing Walsh knew he was on the ground with his guts ripped open by shrapnel.

An ambulance carried Walsh back to a hospital twenty kilometres to the rear. He remained conscious during the entire body-battering drive. At the hospital he longed for unconsciousness. There was no X-ray equipment. A harried doctor tried to locate the shrapnel by digging about in the wound with his fingers. Walsh painfully watched the man yank his intestines out and pick them free of shards of shrapnel. When he had done all that he could, the doctor folded the ropes of intestine into an untidy bundle and shoved it back into his guts. Next, Walsh's lower abdomen was surgically opened so the doctor could continue his shrapnel quest. Finally, as he stitched the incision closed, the doctor told Walsh that he had managed to remove only some of the shrapnel—the rest was beyond reach.

Walsh was taken to a ward brimming with wounded. With each passing day more bloody, battered, and dazed soldiers flooded into the field hospital. When he was transferred to a hospital near Barcelona, Walsh was merely one of hundreds wounded in the Ebro offensive.

Three days into the attack, Jimmy Higgins was part of a detachment of Mac-Paps moving past Corbera, taken earlier by the Dombrowski Brigade. Their goal was Gandesa. A small battery of Republican artillery arrayed on the town's outskirts was snapping out rounds. In the distance the fierce fighting at Gandesa could be heard.

The Canadians were to replace the Catalan troops who had carried the direct assault all the way to Gandesa's outskirts. Those troops were already out of the line; they lay scattered around Corbera in exhausted and bloody clumps.

The XVth International had also had a bad time. They had followed a different route toward Gandesa than that opened by the Catalonian assault. Heavy casualties had been the price paid for opening a new path from the Ebro.

As Higgins approached Corbera, a squadron of fascist planes flew over. No air-raid sirens wailed an advance warning of the attack. A rain of bombs just started exploding in the streets. Buildings collapsed, others burned fiercely. People ran screaming. Shrapnel tore them to pieces, and concussion threw bodies about like leaves caught in a wind.

Repeated waves of bombers roared over and showered the town with bombs. The Canadians huddled on the outskirts, watching the carnage, waiting for the attacks to end. During a lull, Higgins was ordered to go into the town and see if any civilians required assistance. Higgins and his Spanish friend José found a first-aid station already operating in the remains of the town's brick winery. Catalan doctors and orderlies were looking after the wounded. In the streets, people sought relatives and loved ones among the dead lying on the broken paving stones and inside the ruined buildings.

Higgins and José decided they should check on the majority of the civilians who had sought shelter in the adjacent olive groves. As they approached the town's large water reservoir, an enemy plane flew over spewing bombs in its wake. One scored a direct hit on the reservoir, breaching the enclosing wall.

Through the gap, a wall of water tore down onto the road with the ferocity of a flash flood rushing down a *barranca*. Luckily the road worked as a canal, channelling the water directly into a nearby streambed.

José pointed at something rushing along in the flood. Higgins realized it was a child. Jumping into the stream, he fought his way through the water and managed to grab the body with one hand. Higgins dragged the body of a boy of about twelve years of age to him. The lad was choking fitfully on swallowed water.

Draping the boy over his shoulder, Higgins waded ashore. On the terrace slope above the road, he sat down and cradled the child against his chest. More bombers came over and hammered Corbera, so Higgins and José decided it was best to stay put until the attack ended.

When the planes left, Higgins set the boy down. He looked pretty badly beaten up. His knee was bleeding heavily and his left foot was broken. The fingers of his left hand were also wildly askew. Blood ran from his nose, mouth, and deep wounds on his cheek. In fact, the boy seemed to be bleeding just about everywhere. Higgins smiled, hoping to reassure him. Then the soldier hefted the boy on his back piggyback-style.

The two soldiers squelched down the muddy track of the flood-damaged road, heading toward town. Higgins kept looking back over his shoulder at the boy. "*Yo Canadiense,*" he repeated. "I am Canadian." It was all that his poor Spanish could manage. The boy's blood drenched his shirt and clung to his skin. "My name is Jim," he added in Spanish.

As they passed the ruined water reservoir, Higgins saw the corpse of a young woman of about eighteen lying against a block of concrete. She was dead, her back broken and her head almost torn off.

"Rosita, Rosita," the boy cried. Higgins kept going. "*Yo Canadiense,*" he said. "*Yo Canadiense.*" The words were like a canticle. They seemed to soothe the boy. He stopped struggling, stopped trying to go back to the dead girl. Higgins wondered who she might have been. A sister? Too young to be the boy's mother. A cousin? Who could know.

Finally, after dodging more air raids, they reached the winery and turned the boy over to the first-aid attendants. A doctor gave the boy an injection. Higgins left thinking that the boy would probably die of shock. [The boy, whose name was Manuel Alvarez, survived. In 1956, he emigrated to Canada, where he continued what had already been a long search to find the Canadian who saved his life. In 1978, he found Higgins in Peterborough, Ontario.]

William Beeching and the surviving XVth International brigaders could go no farther. They had advanced through a maelstrom of fire for almost forty kilometres from the Ebro River to Gandesa. They had destroyed and overwhelmed countless heavily entrenched fascist positions. All of this had been done with virtually no air, artillery, or armoured support. They had bought the ground with the lives of hundreds of infantrymen.

By the evening of July 29 more than three hundred Lincolns had fallen. Of these about fifty were dead, 250 wounded. Many of their officers were gone. Platoons were commanded by *soldatos,* companies by sergeants, battalions by lieutenants.

The hills and *barrancas* lying between the river and Gandesa were littered with corpses. In the mounting heat, the sickening smell of rotting flesh hung over the battlefield. Scavenging birds and animals fed on the dead. The living had no time to waste with burial details.

Repeatedly the XVth's battalions crawled out from behind their defences and into the jaws of the opposing fascist machine-gun and anti-tank gunfire. All along the fascist line the enemy had deployed Germany's newest military innovation—the eighty-eight-millimetre all-purpose artillery piece. The fire from these high-velocity, rapid-firing weapons was devastating. When a handful of Republican tanks came up on July 29 to provide support, Beeching briefly hoped they could break through. But the 88s were waiting as the tanks went forward across the open ground. A rain of shells from the German guns punched holes through the thin armour as easily as a fist might pass through paper. Their crews perished inside the tanks' burning hulls. That attack failed. As did all that followed.

On the XVth's far flank, the Mac-Paps managed to capture a few houses inside the town itself. This was as close as any Internationals came to achieving the objective of wresting Gandesa from the fascists.

There was virtually no protective cover other than a few *barrancas*. On either side of the *barrancas* stretched plains that were flat and bare of vegetation. Only a few centimetres of soil covered impenetrable bedrock. Digging trenches proved impossible.

Between futile, bloody attacks, Beeching and the rest of the XVth huddled in the *barrancas*. They had gone into the offensive confident that the Republic could succeed. But on the outskirts of Gandesa their optimism was smashed. At midnight on August 6, the XVth was relieved by the Republican 27th Division. On their way to the rear they passed through the town of Corbera. Hardly a building remained. The Internationals walked through the ruins in silence. On the edges of the moonlit streets and in the shattered buildings they caught glimpses of the corpses of old men, women, and children.

For eight days Beeching and the other Internationals rested. Then they marched again to battle. From August 15 to 26 they held a line at Sierra Pandolls, known as the Mountains of the Moon. The Mac-Paps were to the front, the Lincoln and British battalions in immediate reserve. The naked hilltop positions were as dangerous as any they had ever occupied. The men built walls from sandbags, but they offered little protection from artillery shells and aerial bombs.

Beeching was always tired. One endless day followed another as the fascists hammered the hills with shells and hurled infantry attacks against

the XVth's positions. The men threw the attacks back with rifle and machine-gun fire. After eleven days they withdrew to ready reserve status only
to be rushed to a new front line on September 4.

There were so many things that could get you killed, Konstantin Olynyk
often thought. There was the case of the Swedish volunteer. The machine
gunner had spent seven years in prison for political dissidence. He was
very politically motivated. But he also wore glasses that he refused to remove despite the fact that the sunlight reflecting back from their lenses
undoubtedly exposed his position to every fascist artillery spotter within
several kilometres. Little surprise that a direct hit soon destroyed the machine gun and killed the man.

That was what happened. Little mistakes got you killed. And small
flukes also kept you alive. The Dombrowskis were holding a line of trenches
backed up against a group of high hills. Tunnels ran through the hills to
connect different sections of open trench. It was a good position and they
had held it for weeks against countless fascist assaults.

During one such assault, however, the fascists overwhelmed the forward trench line. Olynyk's machine-gun position was dug into one of
the tunnels. When the fascists filled the trenches around him and began
killing his comrades or taking them prisoner, Olynyk realized further resistance would only cost him his life. He shrank away from the opening,
taking refuge in the darkened tunnel. It was pure fluke that his machine-
gun position had been so concealed, while his comrades had been left in
the open.

From where he hid, Olynyk watched the fascists drag several prisoners
out before the trenches and gun them down. Fearful of discovery, Olynyk
abandoned his gun and crawled deeper into the tunnel system. He soon
encountered another fugitive Dombrowski. The two men decided to run
for it.

They burst out of the tunnel, slid down a steep slope, and ran like hell
toward the second trench line, which was still in Republican hands. Enemy
fire nipped at their heels as they dodged through a grove of trees and
shrubs. About four metres from the trenches the other man was hit in the
shoulder. Some men ran out and helped Olynyk pull the wounded soldier
to safety.

Olynyk's Hungarian captain was happy to see him but groused about
how it meant changing the day's records. He had already listed Olynyk

as killed in action. As reward for surviving, he gave Olynyk a bottle of wine, and another machine gun, and sent him back into action.

By now the Internationals were all but finished as military units. The XVth could barely muster battalion strength. Many commanders had fallen. The Mac-Paps were commanded by Finnish-Canadian Capt. Gunnar Ebb. Maj. Edward Cecil Smith had been evacuated after shooting himself in the leg with his pistol. A nasty rumour circulated that the wound was deliberately inflicted. Beeching had little time for what he considered unwarranted slander. Smith had been wounded at Brunete and had fought in almost every major Mac-Pap engagement. He had shown ample courage before. It was probably just dumb luck that he had accidentally discharged his pistol. Things like that happened when a man was hungry and exhausted. [The rumours were officially sanctioned. In their reports to International Brigade command, both American commissars Frank Rogers and John Gates claimed Smith had deliberately shot himself. They admitted there was no proof to support this allegation. Rogers and Gates also harshly criticized Smith for having a capricious nature, being individualistic, and often criticizing Communist Party dogma during debates.]

On September 21, Beeching and the other brigaders received welcome news. They learned that Négrin had formally announced the immediate withdrawal of all foreign volunteers from the front lines.

Early the following morning squadrons of German bombers zeroed in on the *barrancas* and hills held by the XVth International Brigade. Dozens of men were killed and wounded. Some Lincolns were buried alive when the walls of a trench collapsed upon them.

For two more terrible days the XVth held off a series of frenzied fascist attacks. On September 29, following a long day of mutual butchery, the front fell silent for the night and the XVth International Brigade withdrew from the battle lines for the last time. Only a handful walked out unassisted. Thirty-five Mac-Paps were left. The Lincolns were little better off.

Beeching was one of those who walked out. As he crossed a battered Ebro River bridge, he recognized a man behind one of the anti-aircraft guns. It was Bruce McEwan of Vancouver, whose father, Tom McEwan, had been one of the principal recruiters for the volunteer force. In the face of continual bombing and artillery barrages, McEwan and the other anti-air gunners had staved off fascist bombers for almost sixty days. When Beeching told him the Internationals were to be withdrawn, the man seemed neither to understand nor care. Beeching left him there, crouched behind his gun, gazing watchfully up at a sky that was blessedly clear of enemy airplanes. Beeching wondered if McEwan knew whether he was alive or dead. The man was ghostly pale and almost transparently thin. His skin clung like parchment to a skeletal frame. To Beeching, McEwan seemed a symbolic representation of the beleaguered Republic.

Fifteen

*N*o Flags Flew

THE CONSTANT BOMBING WAS FRAYING RONALD LIVERSEDGE'S already threadbare nerves. For several weeks the government had been concentrating the Internationals isolated in southern Spain at Valencia in preparation for a planned mass exodus to the Barcelona area and thence across the French frontier. Although Valencia was still well back from the battle lines, the city was a dangerous place. Every day squadrons of Mussolini's bombers droned overhead and pummelled the city with high explosives.

With the bases on the fascist-held Balearic Islands only a fifteen-minute flight away, the squadrons could fly several sorties a day. To improve their odds of surprising the city's civilians outside the safety of air-raid shelters, the bomber pilots had taken to gliding in at maximum altitude with their engines off. The first warning of an attack came only when the bombs from the planes passing soundlessly overhead started detonating.

After each attack the streets echoed with the screams of fire truck, ambulance, and inhalator siren. Liversedge and the other Internationals rushed to join the rescue workers frantically digging people out of the rubble of collapsed buildings.

Organizing the transfer of the volunteers north had been under way for months, progressing by inexplicable fits and starts that seemed to achieve little. With nothing to do but hang around Valencia's battered streets, the volunteers were becoming increasingly demoralized. Although few had any desire to return to the fight, Liversedge and his comrades were also fed up with helplessly standing by while Republican Spain slowly bled to death before their eyes.

There was never any good news. The fronts were collapsing, the fascists everywhere advanced. Like Valencia, Barcelona was undergoing an airborne blitz. The fascists on the northern front slowly pushed more deeply into Catalan, closing on the provincial capital. Only Madrid, on the battle line since the beginning, held firm.

It was obvious nobody was coming to Republican Spain's rescue. The League of Nations confined itself to impotent hand-wringing. While Germany and Italy openly flouted the terms of the Non-Intervention Agreement, the committee offered only the mildest rebukes. America, fearing embroilment in another European war, had shrunk ever further into isolationism. Republican Spain was being left to die alone.

Across all of Republican Spain cities were enduring daily attacks by fascist bombers. After each air raid rescue crews moved into the destroyed buildings to search for survivors. (NAC PA194402)

On September 30, 1938, British prime minister Neville Chamberlain, still convinced Hitler's voracious appetite for neighbouring territory could somehow be appeased, joined French premier Edouard Daladier in signing the Munich Pact, which handed over Czechoslovakia's Sudeten regions to Germany. The pact's other signatories were Hitler and Mussolini.

When word of the Munich Pact reached Valencia, French volunteers openly wept with rage and humiliation. The Canadians joined their French compatriots in a grim drunken wake—fuelled with vermouth and anisette—for martyred Czechoslovakia.

As the days of autumn shortened and the news worsened, Liversedge spent greater parts of his day getting drunk. Food was in short supply, but the bars always had liquor. Liversedge and fellow Canadian Joe Mitchell searched far and wide for a bar offering a small dish of snails as accompaniment for the drinks. Although it was Spanish custom to serve a snack with each drink, the tradition had suffered due to the food shortages. But every day a few bars managed to scrounge a few snails. The quest to find those that were so blessed served to occupy otherwise meaningless hours.

The equally meaningless days being endured by the Canadians in northern Spain were relieved by three parades. In Marsa, the Mackenzie-Papineau Battalion mustered for the last time as an armed unit to mark the battalion's transition into an all-Spanish contingent. In Ripoll, on October 15, the battalion had its last formal parade before its commanders. This was followed by the final October 29 farewell parade in Barcelona for all Internationals.

After this parade, the Canadians confidently expected to be home for Christmas. But the Yule season found them still at their base in Ripoll, a gloomy village in the Pyrenees foothills. The British and Americans were both gone. But the Canadians still waited for permission to come home.

The Friends of the Mackenzie-Papineau Battalion reported regularly on the Canadian government's endless bureaucratic foot-dragging. The Royal Canadian Mounted Police, claiming the Mac-Paps were mercenaries and communists who would foment armed revolution upon their return, vigorously opposed their repatriation. Prime Minister King dithered, worrying inordinately over whether the government might be left holding the financial bag for costs incurred bringing the men back to Canada. The Department of Immigration demanded assurance that only returnees with full claim to Canadian citizenship would be accepted.

In Marsa, the Mackenzie-Papineau Battalion mustered for the last time as an armed unit and participated in a final parade. (NAC PA 193629)

To get the process under way, the Friends reached an agreement with the Canadian Pacific Railway Company that guaranteed the reimbursement of fares for all volunteers brought home on the company's ocean liners. The Friends had enough money to immediately cover the transportation costs of 120 volunteers. To raise more funds, Tim Buck ordered all of the Canadian Communist Party's property mortgaged.

The Canadian Committee to Aid Spanish Democracy launched an intensive fund-raising campaign. But it had always been the blue-collar workers, the unemployed, the students, and the countless ranks of Canada's poor who had been the committee's primary supporters. Raising money from people who had little, required time—time the volunteers might not have. Republican Spain was falling, and the Canadians had to be brought out soon or they might not get out at all.

The CPR expressed satisfaction with the Friends' guarantee, but it was up to the Canadian government to organize the movement of the volunteers from Spain to Le Havre and other French ports. Without a statement on the part of the Canadian government that it would accept the volunteers being boarded on CPR ships, the French government was unwilling to allow the men to cross the frontier.

For his part, William Beeching believed the primary blame for Canada's slow processing of the volunteers' return rested at the feet of Col. Andrew O'Kelly, assistant commissioner of the London office of the Canadian Immigration Service. Since his arrival at Ripoll in November, O'Kelly had spent weeks systematically interviewing every Canadian volunteer.

The International Brigades' records were trapped in southern Spain at Albacete. Few of the men had either their passports or other Canadian identification papers. O'Kelly appeared to believe the absence of papers was part of some dark, sinister plot rather than the misfortune of war. No doubt he suspected the Soviet Union was trying to infiltrate *agent provocateurs* into Canada disguised as Mac-Paps.

To lead the unwary foreign spy into self-incrimination, O'Kelly had devised a list of questions. A favourite demand was to name a famous Canadian. Much to O'Kelly's chagrin, most volunteers replied by naming Tim Buck.

Unable to ferret out the spies through interrogation, O'Kelly set to determine their identity by classifying them according to probable national loyalties. To this end, he divided them into three groups: Canadians by birth, Canadian citizens who were either British-born or naturalized Canadians, and those he denoted as aliens. Anyone who claimed to have been legally landed in Canada for five years or more before departing for Spain fell into the alien category. Most of these men were of Ukrainian, Finnish, Polish, or other Eastern-European extraction. O'Kelly appeared to reason that it was among these aliens that the spies were lurking. Consequently he spent hours grilling each alien-categorized volunteer.

But even Canadian-born volunteers such as Beeching were not spared. One afternoon when O'Kelly was busily interrogating Beeching, the interview was interrupted by a squadron of overflying fascist bombers. O'Kelly

excitedly rushed from his desk to the window, exclaiming his wish to witness an air raid. Later that day, as O'Kelly and his chauffeur were en route
to his private quarters, the car was strafed by an enemy plane. Thereafter,
O'Kelly would only travel under cover of darkness. Beeching added cowardice to his growing list of grievances against O'Kelly.

In southern Spain, Liversedge was also enduring endless interviews. The
three thousand volunteers stranded in the south had been divided into
groups and transferred to the nearby countryside. Liversedge was with
a group in Villanueva de Castellón, about thirty kilometres from Valencia. The League of Nations Commission, led by Finnish general Bruno
Freidrik Jalander, came to enumerate the volunteers and confirm their
nationality.
     The Finnish general was a talented linguist who delighted in inter-
viewing the volunteers in groups designated by native tongue—all of which
he spoke. Each interview session Liversedge attended was interminably
long. When everyone in the room was yawning and nodding their heads
tiredly, the general would suddenly round on one volunteer and snap out a
terse question in Russian. Although everyone in the room immediately woke
up sufficiently to mock the general with their laughter, no Russian spy ever
tripped over his tongue.
     As the interrogations dragged on into the new year, the Republic en-
tered its final death throes. Everyone knew Franco would soon overrun
Barcelona, and the wedge between northern and southern Republican Spain
was widening at an alarming rate. More than two hundred kilometres of
coastline were now in fascist hands. The volunteers in the south were deeply
afraid their repatriation would be approved too late for them to escape
from Spain. Sooner or later they had to be moved north if any evacuation
was to be undertaken. With each passing day, the chance of a Republican
ship managing to get to Barcelona from the south lessened. Yet nobody in
charge seemed anxious to start this necessary exodus.
     Finally on January 20, 1939, almost three thousand Internationals
queued on the docks of Valencia harbour and stared apprehensively at two
small, dirty, coastal tramp steamers flying the French flag. The harbour was
a scene of terrible devastation. Everywhere Liversedge looked there was
nothing but rubble and shattered buildings. The docks were a tangle of
twisted steel girders and charred decking. Rusting hulls and skeletal masts
of sunken ships thrust out of the water alongside the shattered docks.

Liversedge thought of his terrible ordeal following the *Ciudad de Barcelona* torpedoing and wished fervently he would not once again have to travel on dangerous waters. But it was the only way to reach safety.

Ross Russell limped aboard one of the tramp steamers. Surely the ship was designed to carry only about two hundred men, not the fifteen hundred currently cramming its holds. Russell found himself tangled up with several other volunteers in a hopeless jumble of arms and legs. There was so little room that it was impossible to shift into a comfortable position. Then the hold's hatches were battened down and the men were plunged into darkness.

The trip took fifteen hours. Russell's still-healing foot throbbed mercilessly the whole way. It was terribly hot in the hold because of the press of men, and there seemed to be too little oxygen. Russell felt this discomfort all the more acutely because the shrapnel still lodged in his lung sometimes made breathing difficult.

Finally, when the ship was within sight of Barcelona, the crew opened the hatches and let the men go topside. Russell was overwhelmed by the sickening stench of sweat, feces, and urine that came off him and the others as they emerged wearily from the hold. Fresh air had never seemed so sweet.

On either side of the steamers, a Republican submarine quietly surfaced and the men gave the cigar-shaped craft a ragged cheer. Russell realized they must have been there for the entire fifteen hours, carefully shepherding the two freighters up the coast.

When they got off the ships, the men formed at one end of the harbour to hear a rousing speech from Prime Minister Juan Négrin. He vowed that Spain would fight on, that surrender was unthinkable. Russell decided to believe him. It was better than coming to terms with reality.

Finally O'Kelly started letting the Canadians leave. Beeching was one of three hundred sent in the first group. On January 25, 1939, Beeching and Joe Schoen, who had come to Spain aboard the ill-fated *Ciudad de Barcelona,* hauled down the Mackenzie-Papineau Battalion flag for the last time so they could take it home to Canada. They left by train for Perpignan, France. It was a harrowing trip. Other trains were racing for the border crossing at Port Bou. Both the train before them and the one following were knocked from the tracks by fascist bombs.

Port Bou was a smoking ruin. Everywhere Beeching looked there were children in rags, all helplessly begging for food and shelter. Beeching saw not a single adult on the streets of Port Bou as the train rolled past and entered the tunnel that passed under the Pyrenees to reach the French border. It was a long run through the tunnel's darkness and in that inky blackness Beeching felt tears stream freely down his cheeks. It was the first time in his adult life that Beeching, overwhelmed by a terrible sense of futility and loss, had allowed himself to weep.

After crossing the frontier, the men disembarked from the train. They were immediately surrounded by armed French soldiers and transferred to sealed railway cars. The windows were shuttered and securely bolted, the doors locked. The train carried them to Le Havre without stopping. There the Canadians found themselves waiting yet again.

It was a Sunday night when the phone rang in *Toronto Daily Star* reporter Matthew Halton's London apartment. On the other end was a friend in Paris who had been working on the problem of getting the Canadian volunteers home. He told Halton that about three hundred Mac-Paps were coming out of Spain and would soon be in Le Havre, but the French government was threatening to send them back to Perpignan's camps for Spanish refugees unless ten thousand dollars was made immediately available. The money was needed to pay their passage on Canadian Pacific Railway Company ships to Canada. They had to have the money in three days. Could Halton help? There was no time to get the money from the committee in Canada.

Feeling sick at heart, Halton promised to try. After he hung up, Halton sat beside the telephone wondering how it had come to the point where the volunteers were to be treated like criminals rather than heroes. And where was he to raise ten thousand dollars?

Halton first approached former prime minister Richard Bedford Bennett, who had gone into self-imposed exile from Canada in early 1938. Bennett now lived on an estate in England. Halton phoned and started relating the plight of the Canadians in Le Havre. He did his best to eloquently present his case. "Whether or not you agree with the cause for which they fought you must admit that they are young Canadians animated by motives as unselfish as those that drove the men of Vimy Ridge and Passchendaele. When they volunteered they knew their only reward would be blood and obloquy, though perhaps posterity would notice them. The survivors are

The first group of Canadian volunteers to reach Canada was the largest.
It numbered about three hundred.   (NAC C67458)

wounded, ragged and starving. Will you help me to get them home?"

"I am sure their motives were as high as you say," Bennett replied. "I
have a good deal of admiration for these young men, whether they were
misguided or not." Halton's hopes started to rise. "But I am sorry to say that
I cannot contribute anything just now. I have recently undergone some
unusual expenses." Bennett offered no further elaboration. Halton rang off,
cursing himself for even bothering.

He hoped for better luck with the only British-based Canadian Halton
could think of who had both money and some left-leaning political sentiment—a young businessman named Garfield Weston. Stopping Halton
before he got his pitch even rolling, Weston promised a cheque for five
thousand dollars first thing in the morning.

The remaining five thousand dollars was raised by sources other than
Halton, and the Canadians were released by the French on January 27,
1939. They travelled across the English Channel to the port city of Newha-
ven. Halton was there to greet them and win a major scoop for his paper.
With the time difference working to his advantage, Halton wired a story to
Toronto in time for the morning edition. He wrote:

No flags waved, no bands played at the little English harbour of New-haven in the cold darkness of 3 o'clock this morning as some 300 Canadian members of the famous International Brigade . . . landed in England on the last stage of their odyssey of courage and ideals. . . . As I write, they are en route to Liverpool in sealed trains like so many lepers. . . . Three newspapermen, including myself, formed the only reception committee for Canada's returning crusaders at Newhaven. We travelled with them to London, and I had two hours I won't soon forget. . . . A few of them, no doubt, are soldiers of fortune and aliens, but most are intelligent Canadians who saw what everyone is begin-ning to see now that it is too late; and who had the courage to do something about it. Many of them are even Communists. But today France and Britain wouldn't be so afraid if Spain were Communist instead of fascist.

Not all of Spain had yet fallen to the fascists. At the coastal town of Cassá de la Selva, Ross Russell and a small number of other Canadians were still hoping to get out before the Republic's small remaining toehold in Catalo-nia was lost. They had arrived at the village to find that the other Canadi-ans, most of those who had not been isolated in the south, had all left for France only days earlier.

Cassá de la Selva was crowded with refugees and soldiers of all nation-alities. To the south, merely thirty-five or forty kilometres from Barcelona, the sound of a terrific battle being waged often drifted in on the wind. All day long the Canadians sat by their billets watching refugees flow north for the French border. They came in every kind of vehicle, including Barcelo-na's garbage trucks. Most, however, came on foot. There were old men, women, and children. One cortege included many of the city's prostitutes. The women proceeded with studied dignity on their high-heeled shoes while taking turns carrying babies for mothers who were near dead with exhaustion. The refugees moved through Cassá de la Selva in an unending line. On either side of the village the fascist planes swooped down to strafe and bomb the long column, as they did from Barcelona to the border.

After a few days in Cassá de la Selva, the Canadians moved to an old border fort. Again there was an inexplicable wait that lasted for ten days. The tension was terrible, for on January 26 Barcelona had fallen. Franco's army was rushing northward, driving the remnants of the Republic's northern army across the French border.

One day about three thousand Spanish troops straggled in. They were in dreadful shape. Almost all were barefoot. They had no guns. Most were supporting themselves with canes cut from trees or old boards; others hobbled on improvised crutches. Their clothes were in tatters and they were all half-starved. The men told Russell of their retreat, of how they had tried to fight but had run out of everything. Their artillery finally had no shells, there was no food, no ammunition for the rifles. They were as beaten an army as Russell ever hoped to see.

A couple of days later Russell's group made for the border. There were no trains or trucks. The men walked, entangled with the refugees. On the other side of the tunnel that led into France a representative of the Canadian Pacific Railway Company guided them to a train. The train windows were unshuttered, and Russell could barely believe his eyes as it rattled north from Perpignan toward Paris. For kilometre after kilometre the railroad sidings at every town were jammed with boxcars and flatcars bursting with arms. Russell saw disassembled planes, anti-tank guns, artillery pieces, anti-aircraft guns, huge stocks of ammunition in boxes marked with Russian lettering. Seeing these weapons that had been denied the Republic by the Non-Intervention Committee, Russell was too angry even to weep. Suddenly he wanted nothing more than to quit Europe and return to Canada. Europe did not deserve to be saved from its own folly.

Hans Ibing found himself declared a stateless person. Under Canadian immigration law, the residency status of an alien was automatically revoked after a one-year absence from Canada. Ibing had been gone almost two years. Representatives of the Committee to Aid Spanish Democracy in Paris and the Friends of the Mackenzie-Papineau Battalion were scrambling to arrange papers that would allow Ibing back to Canada, but it was a race against time.

If they failed to come up with papers soon the French were going to deport Ibing to Germany, the former Winnipeg truck driver's country of birth. Everyone knew such a deportation for a Communist and International brigader amounted to a death sentence, but the French officials seemed not to care. One French officer suggested that Ibing might apply at the German consulate for a passport. If successful he could use it to travel to Mexico, which was taking in stateless Internationals.

Desperate, Ibing rushed immediately to the German consulate. Swastika flags hung over the entryway, swastika armbands were worn by all the

253

soldiers and many of the civilian staff. Everywhere Ibing looked men and women sternly traded the straight-armed salute of the Nazi Party, loudly exchanged Heil Hitlers, and clicked heels together so sharply it sounded as if guns were being constantly fired in the consulate halls.

Dressed in the shabby civilian clothes and beret he had worn since coming out of Spain, Ibing felt the consulate staff had his number pegged from the moment he walked into the building. The consular official behind the counter confirmed this impression by immediately asking Ibing if he had been in Spain. Ibing confessed that he had. The German replied with a grim, self-satisfied smile that the only passport he was entitled to was valid for one-way travel to Germany. Although such a passport was little more than a ticket to certain death, Ibing asked for it anyway. The official drew up a passport with the travel restriction stamped on its front.

Possession of an official German document prompted the French to grant him identity papers that declared his stateless citizen status. But neither document prevented them from telling him to be out of France by morning or face deportation to Germany.

As the clock ticked down on Ibing's life, a Canadian Pacific Railway Company official arrived at Ibing's quarters and told him that the Canadian Committee to Aid Spanish Democracy had come up with funds for his transport to Canada. He bustled Ibing to the railway station and they caught a night train to Le Havre, where a CPR vessel was preparing to sail on the morning tide.

Ibing still had no official papers authorizing his travel to Canada, so he would never clear customs. With thousands of Jews trying to escape Europe, people without proper papers were being turned back every day by customs officials. The CPR official said he had no connections that would help Ibing circumvent the customs process. But he did have a plan.

Ibing and the CPR official huddled behind a freight shed on the edge of the pier, watching the other passengers board. At the man's insistence, Ibing carried a large, virtually empty suitcase. When the last passengers were aboard, the customs officers had departed, and two sailors started pulling up the gangplank, the CPR man told Ibing to run for it. Ibing pelted down the pier and scrambled onto the ship, waving his suitcase about, playing the flustered late passenger. The two sailors, concerned only with getting the ship under way, waved him below without bothering to check his papers.

Later that day all the passengers were required to turn their passports

Hans Ibing (far left) found himself declared a stateless citizen and facing deportation to Hitler's Germany, where an International brigader could expect certain death. (NAC PA195504)

into the chief purser's office. Ibing handed in his worthless German passport and the French stateless citizen document. A few minutes later, a steward came and escorted him back to see the purser. The man was furious, raving at Ibing that had he seen these papers before they sailed Ibing would have been thrown off. If it were not for the fact that the ship was making no stops until it reached Canada, the purser would have prevented his reaching Halifax.

But there was nothing the purser could do short of casting Ibing overboard. In Halifax, however, he was detained and taken before a special immigration enquiry. A French-Canadian immigration officer grilled Ibing for hours. Several cables were sent to Winnipeg to confirm that Ibing had lived there. Ibing was getting increasingly nervous. He could still face deportation to Germany. Eventually, the immigration officer reported that Ibing's residency in Winnipeg had been confirmed, but that his arrival in Canada was still illegal and he had no entitlement to admission. Ibing felt sick with apprehension. He almost shouted with joyous relief when the officer said he did not want to be responsible for deporting Ibing to a dire fate in Nazi Germany and was consequently issuing him with a landing permit. Ibing knew he would never be able to adequately thank either the man or his adopted nation enough for this act of mercy and kindness. Nor could he thank the CPR official, for he had never learned the man's name.

James Walsh knew there would be no kindness for him if the fascists overtook the column marching toward the French border. He and four other hospitalized Canadians had joined the other ambulatory patients in a race for the Pyrenees. Behind them the fascist army was closing on the border. Walsh was determined to be in France before it got there. So despite the open shrapnel wound in his stomach, Walsh walked painfully northward. The only thing holding his lower organs inside was a large bandage.

Walsh and the other refugees won the race against the fascists. But the border guards were demanding papers from everyone crossing. Walsh had nothing to prove his citizenship or even his identity. Neither did the other Canadians. The French police threw them in the city jail for the night.

In the morning they were moved to the internment camp for Spanish refugees near Perpignan. It could only be described as a concentration camp: rough bunkhouses, walls of barbed wire, armed guards, and virtually no hygiene facilities or fresh water. The camp made the relief camps in Canada look like holiday resorts.

Walsh had no way to clean up, no way to keep the bandage from getting dirtier. There were no doctors or nurses in the camp to provide a fresh bandage or treat the wound. Walsh knew the risk of infection was great, but there was nothing he could do. The French guards ignored the plight of the people they watched over.

Finally someone from the British consulate in Paris came and took the Canadians out. A police escort stayed with them all the way to Le Havre, where they crossed to England. During the short trip to Liverpool they were closely guarded by British police. Upon arriving in the city the men were locked up in a CPR immigration shed on the docks. Here they waited for two weeks for the arrival of a ship bound for Canada. Throughout this time, Walsh's requests to see a doctor or get a fresh bandage were refused.

The first thing he did on boarding the CPR liner was ask a steward to get him to the ship's doctor. The doctor was less than sympathetic. He tore off the old dressing, swabbed the open wound with alcohol, and slapped on a new bandage. "This'll keep your guts in until you get to Halifax," the doctor said.

Konstantin Olynyk was beginning to think that his chances of returning to Canada were almost nonexistent. He and a number of other ethnic Canadians were detained in a concentration camp on the French border. Col. Andrew O'Kelly was looking for proof that Olynyk qualified for return to Canada. Olynyk had little to offer. He spoke fractured English with an awkward tongue. His Spanish military book cited his domicile as Romania. Under "next of kin" was the address of his Romanian wife.

Making matters worse, he had lied to Canadian customs and immigration officers to smooth his departure from Canada for Spain. Olynyk had used his Romanian passport instead of seeking a Canadian one and had stated his reason for travelling to Europe was a return to Romania. His passport had accordingly been stamped as invalid for return to Canada. That the use of his Romanian passport had been a ruse to enable his leaving Canada for the illegal trip into Spain did nothing to improve things in the eyes of Colonel O'Kelly.

Olynyk felt desperate. The Canadians were all going home. There were fewer around every day. O'Kelly would soon make a decision, and if he decided Olynyk should be repatriated to Romania his future was bleak. Communists returning from Spain were rumoured to be facing imprisonment, torture, even execution at the hands of the Romanian government.

Finally O'Kelly called Olynyk into another meeting. O'Kelly was armed with a Canadian map. He told Olynyk to show him where South Porcupine was located. Without hesitation Olynyk pointed out the tiny village near Timmins. He proceeded to describe the region in great detail, even providing a list of people he knew. Among those was the chief of police. O'Kelly seemed impressed. It was March 6, 1939. A few days later Olynyk was put on a sealed train to Le Havre. When he boarded a ship there he was given a Canadian Immigration Identification Card.

On January 23, 1939, the fascist guards singled out the 106 British and Canadian prisoners still alive in the prison outside Burgos. The men were marched through Franco's capital the next morning. Their feet were sore and covered with blisters, their clothes were ragged and filthy. On either side of the streets down which they marched stony-faced civilians watched in hostile silence. This was the land of the Requetes. There was no sympathy in Burgos for the Republic or the men who had come from other countries to fight for Spanish democracy. Jules Päiviö and the other prisoners held their heads high, kept their backs straight, and marched as if they were on military parade.

Rumour had it the prisoners were being moved north for release across the French border. Perhaps this was true, perhaps not. Päiviö refused to allow his hopes to rise. He focussed instead on surviving for another day.

From Burgos the men were transported in closed boxcars to San Sebastian on the Bay of Biscay. They arrived in the early evening and were paraded through the city—a former bastion of Republican resistance that since its fall to the Nationalists on September 13, 1937, had been suffering under Franco's heel. The fascists had a truck mounted with loudspeakers leading the parade. Over the loudspeakers, a man shouted that the prisoners were barbaric Red foreigners.

The streets thronged with people, but unlike in Burgos, this was no hostile crowd. At every opportunity, people jostled forward to walk alongside the prisoners and talk with them. Some of the Spanish girls gave men their addresses and asked them to write when they were repatriated. The fascist guards tried to stop the contact between the prisoners and the people, but there were too few of them to be effective. The parade was often stalled by the press of the crowds.

During one of these delays, Päiviö saw two young children staring at him with big, wide eyes. He asked them if the *Rojos* [Reds] looked as terrible as the man on the public address system said they were. The children's young mother approached Päiviö. She told him that she knew what he was and that she was one also. The Italians had killed her husband on the Basque front, she said. Her brother still fought in Catalonia, but she had received no word from him since San Sebastian had fallen. She wondered if Päiviö might have met him. Päiviö tried to tell her gently that there had been so many thousands of soldiers that it was almost impossible he and her brother could have met. At this the young woman burst into dry sobs and started leading her children away. Over her shoulder she cried, "*Salud y bueno suerte, camarada!*" Päiviö translated this as meaning roughly, "Goodbye and good luck, comrade!" He shouted the same back to her.

For many of the volunteers, all the horrors they had witnessed while fighting for a doomed cause would haunt them for the rest of their lives. Most, however, remained convinced to the end of their days that by going to fight in Spain they had done something honourable and meaningful. (NAC C67448)

At the parade's end, however, the iron gates of the basement cells in San Sebastian Provincial Prison closed behind them and Päiviö wondered if his luck had run out. This was the worst hellhole yet. The walls were eternally damp. Their rations were seldom anything but bread and water. They were never allowed out of the cells for any exercise. The prisoners were held there until April 5, 1939, when they were taken by bus to the border crossing at Irun and walked over the International Bridge into Hendaye, France. All the men were in terrible shape. Päiviö was suffering from a bone rheumatism due to vitamin deficiencies and his body was covered with scurvy sores.

But after a year in prison he was free. Never had a word sounded so sweet. Looking back across the bridge toward Spain, he remembered everyone he knew there. People who were free no longer.

259

Epilogue

The Cause of
the Century

JULES PÄIVIÖ AND ABOUT THIRTY OTHER CANADIANS WHO HAD
been prisoners of war in Spain returned to Canada in early May 1939. They
were the last Canadian volunteers to come home. They did not arrive un-
noticed. As had been the case for each small group of homecoming survivors, they were met by well-wishers, family, and friends.

In Halifax, Montreal, Toronto, Winnipeg, Vancouver—wherever veterans stepped off ships or trains, crowds of people were there to greet them.
The largest reception naturally enough was held when the group with the
greatest number of veterans reached the nation's most populous city.

On February 5, 1939, 272 men, led by Edward Cecil Smith, arrived at
Toronto's Union Station. More than ten thousand people braved a bitter
winter night to celebrate their homecoming. It was a wild, tumultuous
scene, with everyone trying to touch the volunteers.

Families of those who were missing searched for news of their loved
ones. All too often, the news they received brought only sorrow, which was
the case for the parents of Thomas Beckett. After endless months of hoping
for proof that their son—the first Canadian lost in Spain—might emerge
from some forgotten prison camp, there was only further heartbreak.

It took three hours to calm the crowd sufficiently to allow the inevitable speeches to proceed. There was no message from the federal government to read or any government representative there to speak. On this
evening, the only government presence in Union Station was a small knot
of Royal Canadian Mounted Police who took pictures and scribbled notes,

Major Edward Cecil Smith (standing) addresses a crowd of ten thousand who clogged Union Station in Toronto to welcome the first group of Canadian volunteers home. (NAC C67441)

searching even now among the veterans for subversive elements.

Smith spoke on behalf of the men. It was a thoughtful speech about the nature of causes and those who answered their call.

Rev. Salem Bland, the renowned Methodist social reformer, had the last word. In one sentence he captured the essence of the experience of sixteen hundred Canadians who served the cause of the century: "Canada didn't understand at first what you were doing, but understands now, and as time goes on, you will have more friends, more honour, because you have done one of the most gallant things done in history."

Bibliography

Books

Academy of Sciences of the USSR. *International Solidarity with the Spanish Republic, 1936–1939.* Moscow: Progress Publishers, English edition, 1974.

Allan, Ted and Sydney Gordon. *The Scalpel, The Sword: The Story of Dr. Norman Bethune,* rev. ed. Toronto: McClelland and Stewart, 1989.

Alvarez, Manuel. *The Tall Soldier.* Vancouver: New Star Books, 1983.

Angus, Ian. *Canadian Bolsheviks: The Early Years of the Communist Party in Canada.* Montreal: Vanguard Publication, 1981.

Beeching, William C. *Canadian Volunteers: Spain, 1936–1939.* Regina: Canadian Plains Research Center, 1989.

Beeching, William, and Dr. Phyllis Clarke. *Yours in the Struggle: Reminiscences of Tim Buck.* Toronto: NC Press Limited, 1977.

Bessie, Alvah. *Men in Battle.* New York: Pinnacle Books, 1977.

Betcherman, Lisa-Rose. *The Swastika and the Maple Leaf: Fascist Movements in Canada in the Thirties.* Toronto: Fitzhenry & Whiteside, 1975.

Bethune, Norman. *The Crime on the Road: Málaga to Almería.* Madrid: Publicaciones Iberia, 1937.

Bolloten, Bernard. *The Spanish Civil War: Revolution and Counterrevolution.* New York: The University of North Carolina Press, 1991.

Brome, Vincent. *The International Brigades: Spain, 1936–1939.* London: William Heinemann Ltd., 1965.

Broue, Pierre, and Emile Temime. *The Revolution and Civil War in Spain.* Translated by Tony White. London: Faber & Faber, Inc., 1970.

Buck, Tim. *Our Fight for Canada: Selected Writings (1923–1959).* Toronto: Progress Books, 1959.

Buck, Tim. *Thirty Years 1922–1952: The Story of the Communist Movement in Canada.* Toronto: Progress Books, 1952.

Carr, E. H. *The Comintern and the Spanish Civil War.* New York: Pantheon Books, 1984.

Colodny, Robert Garland. *The Struggle for Madrid: The Central Epic of the Spanish Conflict (1936–37)*. New York: Paine-Whitman, 1958.

Cunningham, Valentine. *The Penguin Book of Spanish Civil War Verse*. London: Penguin Books, 1980.

Dallet, Joe. *Letters from Spain*. Toronto: New Era Publishers, 1938.

Esberey, Joy E. *Knight of the Holy Spirit: A Study of William Lyon Mackenzie King*. Toronto: University of Toronto Press, 1980.

Fraser, Ronald. *Blood of Spain: An Oral History of the Spanish Civil War*. New York: Pantheon Books, 1979.

Griffin, Frederick. *Soviet Scene: A Newspaperman's Close-ups of New Russia*. Toronto: The Macmillan Company of Canada Limited, 1932.

Hills, George. *The Battle for Madrid*. New York: St. Martin's Press, 1977.

Howard, Victor. *We Were the Salt of the Earth: The On-to-Ottawa Trek and the Regina Riot*. Regina: University of Regina, Canadian Plains Research Center, 1985.

Howard, Victor with Mac Reynolds. *The Mackenzie-Papineau Battalion: The Canadian Contingent in the Spanish Civil War*. Ottawa: Carleton University Press, 1986.

Johnston, Verle B. *Legions of Babel: The International Brigades in the Spanish Civil War*. University Park: The Pennsylvania State University Press, 1967.

Kardash, William (Lt.). *I Fought for Canada in Spain*. Toronto: New Era Publishers, 1938.

Kurzman, Dan. *Miracle of November: Madrid's Epic Stand, 1936*. New York: G.P. Putnam's Sons, 1980.

Landis, Arthur H. *The Abraham Lincoln Brigade*. New York: The Citadel Press, 1968.

Landis, Arthur H. *Death in the Olive Groves: American Volunteers in the Spanish Civil War—1936–1939*. New York: Paragon House, 1989.

Liversedge, Ronald. *Recollections of the On to Ottawa Trek*. Edited by Victor Hoar. Toronto: McClelland and Stewart, 1973.

Matthews, Herbert. *Ten Years to Alamein*. Toronto: S. J. Reginald Saunders and Company Ltd., 1944.

Montero, Gloria. *We Stood Together: First-Hand Accounts of Dramatic Events in Canada's Labour Past*. Toronto: Lorimer & Co., 1979.

Nelson, Steve. *The Volunteers*. New York: Masses and Mainstream, 1953.

Orwell, George. *Homage to Catalonia*. Harmondsworth, England: Penguin, 1938.

Orwell, George. *Looking Back on the Spanish Civil War.* Harmondsworth, England: Penguin, 1938.

Payne, Stanley G. *Spain's First Democracy: The Second Republic, 1931–1936.* Madison, Wis.: The University of Wisconsin Press, 1993.

Peck, Mary Biggar. *Red Moon over Spain: Canadian Media Reaction to the Spanish Civil War, 1936–1939.* Ottawa: Steel Rail Publishing, 1988.

Penner, Norman. *Canadian Communism: The Stalin Years and Beyond.* Toronto: Methuen, 1988.

Potvin, Rose, ed. *Passion and Conviction: The Letters of Graham Spry.* Regina: Canadian Plains Research Center, 1992.

Preston, Paul. *The Coming of the Spanish Civil War: Reform, Reaction and Revolution in the Second Republic.* New York: Methuen & Co., 1978.

Richardson, Dan R. *Comintern Army: The International Brigades and the Spanish Civil War.* Lexington, Ky.: The University Press of Kentucky, 1982.

Robin, Martin. *Shades of Right: Nativist and Fascist Politics in Canada: 1920–1940.* Toronto: University of Toronto Press, 1992.

Rolfe, Edwin. *The Lincoln Battalion: The Story of the Americans Who Fought in Spain in the International Brigades.* New York: Veterans of the Abraham Lincoln Brigade, 1939.

Ryan, Frank, ed. *The Book of the Fifteenth Brigade: Records of British, American, Canadian, and Irish Volunteers in the XVth International Brigade in Spain 1936–1938.* Madrid: The Commissariat of War XV Brigade, 1938; reprint, Newcastle upon Tyne: Frank Graham, 1975.

Ryan, Oscar. *Tim Buck: A Conscience for Canada.* Toronto: Progress Books, 1975.

Stacey, C.P. *A Very Double Life: The Private World of Mackenzie King.* Toronto: Macmillan of Canada, 1976.

Stewart, Roderick. *Bethune.* Toronto: New Press, 1973.

Stewart, Roderick. *The Mind of Norman Bethune.* Toronto: Fitzhenry & Whiteside, 1977.

Thomas, Hugh. *The Spanish Civil War.* London: Penguin Books, 1968.

Wejr, Patricia and Howie Smith, eds. *Fighting for Labour: Four Decades of Work in British Columbia, 1910–1950.* Victoria, B.C.: Aural History Program, B.C. Ministry of Provincial Secretary and Government Services Provincial Archives, 1978.

Wyden, Peter. *The Passionate War: The Narrative History of the Spanish Civil War.* New York: Simon and Schuster, 1983.

Addresses

Bethune, Norman. "Reflections on Return from, 'Through the Looking-Glass' " Address to Montreal Medico-Chirurgical Society. Bethune File. Metropolitan Toronto Reference Library, December 20, 1935.

Bethune, Norman. "Symposium on Medical Economics, Discussion." Address to Montreal Medico-Chirurgical Society. Metropolitan Toronto Reference Library, April 17, 1936.

Magazines

Bethune, Norman. "Red Moon." *Canadian Forum* 17 (July 1937).

"Commander Bids Farewell to Internationals." *Volunteer for Liberty*, November 7, 1938.

Farha, Ted. "Canada's Blood Trust in Spain." *The Canadian Magazine*, August 1937: 2–3, 43.

"The History of the Mac-Paps." *Volunteer for Liberty*, November 7, 1938.

"The Mackenzie-Papineau Battalion in Spain." *The Marxist Quarterly* (summer 1966): 1–66.

Momryk, Myron. " 'For Your Freedom and for Ours': Konstantin (Mike) Olynyk, A Ukrainian Volunteer from Canada in the International Brigades." *Canadian Ethnic Studies* 20, no. 2 (1988): 124–34.

Momryk, Myron. "Ukrainian Volunteers from Canada in the International Brigades, Spain, 1936–39: A Profile." *Journal of Ukrainian Studies* 16, nos. 1–2 (summer-winter 1991): 181–94.

Ryan, Larry. "Over the Top." *New Advance* (November 1937).

Spencer, David. "Old Soldiers." *Vancouver* (November 1988): 60–61.

"Trek Will Resume: Bennett Gov't Refuses Demands." *Relief Camp Worker*, June 28, 1935: 1, 5.

Williamson, Bill. "Spain, 1936–1939: An Early Volunteer." *Veterans of the Mackenzie-Papineau Battalion Newsletter*, n.d.: 17–18.

Newspapers

Bethune, Norman, "With the Canadian Blood Transfusion Unit at Guadalajara." *The Daily Clarion*, July 17, 1937.

"Emissaries of Spanish Loyalists in Toronto on Speaking Tour of Canada and the United States." *The Toronto Daily Star*, October 20, 1936.

Griffin, Frederick, *The Toronto Daily Star*, December 7–December 21, 1936.

Halton, Matthew, *The Toronto Daily Star*, January 27, 1939.

Kirkland Lake (Ontario) Northern Daily News, July 6, 1937.
Saskatoon Star-Phoenix, August 23, 1937.
Taylor, Fabrice, "Plaque Unveiled in Honour of Mac-Pap Battalion." *The Globe and Mail,* June 5, 1995.
Winnipeg Free Press, July 20, 1937.

Pamphlets

Canadian Committee to Aid Spanish Democracy, *Canada's Adopted Children,* n.d.
Canadian League Against War and Fascism, *Report: First Canadian Congress Against War and Fascism—October 6th and 7th, 1934,* n.d.
Smith, A. E. Friends of the Mackenzie-Papineau Battalion, *Hello Canada! Canada's Mackenzie-Papineau Battalion: 1837–1937—15th Brigade I.B.— "Fascism Shall be Destroyed.",* n.d.
Stephen, Alexander Maitland. Canadian League Against War and Fascism, *Hitlerism in Canada,* n.d.

Unpublished Materials

Interview with Lucien Tellier, Member of the English Battalion, n.d., Mackenzie-Papineau Battalion Collection, MG30 E 173. National Archives of Canada, Ottawa.
Beckett, Thomas. "Letter to Audrey," January 17, 1937, Mackenzie-Papineau Battalion Collection, MG30 E 173. National Archives of Canada, Ottawa.
Beckett, Thomas. "Notebook," n.d., Mackenzie-Papineau Battalion Collection. Metropolitan Toronto Reference Library.
Beckett, Thomas. "Somewhere in Spain: Letter to Family," January 31, 1937, Mackenzie-Papineau Battalion Collection. Metropolitan Toronto Reference Library.
Bethune, Norman. "Letters to Rev. Ben Spence," December 17, 1936 and January 11, 1937, Metropolitan Toronto Reference Library.
Higgins, H.J. Reminiscence contained in "Mac-Pap Reminiscences, A-J," n.d., Mackenzie-Papineau Battalion Collection, MG30 E 173. National Archives of Canada, Ottawa.
Ibing, Hans. Reminiscence contained in "Mac-Pap Reminiscences, A-J," n.d., Mackenzie-Papineau Battalion Collection MG30 E 173. National Archives of Canada, Ottawa.

Kardash, Bill. "Tanks," n.d., Mackenzie-Papineau Battalion Collection, MG30 E 173. National Archives of Canada, Ottawa.

Kashton, Bill. Interview Transcript, n.d., Mackenzie-Papineau Battalion Collection, MG30 E 173. National Archives of Canada, Ottawa.

King, William Lyon Mackenzie. Diaries 1926–39, National Library of Canada, Ottawa.

Komodowski, Edward. "The Story of Fuentes de Ebro," n.d., Mackenzie-Papineau Battalion Collection, MG30 E 173. National Archives of Canada, Ottawa.

Lindstrom-Best, Varpu, trans. Selected passages of "Meidan Poikamme Espanjassa—Our Sons in Spain," 1939, William Lahtinen, ed. USA, Finnish Workers Federation, Mackenzie-Papineau Battalion Collection, MG30 E 173. National Archives of Canada, Ottawa.

Liversedge, Ronald. "Memoirs of the Spanish Civil War," n.d., Special Collections. University of British Columbia.

Moscow Records, Mackenzie-Papineau Battalion fonds, Microfilm, 1936–41. Reels K-257 to K-265. National Archives of Canada, Ottawa.

Päiviö, Aku. "To my son in Spain," 1938, Mackenzie-Papineau Battalion Collection, MG30 E 173. National Archives of Canada, Ottawa.

Päiviö, Jules. "My Experiences as a Volunteer in Spain," September 26, 1939, Mackenzie-Papineau Battalion Collection, MG30 E 173. National Archives of Canada, Ottawa.

Ryan, Larry. "Letter to Mrs. R. E. Beckett," October 21, 1938, Mackenzie-Papineau Battalion Collection, MG30 E 173. National Archives of Canada, Ottawa.

Ryan, Larry. "Memories of a Year Ago: The First Canadians and Americans Take their Places in the Trenches in Spain," n.d., Mackenzie-Papineau Battalion Collection, MG30 E 173. National Archives of Canada, Ottawa.

Sise, Hazen. Personal Correspondence and Diary, MG30 D 187. National Archives of Canada, Ottawa.

Smith, Edward C. "The Mac-Paps," n.d., Mackenzie-Papineau Battalion Collection, MG30 E 173. National Archives of Canada, Ottawa.

Sorenson, Henning. Reminiscence quoted in "Mac-Pap Reminiscences, K-Z," n.d., Mackenzie-Papineau Battalion Collection, MG30 E 173. National Archives of Canada, Ottawa.

Taylor, J. Secretary of the Friends of the Mackenzie-Papineau Battalion in Spain, Rehabilitation Fund, "Letter to R.E. Beckett." March 27, 1939,

Mackenzie-Papineau Battalion Collection, MG30 E 173. National Archives of Canada, Ottawa.

Ukrainian-Canadian Correspondence from Ukrainian Volunteers in Spain, 1937–38, Mackenzie-Papineau Battalion Collection, MG30 E 173. National Archives of Canada, Ottawa.

Williamson, Bill. "Letter to Wally Dent," March 2, 1981, Mackenzie-Papineau Battalion Collection, MG30 E 173. National Archives of Canada, Ottawa.

Film

Los Canadienses. Tom Daly and Colin Low. National Film Board of Canada, 1987.

Taped Interviews

Taped interviews are drawn from the following sources and are cited by acronyms: the British Columbia Archives and Records Service (BCARS), Canadian Broadcasting Corporation Radio Archives (CBC), National Archives of Canada (NAC). They are identified purely by name of interview subject. CBC interviews are all conducted by Mac Reynolds; other interviews are by miscellaneous and often unidentified interviewers. Multiple listings indicate distinctly different interviews available at different archives.

Bailey, Thomas (CBC)
Beeching, William (CBC, NAC)
Cook, Gerald (NAC)
Copeman, F. (NAC)
Doyle, Bob (NAC)
Edwards, Lionel (CBC)
Geiser, Carl (NAC)
Hilton, Perry (CBC)
Jackson, William (CBC)
Krehm, William (CBC)
Liversedge, Ronald (CBC)
Norris, Len (NAC)

Päiviö, Jules (CBC)
Penn, Marvin (CBC)
Phimister, Zac Sinclair (CBC)
Salsberg, Joseph Baruch (CBC, NAC)
Smorobin, Abe (NAC)
Russell, Ross (CBC, NAC)
Tellier, Lucien (CBC)
Turner and McElliogott (NAC)
Walsh, James "Red" (BCARS)
Watt, George (NAC)
Watts, Jean (BCARS)
Weismann, Irving (NAC)

Index